FIVE MINUTES
WITH
God

PASTOR DAN BUTCHER

BookWise
publishing

FIVE MINUTES

WITH

God

Daily Lessons in the
School of Wisdom

BookWise Publishing
bookwisepublishing.com
chrisbizzz@comcast.net

Interior Design by: Francine Platt, Eden Graphics, Inc.

edengraphics.net

Contact the author at:
dlbutcher2@aol.com

Library of Congress Control Number: Pending

ISBN 978-1-60645-270-7 Paperback $14.99

12/7/2020

For Elissa and Daniel
As I've always said, read a Proverb daily.
This book will help.

— Dad

In loving memory of Mom and Dad

Left to right, Dan, brother Rod (standing), brother Randy (seated), Mom and Dad.

Acknowledgments

*A*ll scriptures are from the *New King James Version* of the Bible or *The Living Bible*. Many excerpts are from Paul Lee Tan's book, *Encyclopedia of 7700 Illustrations* (noted wherever you see the superscript [1] (1. Tan, P. L. (1996). *Encyclopedia of 7700 Illustrations: Signs of the Times.* Garland, TX: Bible Communications, Inc.) and used with permission . There are other attributions noted at the page bottoms and within the text.

PROVERBS 1:32

". . . and the complacency of fools will destroy them."

COMFORTABLY COMPLACENT

*I*n 1934, a railroad worker filed a $100,000 damage suit against his company, claiming he had been jolted off a train and, because of the fall, his legs had become paralyzed.

Knowing it was a false legal action, the company hired two detectives who opened a crystal-gazing parlor in his hometown. Their advertisement of *Home Readings for Shut-ins* brought a request from the faker to call and tell his fortune. During the visit, the crystal-gazer "saw a lawsuit" in his ball and predicted that, to win it, his client would have to carry a log across a nearby railroad track at dawn the next morning, hopping over on one foot and back on the other. He did, and the detectives, hiding in the bushes, took a movie of his performance.

Our Proverb today deals with "complacency" defined as "feeling of smug or uncritical satisfaction with oneself or one's achievements." It teaches that the complacent are deceived, for their achievements, whether they be real or imagined, "will ultimately destroy them!" Harsh words, but so true. Some of the hardest people to recognize their personal sin and thus a need for a Savior are those who believe their success will carry the day before God. The thought of Jesus Christ being the only way to God, John 14:6, is offensive to them and they are better satisfied with their own view of salvation. I've heard them say, "God will see it my way," or "all roads lead to heaven."

Some people have just enough success to believe *they* can re-write the Bible and its clear teaching.

⇝ PRAYER ⇜

"Lord, keep us from believing that any mount of success on earth will somehow approve us in heaven. In Jesus' name. Amen."

PROVERBS 2:10–11

*When wisdom enters your heart,
and knowledge is pleasant to your soul,
discretion will preserve you; understanding will keep you.*

TWIN SISTERS

*J*oseph Papp had a problem. His homemade submarine would not function. He had worked for six years on it; he had spent all his savings building it. How then could he ever admit failure to his friends? He dreamed up a stunt. He spanned the ocean on the Dutch airline KLM, and went to Brest, France, where he told police he had crossed the Atlantic in some twelve hours in his submarine. Yet it was all a desperate and vain, glorious attempt to save face. *The London Daily Mirror* said that the Hungarian-born Canadian, Joseph Papp, "confessed that his tale of crossing the Atlantic in a homemade submarine was a hoax."

Discretion is defined as "speaking in such a way as to avoid revealing private information." This poor soul would have been better off if he had made his claim and stayed silent. This Proverb is not advocating deception, but the point is well made: wisdom will keep you from revealing private information that will harm you in the end. Truth needs to be spoken, but some facts need not always be spoken all the time. Wisdom will help you navigate these coral reef seas and keep you from shipwreck.

Wisdom's twin sisters—discretion and understanding—will preserve and keep you.

⟶ PRAYER ⟵

*"Lord, teach me that it's not necessary to say everything I know
if it will injure myself or the recipient. In Jesus' name. Amen."*

PROVERBS 3: 9–10

"Honor the Lord with your possessions,
and with the first fruits of all your increase;
so your barns will be filled with plenty,
and your vats will overflow with new wine."

INDIAN GIVER

*O*ne man asked another, "If you had a thousand hogs, would you give me half of them?" "Sure!" came the reply." "Well, if you had a hundred hogs, would you give me half of them?" Again, "Sure!" was the answer." "Okay, if you had two hogs would you give me half of them?" "That isn't fair!" came the reply. "You know I have two hogs!" The man was generous with what he did not have but was miserly with what he did have.

Giving is the means by which God develops His people. To give away that which sustains your very existence is to say, "I believe God is the giver of all things (my health, my mind, my abilities). Yes, you have worked hard and developed your skills, just remember that you had nothing to do with your development in the womb of your mother, but God did. He grew your body so that you may now give Him His due glory.

Give to God's cause, because it is not just for your causes alone.

⁓ PRAYER ⁓

"Lord, teach me to honor You by giving to you Honor.
In Jesus' name. Amen."

PROVERBS 4:11–12

"I have taught you in the way of wisdom;
I have led you in right paths.
When you walk, your steps will not be hindered,
and when you run, you will not stumble."

HUMBLE CONFIDENCE

A salesman selling vacuum cleaners knocked on the door of a remote farmhouse. When the lady of the house opened the door, he walked in and dumped a bag of dirt on the floor. "Now," boasted the salesman, "I want to make a bargain with you. If this super-duper, new vacuum cleaner does not pick up every bit of this dirt, I'll eat what's left."

"Here's a spoon," said the farmer's wife. "We don't have any electricity."

Self-confidence in self is not what this Proverb is describing, much to the chagrin of our dirt-eating friend above. This confidence stems from wisdom that has its origin in God and God's ways. He will not betray you. His word (the Bible) is His bond to you.

Remember, confidence is not about you, but God.

☙ PRAYER ❧

"Lord, my confidence in life comes from you,
the giver of life. In Jesus' name. Amen."

PROVERBS 5:22

*"His own iniquities entrap the wicked man,
and he is caught in the cords of his sin."*

GRAPPLING

A ladybug was crawling across the floor when it came head to head with a spider. The ladybug remained motionless, frozen by fear. Slowly the spider reached out with one leg and touched the ladybug. The ladybug remained still. A second time, the spider reached out and attached a second web to the bug. Again, no movement. Again and again the spider reached over to the ladybug with another and another web. Finally, the ladybug became alarmed and started to move, but alas, it was too late. He was firmly in the grip of his master.

This is the nature of sin. As our Proverb teaches, "caught in the cords of sin." Sin slowly deals with you. Its objective is to control, and control it will. It will bind you and enslave you as surely as if you were in chains. It will dictate how you spend your money, your time, and ultimately your life. The solution is simple but drastic—cut off immediately the iniquities that are binding you. Those sins that are clearly against God and the Bible. Spare no pain and free yourself. It has cost you your job, your family, and eventually your life. The time has come to act. The good news is, sin binds but Christ will free you.

⮞ PRAYER ⮜

*"Lord, may I find my freedom in Christ
before I find my bondage in sin.
In Jesus' name. Amen."*

January 6

PROVERBS 6:20–22

*"My son, keep your father's command, and do not forsake
the law of your mother. Bind them continually upon your heart; tie
them around your neck. When you roam, they
will lead you; when you sleep, they will keep you;
and when you awake, they will speak with you."*

PARENTAL ADVICE

*L*atimer was raised to the bishopric of Worcester in the reign of
Henry VIII. It was the custom of those days for each of the bishops
to make presents to the King on New Year's Day. Latimer went with
the rest of his brethren to make the usual offering; but, instead of a
purse of gold, he presented the King with a New Testament, in which
was a leaf doubled down to this passage: "Whore-mongers and adulterers God will judge."—Walter Baxendale

Today's Proverb is a shot across the bow if your ship is heading for
adultery. The warning links the words of a mother and father to their
son regarding sexually immorality. They urge him to bind their words
around his neck, to have them continually upon his heart. The promise
is when he roams, they will lead him, they will keep him, and they
speak to him.

In this darkened world with its darkened ways, a young man needs
to be spoken to about the dangers of adultery. The best advice is from
godly parents who have his best interest in mind.

You can be led by the way of darkness or by the way of light. One
way will bind you, the other will free you.

PRAYER

*"Lord, may I follow the light, lest I be bound by
the darkness. In Jesus' name. Amen."*

PROVERBS 7:21–23

*"With her enticing speech she caused him to
yield, with her flattering lips she seduced him . . .
he did not know it would cost his life."*

AS AN OX TO THE SLAUGHTER

A man was a prime suspect in a brutal murder, but all the evidence was circumstantial. Therefore, the man was never arrested nor tried for the crime.

One night, the man was traveling on an interstate highway. Apparently, he became drowsy and pulled off the pavement for a short nap. As he slept, a truck loaded with logs came along. Just as the truck passed the man's vehicle, the chain holding the logs in place broke. The logs fell on his car and crushed him to death!

Was it an accident? Or was it the principle of divine justice doing what humanity's system of justice could not do? No one can say with certainty, although it *is* worthy of thought.

But one thing is certain. A person may escape humanity's system of justice, but he or she cannot escape God's justice. "For we shall all stand before the judgment seat of Christ." (Romans14:10b). And from His verdict there is no appeal.

Proverbs deals extensively with adultery and fornication, Chapters 5, 6 and 7. Today's Proverb sends out a pellucid (translucently clear) warning of this sin's consequences: ". . . he did not know it would cost his life." As a bird hastens to a snare or an ox to the slaughter, fornication and adultery have devastating consequences. Therefore, to be forewarned is to be forearmed. Stand clear; do not play the fool.

PRAYER

*"Lord, remind me that a moment's pleasure
is not worth a life of regret. In Jesus' name. Amen."*

PROVERBS 8:1–3

*"Does not wisdom cry out, and understanding lift up
her voice? She takes her stand on the top of the high hill,
beside the way, where the paths meet."*

LIMITED ACCESS

A. T. Pierson gives the following illustration: Suppose you had a thousand-acre farm, and someone offered to buy it. You agree to sell the land except for one acre right in the center which you want to keep for yourself. Did you know that in some areas the law would allow you to have access to that one lone spot? And you would have the right to build a road across the surrounding property in order to get to it?

Restrictions, limitations, and no trespassing signs all warn of limited access to no access at all. However, there is an access that is freely given: wisdom from God. Today's Proverbs teaches that the offer of wisdom is like a woman who takes her stand on the "top of the hill." (v.2) and she "cries out by the gates . . ." (v.3). She tells us that the "simple ones will understand prudence and fools will be given an understanding heart, (v.5). She tells us that wisdom's fruit ". . . is better than gold, yes, than fine gold," (v.19), but also states that by wisdom ". . . I may cause those who love me to inherit wealth, that I may fill their treasuries," (v.21). Though wisdom's beginning is "the fear of the Lord," (1:7), and the growth of wisdom is by obedience to God, He also gives financial insight for those who reverence Him.

Wisdom has no restrictions for those who seek God. Its "fruit is better than gold . . ." but He may also see fit to through in a few treasures as well.

⟶ PRAYER ⟵

*"Lord, I rejoice that access to You and the wisdom you offer
is not restricted, but freely given. Jesus' name. Amen."*

PROVERBS 9:6

*"Forsake foolishness and live
and go in the way of understanding."*

A PROPER UNDERSTANDING

*O*ne of the strangest things from Ripley's "Believe-it-or-Not" told was about was the woman in Genoa, Italy, called the "Doughnut Seller." For fifty-two years, Paisanan sold doughnuts on the streets until she had made enough money to have created a beautiful statue of herself to be placed in the cemetery of Genoa. The statue was finished before her death, and she "spent the last three years of her life gazing at it."—Christian Victory

Our Proverb urges us to "forsake foolishness and live." The above story is absurd at best, but still true: to gaze on oneself in statue-form until life ends is truly foolish (lacking good sense or judgment). Just as foolish is to forsake the clear exhortation to live life in the "way of understanding." Proverbs always admonishes the reader to pursue "wisdom"and "understand"through a reverence for God, (cf.1:7). To live in this world with all its marvelous design, the beauty of a rose, or the wonder of a sunset, yet deny its very Designer is to gaze on a statue of yourself, all the while denying there ever was a sculptor who made it.

PRAYER

"Lord, help me to forsake foolishness and all its errant ways, one of which is to deny Your existence. In Jesus' name. Amen."

PROVERBS 10:5

*"He who gathers in summer is a wise son;
he who sleeps in harvest is a son who causes shame."*

OPPORTUNITY KNOCKS

John Wooden, UCLA's legendary basketball mentor, born in Hall, Indiana, knew the rigors and compensations of agrarian living. His father, a rural mail carrier and farmer, made a lasting impression on young John. Upon graduating from the county school in Centertown, Joshua Hugh Wooden gave his son this written creed: "Be true to yourself; make each day your masterpiece; help others; drink deeply from good books, especially the Bible; make friendship a fine art; build a shelter against a rainy day; pray for guidance, count, and give thanks for your blessings every day."

Excellent advice from a caring father. Proverbs (the Hebrew word means an "insightful saying") encourages us to make good use of opportunities, for they sometimes come only once. The wise son gathers in summer, the time of harvest, to make full use of the opportunity. A shameful son sleeps away opportunities. As the saying goes, "if you snooze, you lose." Rightfully so! Make use of the opportunities to save, to give to the less fortunate, to read your Bible, pray and most importantly, to trust Christ as your Savior. Take those opportunities now because it's possible that when they present themselves over and over again, your eyes may not see their value because you passed on them so many times before.

❧ PRAYER ❧

*"Lord, open my eyes to life's opportunities,
lest I close them in shame. In Jesus' name. Amen."*

PROVERBS 11:13

"A talebearer reveals secrets,
but he who is of a faithful spirit conceals a matter."

ENTRUSTED SECRET

An old saying is that a dog that brings a bone also carries a bone. Thus, the hearer of contentious talk must be careful what is said to the person bearing the tale. You may be certain that the person who brought the "bone," will make haste to carry one back to somebody else.

Beware! The person who reveals secrets to you about another, will one day reveal your secrets. I have personally watched a gossip seek out those who had disparaging news about others. It seemed she had a quiver full of negative and destructive information about people in the fellowship. One of the characteristics of a talebearer is they seek out the tales. Our Proverb today admonishes us to keep silent about confidences shared with us. Some people will confide in you with the hope of a listening ear or Godly counsel. Be a true friend and pray about the circumstances, but heaven forbid if you share them with others!

As Christians, we are to build the kingdom, not undermine it.

PRAYER

"Lord, help me not to divulge a proper secret,
lest I destroy another by sharing it. In Jesus' name. Amen."

January 12

PROVERBS 12:10

"A righteous man regards the life of his animal,
but the tender mercies of the wicked are cruel."

PROTECT ANIMALS

Detroit's zoo director hired four new security guards—to protect the animals from man.

In the past years there, a baby Australian wallaby left the protection of its mother's pouch and was stoned to death; a duck died with a steel-tipped hunting arrow in its breast; a pregnant reindeer miscarried after firecracker-hurling youths bombed the frantic animal into convulsions. Visitors have dropped lighted cigar butts on the backs of alligators, laughing at the reptiles' reactions as the ashes burn through their skin. Finally, the zoo's male hippopotamus choked to death when someone responded to his open-mouthed begging for peanuts by rolling a tennis ball down his throat.

The zookeepers wonder: Who should be caged?

A righteous man lives a life of kindness. This kindness extends to everyone, even his animals. A wicked man is cruel to everyone in some manner, even his animals. He has complete control over them, and he exercises that control by being cruel. The Proverb is penetratingly accurate: What type of person is cruel to animals? The wicked. What happens to the wicked? "They are turned into Hell," (Psalm 9:17). These individuals will someday reap the just reward of having a superior power (God) return on them the consequences of their sin; one of which is cruelty to animals.

You cannot sow cruelty and expect mercy.

⇜ PRAYER ⇝

"Lord, remind us that every kind act will be rewarded
as well as every unkind one. In Jesus' name. Amen."

January 13

PROVERBS 13:10

"By pride comes nothing but strife,
but with the well-advised is wisdom."

THE WISDOM OF HUMILITY

*H*ave you ever thought that only the smaller birds sing? You've never heard a note from the eagle in all your life, nor from the turkey, nor from the ostrich. But you have heard from the canary, the wren, and the lark. The sweetest music comes from those Christians who are small in their own estimation and before the Lord.—Watchman-Examiner

Pride has been defined as "an assumed superiority." Pride destroys! In our Proverb for today is the basis of strife (angry disagreement over fundamental issues). A proud person assumes a superior position in conflicts. When he/she is not respected, as *they* see respect, there is conflict—big conflict! How dare you do not see it my way? Why should a proud person receive advice. He is superior in his own mind and does not need it. In contrast, the wise man is willing to receive advice. He is humble enough to have needs. He does not see his way as the only way or his thoughts as the only thoughts. He is humble (showing a modest or low estimate of one's own importance).

The wise are willing to receive advice; the proud are too wise to need it.

PRAYER

"Lord, we're all proud!
Remind us that a wise man is a humble man,
one not so proud as to receive counsel.
In Jesus' name. Amen."

PROVERBS 14:1

*"The wise woman builds her house,
but the foolish pulls it down with her hands."*

WALK AWAY WOMEN

According to the *US News and World Report*, the spread of no-fault divorce in the United States is one reason for the huge rise in overall rates in US divorces. Almost 1.1 million marriages were dissolved in the US in 1976—more than double the 1966 total.

It's so easy these days to get divorce, as the above statistics show, that a new phrase has been born: "Walk Away Moms." These mothers just decided one day they have had enough, and they walk away. They walk from the entanglements of marriage, children, house, and the burden of the routine. Many of them go to the open arms of another marriage, which statistics show, don't fare well either; about 40% of those who divorce and remarry may have their second marriage again end in divorce.

Our Proverb teaches that a "wise woman builds her house." Her priority starts before she even marries with a wise choice of a spouse. As Proverbs clearly teaches, a "wise man is a God-fearing man," (1:7), just as the wise woman would be. They are both orientated toward God and His Word. That is where the wise woman starts. She wants a man who shares the same faith, the same values, and is heading in the same direction. Consequently, she is the type of woman who won't be "walking away" from the marriage; and he won't either. There are exceptions. The foolish woman has no such orientation. A godly man is not her priority. In all honesty, the thought doesn't enter her mind. So, when the weather gets rough, and it always does, she bails. The builder of any good marriage is God.

⇜ PRAYER ⇝

"Lord, help me remember that a good marriage is not a mistake. It takes a wise woman and wise man building on the wisdom of the God. In Jesus' name. Amen."

PROVERBS 15:8

*"The sacrifice of the wicked is an abomination to the Lord,
but the prayer of the upright is His delight."*

HOW TO PLEASE GOD, GREATLY

*T*homas Edison invented the phonograph at age 30, and he was almost totally deaf from childhood. He could hear only the loudest noises and shouts. This kind of delighted him, for he said, "A man who has to shout can never tell a lie!"

His other inventions: the incandescent bulb, microphone, mimeograph, fluoroscope, and movies.[1]

Edison's delight? He had to shout to hear himself speak. Amazing! Our Proverb for today teaches us we can delight the Almighty with our prayers! The word delight means "to please someone greatly." We can please God greatly every day. At the beginning of a New Year, a noble resolution would be to pray daily. This is a resolution that is within reach. Set aside a daily time to pray—not while you are driving, thought that is possible, but a dedicated time of prayer where that is all you're doing—praying. To think it is possible to "please God greatly" by our prayer is unexpected by many. It is not our education that delights Him; not our intellect; not our status; nor our sacrifices for the kingdom. It is prayer. There is one caveat, one stipulation—you must be upright. There is no perfection this side of heaven, but there is forgiveness in Christ and the indwelling Holy Spirit.

A man yielded to Christ is on the upright path to delighting God when he prays.

PRAYER

*"Lord, sometimes I think I need to perform wonders
to delight you when all I need is prayer.
In Jesus' name. Amen."*

PROVERBS 16:25

*"There is a way that seems right to a man;
but its end is the way of death."*

I THINK I'LL GO THIS WAY

All my life I have lived in the presence of fine and beautiful men going to their death through alcohol. I call it the greatest trap that life has set for the feet of genius.

Nothing can make a monkey into a human being. However, alcohol (or other drugs) can make a human being act like a monkey—or worse.

There is, in my humble opinion, no more effective destruction of a person's life than alcohol. Yes, it does make a man act like a monkey. Yes, you would be better off clasping a rattlesnake to your lips than a bottle, for in the end alcohol will wield a deadlier bite. All the while men and women pursue this habit, for it "seems right to a man." The bitterness and broken lives on this long train ride of life are not in view when people drink. "It seems so right for it helps me cope," but all the while the uncontrollable end is one day and one step closer. If people could predict how their drinking might end, what the consequences might be after a habit that has been well-groomed for a lifetime, many would stop. But not having such knowledge, or not caring to know at all, they continue in the path that *seems* right. God knows how this end; He says so in today's Proverb. Our Proverb looks down the long hallway with a divine perspective and declares it will end poorly for most people. There are exceptions, but most likely you are not one of them. Call on God's mercy through Christ to deliver you from drinking; enjoy His power and deliverance today. Do not put it off.

·❧· PRAYER ·❧·

*"Lord, there are some paths I have been warned not to travel;
help me to believe You know better than me.
In Jesus' name. Amen."*

PROVERBS 17:27

"He who has knowledge spares his words,
and a man of understanding is of a calm spirit."

SPARE WILLINGLY

Dayton's C. F Kettering, father of the automobile's self-starter, has a prize story upholding the theory that "ignorance is bliss."

"We had a convention of household electric plant distributors in Dayton some years ago," he relates."Each man was required to tell how much it cost him to wire a room. Finally, one big, breezy fellow named Bill, from Texas, got up and said, "Why, I can wire a room for half of what these fellows are talking about."

"The next day, we took him to a room and told him to wire it his way. To our amazement he merely fastened the wire to the walls with staples.

"But you can't put up electric wiring that way," I said to him when he was done. "It's against the fire underwriters' code."

"What's that?" asked Bill.

"I gave him the code book of the underwriters and told him to study it overnight. The next morning, he laid the book on my desk.

"The more a fellow knows in this country," he ruefully commented, "the less liberty he's got."

According to our Proverb, true knowledge is exercised in restraint! When a man has knowledge when not to speak and does so, he is not only knowledgeable but wise. He spares his words because the circumstances dictate that as the best course. The foolish, however, speak in almost in every occasion and many times without restraint. Proverbs 10:19 states, "In the multitude of words, sin is not lacking, but he who restrains his lips is wise." Why is it that a man of understanding "spares" his words? Because he knows if he keeps talking, eventually he will trip himself up with his own words.

⇝ PRAYER ⇜

"Lord, help me spare my words lest I snare my soul.
In Jesus' name. Amen."

PROVERBS 18:10

*"The name of the Lord is a strong tower,
the righteous run to it and are safe."*

A TOWERING TOWER

*F*alling down a flight of stairs caused a middle-aged Kansas City man not only a broken ankle but also an acute case of embarrassment.

As a judge in a Cub Scout safety poster contest, he had just selected the winning entry. It had read: "Always watch your step while walking on stairs."[1]

True and unfailing safety comes from the Lord. There are those who run for education as their "strong tower." Others prefer money for their safety; while still others prefer pleasure. According to our Proverb, the only worthwhile tower of strength is God. Admittedly, it's hard to cast oneself on the unseen God of the Bible, but our trust is in His Word, such as Deuteronomy 33:27: "The eternal God is your refuge, and underneath are the everlasting arms." The evidence of God's strong tower of safety is seen in how he equips his creation for its own safety. A tortoise's shell is not only hard, but slick. These two features make a tortoise shell very difficult to break, even by much larger predators. Turtles' shells are strong enough that they have been known to withstand bullets, dogs, and even alligators. This obvious design for safety clearly implies that He can protect us as well.

If you are looking for safety during life's storms, run to the "strong tower" of God's Eternal arms.

✣ PRAYER ✣

*"Lord, teach me that safety is not in a place but in a person.
In Jesus' name. Amen."*

PROVERBS 19:11

"The discretion of a man makes him slow to anger,
and his glory is to overlook a transgression.
It does not matter how much money you have;
everyone has to buy wisdom on the installment plan.[1]

SLOW ON THE DRAW

*D*iscretion has been defined as "the ability to avoid an upset." A discrete person behaves and speaks in such a way as to avoid offense. Our Proverb instructs us that a "discreet"person is one who is slow to anger. Patience and restraint are one of the hallmarks of true wisdom. A wise man does not get bent out of shape each time he is slighted, insulted, or ignored. Why is that? Because he has learned that anger usually does not profit. Through hardship of one kind or another, the fight over most encounters that anger us is just not worth it. An old country preacher once said, "A bulldog can whip a skunk, but it just isn't worth the fight." The bullheaded will be easily offended and fight, but the wise of heart has learned that most of what angers us is not worth the fight. Some things yes, most things no. So, he is "slow to anger." The wise man has learned that discretion is a better choice. He speaks, but not at a "right angle" to his opponent. And, when things get ugly, and sometimes they do, the wise man is quick to forgive; he "overlooks a transgression."

❧ PRAYER ❧

"Lord, help me to know when anger justifies the fight,
and the grace to overlook the transgressions when it's over.
In Jesus' name. Amen."

PROVERBS 20:1

*"Wine is a mocker, strong drink is a brawler,
and whoever is led astray by it is not wise."*

SEIZED

All my life I have lived in the presence of fine and beautiful men, going to their death through alcohol. I call it the greatest trap that life has set for the feet of genius.[1]—Upton Sinclair

And there is the verdict! Our Proverb teaches the dangers of drunkenness, the medical society warns us, and Upton Sinclair makes a fine observation: ". . . it (is) the greatest trap that life has set for the feet of the genius." Yet, thousands and hundreds of thousand slowly march toward it precipitous cliffs.

Our Proverb shouts a warning from the crossroads of life: "Whoever is led astray by it is not wise."Wisdom is the successful application of knowledge. To cope with life or to seek alcohol's relaxation from the squeeze of life's pressures, is *not* wise. A foolish man, not a wise man, pursues its embrace. The cure is simple, yet painful for some. Cut off the pursuit. Lay it aside and start dealing with life's harshness through prayer, Scripture and faith. Jesus said in John 6:35, "I am the bread of life. He who comes to Me shall never hunger, and he who believes in Me shall never thirst." Jesus will satisfy your soul's hunger, not the bottle. Simple faith in the pardoning sacrifice of Christ (II Corinthians 5:21) will satisfy the hungry heart.

Drinking, mocking, and brawling are symptoms of a hungry soul. Jesus Christ is the cure.

⟶ PRAYER ⟵

*"Lord, my soul hungers for life's satisfaction,
may I find my satisfaction in the bread of Life.
In Jesus' name. Amen."*

PROVERBS 21:9

"Better to dwell in a corner of a housetop,
than in a house shared with a contentious woman."

NAG UNCEASINGLY

*L*ondon (UPI)—Barbara Peers nagged her boyfriend about getting married. She nagged about buying a house. She nagged about having a family. Doctors said her nag, nag, nagging paid off.

Logan, 25, was knocked unconscious in a 100-mile-an-hour motorcycle accident while practicing for the Isle of Man grand prix." Without regaining consciousness, David's brain would deteriorate and he would become a vegetable," she said.

After 17 days of nonstop nagging, he spoke.[1]

Now that's some serious nagging. After 17 days of this, he came out of his coma and spoke. I'm wondering what he said. He should have said, "Get her out of her!"

No sane man wants to be nagged. Even if the nagging is for his own good. A better approach is to try *prayer*. Ask God to move in his heart, and if he resists God and good reason, try *trust*. Nagging is hard on the woman as well as her man. Though it may get a woman what she wants, there is a lot of resentment that builds up. God is sympathetic; that is why our Proverb teaches that it's *better* to have some space. Some things we just need to get away from.

Stop the nagging or lose the spouse.

PRAYER

"Lord, may I trust the power of prayer,
not the power of nagging. In Jesus' name. Amen."

PROVERBS 22:7

*"The rich rules over the poor,
and the borrower is servant to the lender."*

YIELD TO RULER

*I*t is known that Lincoln had no great admiration for mere financial success. "Financial success," he once said, "is purely metallic. The man who gains it has four metallic attributes: gold in his palm, silver on his tongue, brass in his face, and iron in his heart!"[1]

Iron in his heart! Pity the man who borrows from such a fellow. As Dave Ramsey exhorts, try to get out of debt as soon as possible. Whoever you owe, is whoever controls. The more people you owe, the more people who have control over you. The joy of being debt free is the feeling of being able to control what you have. You are not beholden to the mortgage company, the bank that holds your car title, or the company that has a lien on your home or property. The issue nowadays is not how much you make but *how much you spend*. Proverbs teaches over and over that restraint is one of the hallmarks of the wise person.

So, keep a watchful eye on from whom you borrow, for he may have a heart of iron.

◦❧ PRAYER ❧◦

*"Lord, remind me as I'm tempted to spend myself
into financial servant-hood,
that the wise strive for freedom, not bondage.
In Jesus' name. Amen."*

January 23

PROVERBS 23:9

"Do not speak in the hearing of a fool,
for he will despise the wisdom of your words."

There was a certain nobleman who kept a fool, to whom he one day gave a staff, with a charge to keep it till he should meet with one who was a greater fool than himself. Not many years after, the nobleman was sick, unto death. The fool came to see him.

His sick lord said to him. "I must shortly leave you."

"And whither are you going," said the fool.

"Into another world," replied his lordship.

"And when will you return? Within a month?"

"No."

"Within a year?"

"No."

"When, then?"

"Never!"

"Never?" said the fool. "And what provision hast thou made for thy entertainment there, whither thou goest?"

"None at all."

"No?" said the fool. "None at all? Here, then take my staff; for, with all my folly, I am not guilty of any folly such as this."—Bishop Hall

The book of Proverbs defines the "fool"as one who is morally deficient. A fool can be brilliant,; it's just his morals are blasted. Our Proverb teaches us, "Do not speak in the hearing of a fool . . .." Such fools deny the existence of God. "The fool has said in his heart, there is no God. (Psalm 14:1).

When atheists are confronted with reasoned arguments for God's existence (for example, every design has a designer, every watch has a watchmaker, the earth is clearly designed for man's existence, therefore, there must be a designer), then he becomes uncomfortable. We all feel guilt, at least we should. We all have an innate since of right and wrong, especially if we are the one wronged. What if this unseen God has a sense of right and wrong like I do? Has he been offended by my morals as I have been offended by some others? Am I accountable to Him as others are accountable to me? So, such deniers of God's will despise "your words of wisdom," to eliminate guilt and accountability. The fool has a moral problem that often effects his reason!

∽ PRAYER ∾

"Lord, help me to know when to stop reasoning
with the unreasonable. In Jesus' name. Amen."

PROVERBS 24:11

*"Deliver those who are drawn toward death
and hold back those stumbling to the slaughter."*

HOW SHALL WE ESCAPE?

It was the beginning of a holiday weekend, and the service station was crowded with motorists and cars. Finally, the attendant hustled up to the local minister, who had been waiting in line for quite some time.

"Sorry about the delay," the attendant apologized. "It seems as if everyone waits until the last minute to get ready for the trip he's planned."

The pastor smiled. "I know what you mean," he said. "I have the same problem in my business."[1]—Gospel Herald

Are you ready to meet God? We often put off those duties and responsibilities that do not seem to be pressing us at the moment. A Welsh minister, beginning his sermon, leaned over the pulpit and said with a solemn air, "Friends, I have a question to ask. I cannot answer it. You cannot answer it. If an angel from heaven were here, he could not answer it. If a devil from hell were here, he could not answer it."

Every eye was fixed on the speaker, who proceeded. "The question is this: 'How shall we escape if we neglect so great salvation?'" (Hebrews 2:3)

We cannot escape the judgment of our sins if we neglect God's salvation in Christ. Have you trusted the Savior's sacrifice that brings you to God? "For He made Him who knew no sin to be sin for us, that we might become the righteousness of God in Him." (II Corinthians 5:21) Every serious Christian should take today's Proverb with urgency, "deliver those who are drawn toward death . . .." Have you prayerfully pressed your friends and loved ones about the reality of their sin, the fact of God's love, and the certainty of judgment?

PRAYER

*"Lord, help us remember:
'He who provides for this life, but takes no care for eternity,
is wise for a moment, but a fool forever.' — Tillotson
In Jesus' name. Amen."*

PROVERBS 25:11

"A word fitly spoken is like apples of gold in settings of silver."

WISE OR WILD?

*T*he following story is a humorous version of today's Proverb. This word was intended to be "apples of gold in settings of silver," but I'm afraid it turned out to be a "rotten apple."

In the autumn of 1923, a man arrived from Wales, his native land, with the party of David Lloyd George, famed British Prime Minister. He soon found himself the guest of the African Inland Missionary Home in Brookline, a guest who was a very lonely and homesick. A large group of retired lady missionaries, sensing his loneliness, arranged an afternoon tea to help dispel his gloom. At the close, he was asked to say a word to the assembled ladies, and looking them squarely in the face, he exclaimed, "What language is there to describe my gratitude to you, dear women, for all this kindness? What word can describe my feelings?"

Then in a burst of enthusiasm, he thundered, "I know just the word! You are, without doubt, the homeliest women I have ever met!"

This man learned the hard way that there are words used in the old country that are never used elsewhere, even if homely in Wales does mean wholesome, gracious, kind, loving, and motherly!

I suspect he was not invited back! Choose your words carefully, they can build up or tear down.

PRAYER

"Lord, help us to weigh our words
for our hearers may weigh them even more.
In Jesus' name. Amen."

PROVERBS 26:12

"Do you see a man wise in his own eyes?
There is more hope for a fool than for him."

A FOOL'S WISDOM

Writing in *Power, A New Social Analysis*, Bertrand Russell noted, "Every man would like to be God if it were possible; some few find it difficult to admit the impossibility."[1]

There are those who live as if they are God. They believe they are in control; they make their plans and then execute them all the way to the top of success. Such success can convince some of their superior wisdom, insight, and "wonderfulness." But our Proverb teaches that any wisdom that exalts a man in his own eyes is to say that I'm worse off than a fool, and Proverbs doesn't hold fools in high esteem. Such wisdom can blind the eyes to the wonders of God, while only seeing their own wonders.

A small boy on vacation with his family visited the Grand Canyon. The guide told them that the canyon had a depth of one mile. The boy's parents gazed with rapture on this beautiful marvel of nature. As they turned to leave, the boy spit out over the rim of the canyon. That night he wrote in his diary, "Today I spit a mile."

Many people focus only on what they do and miss God's grandeur that is all about them.

⟶ PRAYER ⟵

"Lord, keep me from believing I'm so wonderful,
and God isn't. In Jesus' name. Amen."

PROVERBS 27:1

"Do not boast about tomorrow,
for you do not know what a day may bring forth."

A VAIN BOAST

In her syndicated column for November 11, 1971, Erma Bombeck reminded us that time hangs heavy over the heads of bored people, eludes the busy, flies by for the young, and runs out for the old. Perhaps we should view it, she counseled, through a child's eyes.

"When I was young, Daddy was going to throw me in the air and catch me, and I would giggle until I couldn't giggle anymore; but he had to change the furnace filter, and there wasn't time."

Well put. There is always something else to do. The problem is perception! I remember reading an article from an Emergency Room physician who said that upwards to ninety-five percent of those who come into the emergency room were not actual life or death emergencies. Yet, people believe they are, so off to the emergency room they go.

Our Proverbs implies that God has a hand in the times of our lives. We are not in control over the days of our life. We may think so, but that is an illusion; that is why some brag about tomorrow. But the bragging is self-centered, not God-centered. Here's a better plan, commit each day into the hands of the Lord. "Commit your works to the Lord, and your thoughts will be established." (Proverbs 16:3) Make prayer and the reading of God's thoughts (the Bible) a priority, and it will keep you from boasting over what you don't control. Just as you have no control over the rising and setting of the sun, know that God does. We really are short-sighted when we brag about tomorrow, for tomorrow is not ours. It is a favorable practice to *trust tomorrow to God.*

Save yourself time and worry by committing the day to the Lord and then trust Him that He has things under control. Nothing will touch our lives unless it goes through the hands of God first (cf. Job 1).

PRAYER

"Lord, I'm not going to boast or worry about tomorrow,
for I know that today and tomorrow are in your hands.
In Jesus' name. Amen."

PROVERBS 28:26

*"He who trusts in his own heart is a fool,
but whoever walks wisely will be delivered."*

SOUND REASON

When Igor Sikorsky was a lad of twelve, his parents told him that competent authorities had already proved human flight impossible. Yet Sikorsky built the first helicopter. And in his American plant he posted this sign: "According to recognized aero-technical tests, the bumblebee cannot fly because of the shape and weight of his body in relation to the total wing area. The bumblebee doesn't know this, so he goes ahead and flies anyway."—James Hastings

Competent authorities, panel of experts, those in the know, do not always know and are not always right. Sometimes, a careful search coupled with diligence often wins the day. Do not allow those who you come to trust, even your own heart's emotions, dissuade you from walking wisely. Your emotions can fool you. Beware, many a travesty has occurred when only the emotions were engaged and not sound reason. Luther said, "Show me from Scripture and right reason." A good model to follow.

Be careful with your heart, safeguard it, for if it leads you contrary to the Bible, you will only play the fool.

∽ PRAYER ∼

*"Lord, keep us so close to you, that we won't be fooled
by our own fickle inclinations. In Jesus' name. Amen."*

PROVERBS 29:7

*"The righteous considers the cause of the poor,
but the wicked does not understand such knowledge."*

LOOK WHAT I'VE DONE

The small village of Humlikon, Switzerland, sustained an unbelievable tragedy September 4, 1963. Forty-three men and women, all dirt farmers, boarded a plane for a one-day excursion to Geneva where they were to inspect a fertilizer plant.

The airplane crashed enroute and all were killed. Imagine one generation from a small community obliterated at once! Jakob Zindel, an elderly town clerk, faced the dreadful task of notifying the next of kin.

The following day, Pastor Konrad Niederer, from the nearby village of Andelfingen, came to help. Day after day, he, his people, and volunteers from as far away as England, assisted with the children and crops.

Jakob Peter, seventy-four, former councilman from Zurich, was chosen leader and coordinator of the bereaved community. More than eighteen-hundred gifts from around the world, totaling three-hundred-fifty thousand dollars, came in as a tidal wave of love. Orphaned children, of course, were given first consideration. Equipment was purchased to expedite the harvesting of potatoes and beets. A Humlikon farmer said, "We have suffered a great misfortune, yes, but we have good fortune, too; for we have learned that the world has a heart."[1]

A good man or woman feels for the unfortunate. It is our obligation to relieve the poor and to help the needy. To hoard our resources or good fortune at the expense of those less fortunate, is to ignore our Creator. The wicked believe what they have, what they have earned, is theirs and theirs only. The thought escapes them that they did not form their fingers in their mother's womb, they had no hand in the development of their mind, no part in the intricacies of their vision, but God did. Without God they would possess nothing—zero, zip.

⁓ PRAYER ⁓

*"Lord, you have allowed us to possess so much,
let us help those who possess so little. In Jesus' name. Amen."*

PROVERBS 30:11–12

"There is a generation that curses its father
and does not bless its mother.
There is a generation that is pure in its own eyes
yet is not washed from its filthiness."

THE BLIND CONDEMNING THE BLIND

Years ago, a mother who had raised six boys to manhood, her work done, had lain down to die. The boys came home to see their mother and her oldest son, a great, powerful man, knelt by her and, wiping the death-dew from her forehead, said to her: "Mother, you have always been a good mother to us boys."

The tired woman closed her eyes and great tears pushed out under the lids and ran down her wasted cheeks. Then she opened her eyes, looked searchingly into the face of her firstborn and said to him:

"My boy, I prayed more that I might be a good mother to you six boys than for anything else. I was afraid that I should fail in some way to be all that I ought to you, and I never knew whether you boys thought I had failed or not until now. Not one of you ever told me I was a good mother until today."

To be ruled by a temperament that does not express thanks, especially to parents, is exactly what our Proverb is warning us about. I understand parents are less than perfect, but neither are we. If you question that, ask your own children. Such people curse their parents but are always justified in their condemnations. Why is that? Because the curse of sin is deceit. Sin misrepresents the truth. In this case, such people believe they are pure in their own estimate, yet the truth is, they are not washed from their own filthiness.

We have entered a generation in which the accuser is committing the very sin they are accusing others of doing! Yet they are blind to it. They misrepresent the truth but do not see it.

·❧ PRAYER ❧·

"Lord, deliver us from our blinders, which condemns others
while we suffer the same. In Jesus' name. Amen."

PROVERBS 31:12

"She does him good and not evil all the days of her life."

THE IDEAL WOMAN

*A*t her Golden Wedding celebration, my grandmother told guests the secret of her happy marriage: "On my wedding day, I decided to make a list of ten of my husband's faults, which, for the sake of our marriage, I would overlook."

As the guests were leaving, a young matron whose marriage had recently been in difficulty asked by grandmother what some of the faults were that she had seen fit to overlook. Grandmother said, "To tell you the truth, my dear, I never did get around to listing them. But whenever my husband did something that made me hopping mad, I would say to myself, 'Lucky for him that's one of the ten!'"[1]

Our Proverb describes the ideal woman> She is morally excellent all her life long. Truly, she is ideal. Our generation has a rash of women who start good and stay good if the husband is good, but if that equation changes, she is good and gone! Most women nowadays will not stay with a bad man. In one regard, I do not blame them. Some men deserve to be publicly horse whipped. But public horse whipping is outlawed. There was a day when abused women would still stay married, miserable as they were, but secretly admired, nonetheless.

"She does him good and not evil all the days of her life." What a woman!

PRAYER

"Lord, deliver good women from bad men,
and good men from bad women. In Jesus' name. Amen."

PROVERBS 1:8–9

"My son, hear the instruction of your father,
and do not forsake the law of your mother;
for they will be a graceful ornament on your head,
and chains about your neck."

THE APPEAL

A judge who had a great number of cases involving families and homes once said: "We adults spend far too much time preparing the path for our youth and far too little time preparing our youth for the path."

In today's Proverb, we hear the voices of two concerned parents "preparing the youth" for life's path. Their advice centers around the father's instruction and the mother's command (laws). It's as though the young man is launching out on the road of life for the first time. Avoid bad company (vv.10–19), they say. Who might that be? Those whose are "greedy for gain," (v.19). The gain is illegal, fraudulent, and underhanded. They say, "It is okay to steal, to deceive, to get ahead; life is such a struggle. Besides, everyone is doing it." What the young man (or woman) does not know, but his parent's do, is to live in such a way, "takes away the life of its owners," (v.19). Choices have consequences, some of which follow us our whole life long. "They lie in wait for their own blood, they lurk secretly for their own lives," (v.18).

Be honest, work hard, always keep your word, reverence God (v.7), don't despise your father's and mother's instruction (v.8), and you'll soon see they'll be a "graceful ornament on your head and chains (of honor) about your neck," (v.9).

⟶ PRAYER ⟵

"Lord, may the parents' life be their children's instruction.
In Jesus' name. Amen."

February 2

PROVERBS 2:7–9

"He stores up sound wisdom for the upright;
He is a shield to those who walk uprightly;
He guards the paths of justice
and preserves the way of His saints.
Then you will understand righteousness
and justice, equity and every good paths."

ABIDING SUCCESS

*A*mong the souvenirs in the Mark Twain Memorial in Hartford, Connecticut, one finds these words written on white paper and neatly framed:

"Always do right. It will gratify some people and astonish the rest. Truly yours, Mark Twain. New York, Feb. 16, 1901."[1]

Always doing right is not easy, but with God it *is* do-able. But there is a caveat (condition), God gives "abiding success" but we must be honest (v.7), God will be our shield, but we must live uprightly (v.7), God will guard us but we must be just (v.8).

If we follow God, every path becomes a path of understanding, righteousness and justice (v.9).

PRAYER

"Lord, keep my feet on the smooth, the straight and the level.
In Jesus' name. Amen."

PROVERBS 3:11–12

*"My son, do not despise the chastening of the Lord, nor detest His
correction; for whom the Lord loves He corrects,
just as a father the son in whom he delights."*

ILLEGITIMATE

Mark Guy Pearse used to tell of the time he overheard one of his children admonishing the other, "You must be good, or Father won't love you."

Calling the boy to him he said, "Son, that isn't really true."

"But you won't love us if we are bad, will you?" the boy asked.

"Yes, I will love you whether you are good or bad," Pearse explained. "But there will be a difference in my love. When you are good, I will love you with a love that makes me glad; and when you are not good, I will love you with a love that hurts me."

Every loving parent knows the difficulty of disciplining a child that has been bad. I told my children when I spanked them, "this hurts me worse than you," but I suspect they thought I was lying! Hebrews 12:8 teaches that any professing Christian who is not disciplined by God in some form for violating his laws, "you are illegitimate and not sons." That means God is not your father! True sons of God are corrected when they rebel against God. Just as a caring father will spank a young child for playing in the road, so will God His children. Serious as the discipline of God is, the lack of discipline is more so.

Have you made a professing for Christ, and then just did your own thing; no real change? Do you live just like the unbelieving, same words, same behavior, same violations? If so, and God hasn't stepped in with his own form of "spanking," it's very possible that you're *not* one of His children.

God disciplines His children for good reason; so they will bear His likeness in their lives. No discipline, no likeness, no son-ship.

◦~ PRAYER ~◦

*"Lord, keep me out of the streets of disobedience,
lest I be 'spanked' for my own good. In Jesus' name. Amen."*

PROVERBS 4:14–15

"Do not enter the path of the wicked,
and do not walk in the way of evil, avoid it,
do not travel on it; turn away from it and pass on."

LORD, DON'T LET THE ICE CREAM MAN COME DOWN OUR STREET

Alexander was trying to save all the pennies he could in order to buy a baseball bat. But he had a hard struggle.

One night when he was saying his prayers, his mother heard him say fervently, "Oh Lord, please help me save my money for a baseball bat. And, God, don't let the ice cream man come down this street!"

This young man had it right. There are some places our feet, our eyes, and our ears should never go. The nature of temptation is if it is not resisted, it soon becomes a necessity. And some necessities are morally destructive (pornography), financially draining (gambling), and rationally devastating (pride).

The solution is to resist as Christ resisted. He quoted the Bible. Yep, the good old Bible. When Satan tempted him to eat bread after forty days of fasting, he said, "Man shall not live by bread alone, but by every word that proceeds from the mouth of God." (Deuteronomy 8:3) Temptation will come to us all. It's intent is to satisfy you with life without God. Such temptation never satisfies; you only think it will. Only God satisfies in this life. All the rest is an illusion.

PRAYER

"Lord, remind me,
"It is easier to suppress the first desire
than to satisfy all that follows it.
In Jesus' name. Amen."

PROVERBS 5:5

"Her feet go down to death; her steps lay hold of hell."

*"One of the horrors of hell
is the undying memory of a misspent life."*

Solomon speaks of the adulterous woman as one whose lips are as sweet as honey and smoother than oil (v.3), but he presses his message with how adultery ends up. "But in the end, she is bitter as wormwood, sharp as a two-edged sword (v.4). The advantage that the elderly have over their youthful sons and daughters, is their experience. They have lived long enough to know the dangers of life. With characteristic love, Solomon pleads with his son, ". . . pay attention to my wisdom; lend your ear to my understanding . . ." (v.1). He continues to say allow me to teach you, for the adulterous woman's feet ". . . go down to death, her steps lay hold of hell," (v.5). Keep the end in mind. He warns, remember that ruin awaits you.

This is not complicated at all, ". . . do not go near the door of her house."(v.8)

⟶ PRAYER ⟵

*"Lord, keep me yielded to my parent's counsel,
so one day they may see a man and not a fool.
In Jesus' name. Amen."*

PROVERBS 6:12–15

"A worthless person, a wicked man, walks with a perverse mouth,
he winks with his eyes, he shuffles his feet, he points with his fingers;
perversity is in his heart, he devises evil continually, he sows discord.
Therefore, his calamity shall come suddenly;
suddenly he shall be broken without remedy."

BROKEN

A certain tribe in Africa elects a new king every seven years, but it invariably kills its old king. For seven years the member of the tribe enjoying this high honor is provided with every luxury known to savage life. During these years his authority is absolute, even to the power of life and death. For seven years he rules, is honored, and surfeited with possessions, but at the end he dies.

Every member of the tribe is aware of this, for it is a custom of longstanding; but there is never lacking an applicant for the post. For seven years of luxury and power men are willing to sacrifice the remainder of life's expectation.

This Africa tribes celebrates today's Proverb a little differently than expected, after seven years of opulent living, their king is executed and another appointed! What is surprising is how many are willing to be the new king. This story illustrates well the certain truth that scores, and hundreds and thousands are willing to be bankrupt through eternity if they may only win their millions here.

Hopefully, you are not one of them! Reverence God, trust Christ for forgiveness, and live your time on earth with eternity in mind.

∼ PRAYER ∼

"Lord, preserve me from being wise for a moment
and foolish for eternity or to be 'suddenly broken
without remedy.' In Jesus' name. Amen."

PROVERBS 7:6–9

*"For at the window of my house I looked through my lattice,
and saw among the simple, I perceived among the youths,
a young man devoid of understanding, passing along the street
near her corner; and he took the path to her house in the
twilight, in the evening, in the black and dark night."*

SHORT ON UNDERSTANDING

The longest flight made by a homing pigeon was the 7,200 miles that one flew in 1931 from Arras, France, to its home in Saigon, Vietnam. To demonstrate that homers are not guided by landmarks, the bird was taken to France in a covered cage aboard a ship that crossed the South China Sea, the Indian Ocean, the Red Sea and the Mediterranean. The pigeon—straight as an arrow and over "unfamiliar" land—returned in just 24 days.

Oh, that men had such instincts and not be so easily distracted. That they would fly to God's commands over every temptation. Today's Proverb describes rather pitifully, the downfall of a youth as he makes his way to a prostitute. Solomon warns the reader in three separate Chapters (5-7), the ensuring disaster of sexual immorality and for good reason. Proverbs describes the danger of the immoral lifestyle as "an ox goes to the slaughter, or a fool to the correction of the stock, till an arrow struck his liver. As a bird hastens to the snare, he did not know it would cost his life," (vv.22–23), "her house is the way to hell," (v.27). Hardly a list of perks! That's why he is described as ". . . a young man devoid of understanding," (v.7). The antidote to such temptation is this,: "Keep my words, treasure my commands within you. Keep my commands and live, (vv.1-2). I love Proverbs!

This is "simple science." Keep God's commands and live, or insist on sexual immortality and gamble with your very life.

⟶ PRAYER ⟵

*"Lord, I am grateful that Your ways are simple and clear and
rewarding. May we never believe that keeping the commands of God are
more burdensome than breaking them. In Jesus' name. Amen."*

PROVERBS 8:34–36

"Blessed is the man who listens to me, watching daily at my gates, waiting at the posts of my doors. For whoever finds me finds life and obtains favor from the Lord; but he who sins against me wrongs his own soul; all those who hate me love death."

FEAST OR FAMINE

In *A Twentieth-Century Testimony*, Malcolm Muggeridge wrote: "The true purpose of our existence in this world, which is, quite simply, to look for God, and, in looking, to find Him, and, having found Him, to love Him, thereby establishing a harmonious relationship with His purposes for His creation."

Our Proverb says it this way, "For whoever finds me finds life . . ." (v. 35). The "me"of this Proverb is wisdom. Wisdom is the "successful application of God's knowledge." Wisdom starts with a reverence for God (cf. 1:7) and continues by obeying Him.

Oh, how happy is the man who daily "listens to me, watching daily at my gates," (v.34). Some things never change—daily in the Word, daily in prayer, daily in His favor (v.35). Jesus put it this way, "It is written, man shall not live by bread alone, but by every word that proceeds from the mouth of God (Matthew 4:4). I got in trouble if I skipped a day from school, likewise, my soul is in trouble if I skip it.

If it's God's favor you're looking for, read or listen daily to His word; otherwise, you will be hating life, (v.36).

PRAYER

"Lord, I choose life and favor. Keep me from famishing my soul through neglect. In Jesus' name. Amen."

PROVERBS 9:1, 5–6

*"Wisdom has built her house . . . come, eat of my bread
and drink of the wine I have mixed. Forsake foolishness
and live and go in the way of understanding."*

TO THE RIGHT OR TO THE LEFT?

*R*obert Folton had only words of discouragement from the crowd as
they watched him work on his steamboat. They derided it as "Fulton's Folly." Today steamboats cross the seas. Mistaken was the crowd.

The crowd thought Charles Goodyear and his wife were misled for
trying to vulcanize rubber. But now the name Goodyear is associated
with rubber.

Benjamin Franklin's prospective mother-in-law hesitated about
permitting her daughter to marry a printer. There were already two
printing shops in the United States, and she was dubious about the
country's being able to support a third.

Many have been ridiculed for forsaking the ways of the world to
follow Christ, to build their house as God commands. Some were
called "fool" and others mocked with "what a waste." But life lived in
consistent love for God and others is never a travesty. The real loss is
for those who believe life consists of one pleasurable experience after
another. These leave in their wake sorrow, regret, and emptiness. To
forsake foolishness (lack of good sense) in order to follow Christ's commands (. . . love God and your neighbor: Matthew 22:37–40) is never
to miss life's true purpose; exactly the teaching of today's Proverb. Too
many figure this out at the end of life's journey only to grieve over the
life they could have had. Heed God's invitation to acquire wisdom:
"Go in the way of understanding, forsake foolishness and live," (v.6).
Trust Christ and follow Him; and do it today.

ᵔ PRAYER ᵔ

*"Lord, there is a tower of utterances inviting us to enjoy their
so-called 'wisdom.' Tune our ears to Your voice
while forsaking all others. In Jesus' name. Amen."*

PROVERBS 10:7

*"The memory of the righteous is blessed,
but the name of the wicked will rot."*

NOW, I'M ONLY A MEMORY

In 1871, the *New York Herald* sent Henry Stanley to Africa in search of the missionary, David Livingstone, who was long overdue. After unbelievable hardships, the journalist found the explorer in central Africa, where he spent four months with him. Stanley went to Africa a conceited and confirmed atheist, but Livingstone's influence, gentleness, genuineness, goodness, and zeal won Stanley over. He became a Christian, saying, "I was converted by him, although he had not tried to do it."

And now for the wicked.

Back in the 1930s, a Chinese guerrilla named Mao Tse-tung often spoke from a rock outside a village in South China. The armies of Chiang Kai-shek forced him to retreat further and further inland. Mao Tse-tung, however, took his ideas with him, teaching people as he went. The day came when nearly a billion people, almost a quarter of the population of the earth, looked to this evil man for leadership.

Make no mistake about it, one person always has and always will make the difference between success and failure—however measured—between good and evil.

So, how will it be for you? When friends and family think back on you or visit your grave, will it be with fondness and longing, love and respect; or will it be with bitterness? What could have been but was not? If she only had been more patient or, if he could only stay sober. Amazingly, the choice is ours! We fancy blaming our family or difficult circumstances or lack of personal skills, but in the end, it's really up to us.

I choose righteousness and life, forsaking the rot that comes from wickedness. This is only possible through Christ. "I can do all things through Christ who strengthens me." (Philippians 4:13)

⁖ PRAYER ⁖

"Lord, as Christ my strength, may my name be remembered as sweet smelling to those left to remember. In Jesus' name. Amen."

PROVERBS 11:14

"Where there is no counsel, the people fall;
but in the multitude of counselors there is safety."

PRUDENT COUNSEL

*J*ohn Wooden, UCLA's legendary basketball mentor, born in Hall, Indiana, knew the rigors and compensations of agrarian living. His father, a rural mail carrier and farmer, made a lasting impression on young John. Upon graduating from the county school in Centertown, Joshua Hugh Wooden gave his son this written creed: "Be true to yourself; make each day your masterpiece; help others; drink deeply from good books, especially the Bible; make friendship a fine art; build a shelter against a rainy day; pray for guidance, count, and give thanks for your blessings every day."

Advice is good, seek it out. How often we have found ourselves wondering what to do next. Our Proverb suggests you seek counsel from a trusted friend. I have such a friend. When I needed counsel on ministry and its difficulties, I would give him a call. He never failed to deliver.

Wondering what to do next? First, always do the next right thing, as God sees it.

Second, call a friend.

⟶ PRAYER ⟵

"Lord, keep me in the safety of wise counsel,
lest I go it on my own and fall. In Jesus' name. Amen."

PROVERBS 12:18

"There is one who speaks like the piercings of a sword,
but the tongue of the wise promotes health."

WILD WORDS

California was leading Georgia Tech 7–6 when Roy Riegels (playing for the University of California) took the ball. He became confused when his teammates began blocking Tech men behind him. He turned and ran in that direction.

The crowd roared in amazement. "Wrong way! Wrong way!" Benny Lom, a fast Cal halfback, started after Riegels who was headed straight for the opponent's goal. "Roy, Roy, stop!" he cried.

But the noise was so great that Riegels thought the crowd was cheering him on. Just as he reached the goal, his teammate pulled him down.

The California team tried to punt from their one-yard line. But Tech blocked the kick and pounced on the ball behind the goal. The play was scored as a two-point safety for Georgia. This proved to be Georgia Tech's margin of victory.

That would leave most people severely depressed! Yet, there is another mistake that is commonly committed daily by multiple thousands. *What they say.* Our Proverb teaches there are those unfortunate souls who, when they speak, it is like being punched in the stomach. They either say what they shouldn't, say it in such a way as to offend, or say it without any discretion. Just a host of missteps when it come to their mouth.

In contrast, there are those souls who know how to encourage, when to encourage, and what words to use to encourage. This is either by gift or practice, but they have a knack of bringing a healing touch with words. It is possible for you, so don't quit. I have run several times toward the wrong goalpost, but things are getting better. God hasn't given up on me, and He won't give up on you.

PRAYER

"Lord, keep me running in the right directions
with my words. In Jesus' name. Amen."

PROVERBS 13:15

*"Good understanding gains favor,
but the way of the unfaithful is hard."*

UNDERSTANDING EQUALS FAVOR

After several pastors had failed to win a condemned criminal to Christ by preaching down to him, a layman went to visit the man. Entering the death row cell, he sat on the cot alongside the man, took him by the hand, and said, "We are in a bad fix, aren't we?" The man broke into tears and soon yielded to Christ. He needed somebody to understand and care.

Understanding can open many doors. Combine it with compassion, and it's a formidable force.

We are so goal-oriented these days that compassion and understanding are considered time-consumers by some. Yet our Proverb teaches that understanding equals favor, and who does not want favor? This favor comes from both God and man. If you do not take time to understand your frustrated spouse, or difficult employee, or troubled child, or just how life works, the Proverb also teaches the way will be "hard."

PRAYER

*"Lord, keep me in the way of understanding,
understanding You, Your ways, and Your world.
In Jesus' name. Amen."*

PROVERBS 14:21

"He who despises his neighbor sins;
but he who has mercy on the poor, happy is he."

HAPPY AM I

In *Les Miserables*, Victor Hugo tells of Jean Valjean, whose only crime was the theft of a loaf of bread to feed his sister's starving children. After serving nineteen years, he was released from the galleys. Unable to find work because he had been a convict, he came to the home of a good, old bishop who kindly gave him his supper and a bed for the night.

Yielding to temptation, he stole the bishop's silver plates and slipped out but was soon caught and returned. The kind bishop said, "Why, I gave them to him. And Jean, you forgot to take the candlesticks." Jean was astounded at such kindness, and this brought about his salvation. A little deed of kindness can turn a sinner to the Savior.

An amazing and beautiful illustration. Mercy extended to anyone will pay rich dividends, especially to the poor. If it were not for the unearned favor of God on our own lives, we might have been born in poverty with very limited resources. The Rescue Mission and Rescue Haven are two homeless shelters in Salt Lake City that are trustworthy services. There is no lack of non-profit organizations if you're looking to have ". . . mercy on the poor . . . ."

So, if you want to experience feelings of pleasure, show mercy, especially to the less fortunate. If you're really into pain and misery, nurture an attitude of contempt.

PRAYER

"Lord, I have received your mercy;
now help me to extend that mercy
to my poor brothers and sisters.
In Jesus' name. Amen."

February 15

PROVERBS 15:15

*"All the days of the afflicted are evil,
but he who is of a merry heart has a continual feast."*

LAUGH MORE, FROWN LESS

Scientists have been studying the effect of laughter on human beings and have found, among other things, that laughter has a profound and instantaneous effect on virtually every important organ in the human body. Laughter reduces health-sapping tensions and relaxes the tissues as well as exercising the most vital organs. It is said that laughter, even when forced, results in beneficial effect on us, both mentally and physically. Next time you feel nervous and jittery, indulge in a good laugh.—*Executives' Digest*

Today's Proverb emphasizes the value of a merry heart. Merry has been defined as "jolly or festive or to celebrate." There is much in our lives that can give us a lift, to celebrate; from the ridiculous to the sublime. We have four cats, and one afternoon summer while relaxing in the backyard, my and wife and I noticed that each of our four cats were being stocked by another cat directly behind it. Each cat was quite unaware that there was a cat directly behind it, hugging the grass, ready to pounce. It made for quite a comical relief.

There is another way to be "merry" throughout your day. Be thankful! "In everything give thanks; for this is the will of God . . .." (Thessalonians 5:18) A thankful heart doesn't have time to complain, and it most certainly keeps you in a good mood. There is an alternative. You can sing the "blues" the whole day, but the song makes for miserable company.

⸫ PRAYER ⸺

*"Lord, remind me that it takes 72 muscles to frown,
but only 14 to smile. In Jesus' name. Amen."*

PROVERBS 16:7

"When a man's ways please the Lord,
He makes even his enemies to be at peace with him."

HOW TO DEAL WITH ENEMIES

*J*udge Kaufman presided at the trial of the Russian spies, the Rosenbergs. They were charged with and convicted of treason against the United States and sentenced to death.

In his summation at the end of the long and bitter trial, the lawyer for the Rosenbergs said animatedly, "Your Honor, what my clients ask for is justice."

Judge Kaufman replied calmly. "The court has given what you ask for—justice! What you really want is mercy. But that is something this court has no right to give."—Selected

Man's court may not always provide mercy, but the court of heaven does. In our Proverb today, we have as a general guideline that teaches ". . . He makes even his enemies to be at peace with him." God in His favor cancels the sinner's debt through Christ, and sometimes adds to it the peace from unexpected sources—our enemies. The one condition is a man's willingness to please God. Most people are forgiving; howbeit, not all. Even an enemy can recognize a changed man, from what he was to what he is now. It may even pique his interest to know what has "happened." A true Christian living a true Christian life will restore, either financially or morally, the relationships sin has destroyed, when possible. Such restoration of relationship is commanded by Christ Himself. "Therefore if you bring your gift to the altar, and there remember that your brother has something against you, leave your gift there before the altar, and go your way. First be reconciled to your brother, and then come and offer your gift." (Matthew 5:23–24) When a man's ways please the Lord, he wants to be reconciled with his enemies. Financial restoration or forgiveness sought has a profound impact on our foes.

PRAYER

"Lord, help me to please You, even to the extent
of being reconciled with my enemies. In Jesus' name. Amen."

PROVERBS 17:1

*"Better is a dry morsel with quietness,
than a house full of feasting with strife."*

BETTER THAN

*I*n one of the "Big Three"conferences during World War II, Roosevelt and Churchill were trying to get Stalin to agree with some proposed strategy. When Stalin gave his reason or excuse for not agreeing with them, they said, "That is no reason for your refusal!" Stalin replied with a story of two Arabs.

One Arab asked the other to lend him his rope. The latter replied, "I can't. I need it to tie my camel." The first Arab reminded his companion that he did not own a camel. To which the companion replied, "I know that. But when you do not want to lend your rope, one excuse is as good as any other."

Excuses offered to God are in the same category. They reveal that we simply do not want to do what He tells us to do.

Some will make any excuse to have a large piece of the world! They would rather have the house, the boat, the bank account, the jewels, the prestige; regardless of how much strife comes with it. The Bible often uses contrasts to communicate its principles. In this case, it is far better to have little with peace of mind than the world at your front doorstep with a house full of contention.

PRAYER

*"Lord, remind us that peace within is better
than prosperity without. In Jesus' name. Amen."*

February 18

PROVERBS 18:2

*"A fool has no delight in understanding,
but in expressing his own heart."*

NO LOVE, NO TRUTH

*A*n old funeral custom that prevailed in Scotland until recent times was to carry out the casket of the deceased, not through the front door, but through an opening made in the side of the house which was walled-up immediately after serving its purpose. Thus, the ghost was prevented from re-entering the house because the only door that it knew was gone.

A fool (a person who lacks good judgment or sense), is a person who believes such nonsense as the above story. Unfortunately, they will reject the truth of the Bible because it is foreign to their thinking or up-bringing. Christians are to be open-minded to "truth claims;" we have nothing to fear. The question has not been asked that will cause the fall of Christianity. James encourages us, "So then, my brethren, let every man be swift to hear, slow to speak, slow to wrath," (1:19). Prejudices and ignorance are not worth expressing, but an open mind to the voice of God should be our delight. All truth is the voice of God. Science, theology, and philosophy—used properly and without prejudice—are all the voice of God.

There is no truth but God's truth. The ultimate expression of that truth is in the person of Jesus Christ, and that truth always expresses itself in love. No love, no truth.

PRAYER

*"Lord, may I delight in understanding, not in expressing.
In Jesus' name. Amen."*

PROVERBS 19:2

*"Also, it is not good for a soul to be without knowledge,
and he sins who hastens with his feet."*

There is no more terrible sight than ignorance in action.

CONTENTEDLY IGNORANT

When Thoreau, the naturalist, was close to death, he was visited by a very pious aunt who asked, "Henry, have you made your peace with God?" "I didn't know that we had ever quarreled," was Thoreau's answer.

And in his answer, he revealed his profound spiritual ignorance. Too many people are like him. They are utterly unconscious of the fact that they have sinned against God, and so have "quarrel"with Him, and are really lost and separated from God. The first step in coming to Christ is to realize one is a sinner—a lost sinner.

Thoreau's answer revealed that he still was a lost man: he did not know he was lost, and so he had never come to Christ to be saved. Here is the truth about man's sin and lost condition by nature.

It is possible to live life without sensing a conflict with God. An individual may believe there is a God but fail to pursue Him. He doesn't have any real "quarrel" with God, he just hasn't settled accounts with Him. The Bible is clear: "for all have sinned and fall short of the glory of God." (Romans 3:23) We have a sin problem, and this sin problem earns us death. "For the wages of sin is death, but the gift of God is eternal life in Christ Jesus, our Lord. (Romans 6:23) Deliverance from the penalty of our sin has always been offered to mankind through simple faith in Christ's death. (Romans 5:1) "Therefore, having been justified by faith, we have peace with God through our Lord Jesus Christ."

Do you have peace with God? Do not be ignorant of God's ways; don't hasten with your feet through life in ignorance of your sin problem and then suddenly find yourself standing before God.

⸙ PRAYER ⸙

*"Lord, I accept that I've sinned against You; bring peace to my heart
through simple faith in Your Son's sacrifice on my behalf.
In Jesus' name. Amen."*

PROVERBS 20:9

"Who can say, 'I have made my heart clean; I am pure from my sin?'"

THE DAINTY SINNER

Eddie Martin met a few people who ad tried to convince him that they were not bad sinners. In Bluefield, West Virginia, a well-dressed woman came forward on the salvation invitation. He took her hand and prepared to give her a prayer to repeat after him.

He said, "Please repeat after me. 'Dear Lord, I know I'm a no-good sinner.'" She never said a word. He looked at her and asked, "Don't you want to be saved?"

She said, "Yes, Eddie, I do want to be saved; but I'm not a sinner."

"Then you can't be saved," He said. "Jesus only died for sinners."

"But, Mr. Martin," she replied, "I'm a good sinner."

"A good sinner! Lady, there are no good sinners. You will have to take your seat. God can't save you until you become conscious that you are a no-good sinner and need His forgiveness."

"But, Mr. Martin, you don't understand. I'm really not a bad sinner."

He told her to go back and sit down. She held on to his hand with a vise-like grip. Finally, she looked him in the eyes and said, "Oh, please forgive me. I know I am a no-good, hell-deserving sinner. I am a proud, no-good sinner. I do need Christ to forgive me of my sins."

"Wonderful! Now, lady, you are ready to do business with God." They prayed together there at the front, thousands of people looking on. The lady came clean with God. God saved her. But she never would have been saved if she had not changed her attitude. None of us are good sinners. We are all big sinners, bad sinners.—Eddie Martin

If you do not believe you are a sinner, there's no use for a Savior. The truth is, "there is none righteous, no not one." (Romans 3:10) Jesus said there is none good but God (cf. Matthew 19:17) Good sinners need Jesus even worse than bad sinners, because they don't believe they're sick. The hardest patient to treat is the one who does not believe he's sick.

PRAYER

"Lord, thank You that I've come to my senses, for I'm a 'good sinner' who desperately needs Jesus. In Jesus' name. Amen."

PROVERBS 21:5

*"The plans of the diligent lead surely to plenty,
but those of everyone who is hasty, surely to poverty."*

PERSEVERING DILIGENCE

What Francis Bacon, the seventeenth-century English philosopher, said about reading in general applies with peculiar relevancy to the Bible: "Some books," he maintained, "are to be tasted, others to be swallowed, and some few to be chewed and digested." That is, some books are to be read only in parts; others to be read, but not curiously; and some few to be read wholly, and with diligence and attention. The Bible belongs in the last group.

My dear children, are you just tasting the Bible, or are you chewing and digesting it?

If I have had any success in this life, as a servant of God, it will be found in my diligent reading of the Bible. No reading, no power; no reading, no reality; no reading, no transformation. If your life lacks power or reality or Christ-likeness, get back to your Bible. Read it daily, read it prayerfully, and heaven's gates will open its arms to you here on earth, and will receive you into its everlasting bliss when you leave this earth.

PRAYER

*"Lord, as Sir Walter Scott well said, 'There is only one Book.'
Keep me diligently in it. In Jesus' name. Amen."*

PROVERBS 22:9

"He who has a generous eye will be blessed,
for he gives of his bread to the poor."

GOD'S FAVOR

The year 1983 marked the five-hundredth anniversary of the great reformer, Martin Luther, whose stature increases with time. Found by his deathbed, scrawled in German and Latin, was this declaration: "We are beggars: That is true."

This statement may have inspired D. T. Niles to say, "Evangelism is one beggar telling another beggar where he can find a piece of bread." Not a sweet roll and a cup of coffee, but a bite of the staff of life—bread!

The church is a fellowship of beggars, receiving and offering love, support, and hope. Committed Christians acknowledge their dependence upon God and their interdependence on one another. They are always in the bread line; if not receiving, then giving.

A good eye is Proverb's way of saying generous. A good eye observes the needs of others first. A bad eye sees only its own selfish interest.

Always be generous, give to the poor, and be grateful for God's good fortune on your life. The result will be God's blessing; God's favor on you.

It's impossible to stay discouraged when you are generous to others.

PRAYER

"Lord, I'm prone to cling rather than give.
Help me as I help others. In Jesus' name. Amen."

PROVERBS 23:15–6

"My son, if your heart is wise, my heart will rejoice-indeed,
I myself; yes my inmost being will rejoice
when your lips speak right things."

WISE OF HEART

Someone has said that the Gospel in the first century was carried by a good system. It was called the teleperson system, and it truly got results, better than we do today with our telephones, televisions, and so on. The woman of Samaria carried the Gospel after her meeting with Christ by the teleperson system. It is said that "many of the Samaritans . . . believed on Him for the saying of the woman." (John 4:39)—Mrs. J. Shields

If you are interested in what will delight God's heart, tell someone about Jesus! You'll be speaking exactly what Jesus commanded us to say. Jesus said in Luke 24:46-47, "Thus it is written, and thus it was necessary for the Christ to suffer and to rise from the dead the third day, and that repentance and remission of sins should be preached in His name to all nations . . .."

So, speak of the love of God in this life and the judgment of God in the next. It will rejoice God's heart and your own.

❧ PRAYER ❧

"Lord, may I be more concerned about what delights Your heart
rather than that of my own. In Jesus' name. Amen."

PROVERBS 24: 5–6

"A wise man is strong, yes, a man of knowledge increases strength;
for by wise counsel you will wage your own war,
and in a multitude of counselors there is safety."

COUNSEL IS THE BROTHER TO SAFETY

The person who knows everything has a lot to learn.

If you want to increase your value and influence, increase your knowledge. If you want to increase your success in life, be humble enough to ask for counsel on difficult decisions. Wisdom abides in the hard-fought battles of others. Learn from their experience, and you'll avoid the heartache of their mistakes.

It is not necessary to find out the stove is hot when another shows you his scar.

⟨ ⊱ PRAYER ⊰ ⟩

"Lord, may I be humble enough to seek Your wisdom,
and wise enough to value it. In Jesus' name. Amen."

PROVERBS 25:26

*"A righteous man who falters before the wicked
is like a murky spring and a polluted well."*

BEWARE THE FALL

*D*uring President Wilson's difficulties in international negotiations he, too, felt the need of divine guidance. When Mr. Wilson arrived at a cabinet meeting, his face wore a solemn look. It was evident that serious affairs of the nation were on his mind. He said to the cabinet members: "I don't know whether you men believe in prayer or not. I do. Let us pray and ask the help of God." The President of the United States fell upon his knees with the members of the cabinet and offered a prayer to the Almighty for help.—Aquilla Webb

That is inspiring to read. Likewise, you can achieve and succeed, and your life can be an example far beyond your present reach. Never underestimate your influence for good. People are watching.

However, be aware if you are tempted to falter, it will give many the right (in their own minds) to falter themselves. If you are someone's inspiration, and you fall before the wicked, you will become a polluted well in their sight. Beware!

No one lives in a vacuum. We are either an inspiration or a disaster before those who love us.

PRAYER

*" Lord, remind me in a moment of temptation,
that heroes are born out of times of desperation.
In Jesus' name. Amen."*

PROVERBS 26:1

*"As snow in summer and rain in harvest,
so honor is not fitting for a fool."*

HONOR HAS A TWIN SISTER

Neither snow nor rain nor heat nor gloom of night stays these couriers from the swift completion of their appointed rounds." That is how Herodotus, the Greek historian, described the Persian postal system of 500 B.C.

They tell a story about the time former Postmaster General Winton Blount sat in on a brainstorming session on the problems of mail delivery. "I've been listening patiently now for three hours," Blount finally said in exasperation, "and all I want is a simple answer to a simple question: If it is neither snow nor rain nor heat nor gloom of night that is holding up the mail, then just what is the trouble?"— Congressional Record

Cute! So, what is holding up the honor we all so covet? Perhaps, as the Proverb says, it's our own foolishness. Some things in life we know *not* to expect. It is not supposed to snow in summer and rain in harvest time. We also should *not* expect people or circumstances to honor us if we act unwisely or imprudently. A wise man carefully considers the consequences of his choices: how he spends his money, who he marries, what job he chooses, and whether he honors God. "The fool has said in his heart, 'there is no God.'" (Psalm 14:1)

Such foolishness will end in disaster. "For what will it profit a man if he gains the whole world, and loses his own soul?" (Mark 8:36)

So, do not be a fool; honor God, and He will honor you.

PRAYER

*"Lord, may I believe that by honoring God,
I am honored. In Jesus' name. Amen."*

February 27

PROVERBS 27:5–6

*"Open rebuke is better than love carefully concealed.
Faithful are the wounds of a friend,
but the kisses of an enemy are deceitful."*

REBUKES OVER KISSES

When a robber broke into a home in Cleveland, Ohio, he discovered that the 81-year-old woman resident was none other than his old schoolteacher. "You were always good to me," said the thief, kissing her tenderly on the cheek. Then he and an accomplice fled with $210. The thief's show of gratitude and affection did not, however, change his way of life.—*Prairie Overcomer*

It is frightening to hold a loved one accountable for an obvious and potentially dangerous sin. To always praise a person without holding them accountable for wrong really isn't love; it's the hallmark of an enemy!

We all stand in need of a rebuke, whether it be for a speeding or outright dishonesty for the Bible says, "there is none righteous, no, not one." (Romans 3:10)

Sometimes true love may be hidden in a rebuke, just as hatred may be hidden in a kiss.

⟡ PRAYER ⟡

*"Lord, to hold back blame, it has been said,
is to hold back love. In Jesus' name. Amen."*

PROVERBS 28:14

*"Happy is the man who is always reverent,
but he who hardens his heart will fall into calamity."*

THE PROSPECT OF HAPPINESS

The late Robert Horton said the greatest lesson he learned from life was that people who set their minds and hearts on money are equally disappointed, whether they get it or whether they do not.

I have a simple solution to happiness. It is not money; it's doing life God's way! Just as our Proverb says, "if you keep your relationship with God your priority, God will bless you, make you happy." (Psalm 1:1–3) "Blessed (oh, how happy) is the man who walks *not* in the counsel of the ungodly, nor stands in the path of sinners, nor sits in the seat of the scornful; but his delight is in the law of the Lord, and in His law he meditates day and night . . . and whatever he does shall prosper."

There is an alternative. You can harden your heart over life's injustices, heartaches, and sorrows, but that will only lead to more injustices, heartaches, and sorrows; only this time, it will be by you. Ultimately, you fall into calamity, depression, and despair; and finally you'll perish. "But the way of the ungodly shall perish." (v.6)

⟶ PRAYER ⟵

*"Lord, how prone I am to forget that my greatest good is You. Keep
me from hardening my heart over life's disappointments.
In Jesus' name. Amen."*

PROVERBS 29:5

"A man who flatters his neighbor spreads a net for his feet."

INSINCERE

The chances are about ten to one that when a man slaps you on the back, he wants you to cough up something.—*The Bible Friend*

If a man listens to such flattering words, and is influenced by them, he works his own ruin; self-deceived, he knows not his real condition, and accordingly makes grievous disaster of his life.

Be careful with flattery: a "smooth"word about someone's abilities or gifts. It may not be sincere, and the person who flatters may only have a self-centered purpose in mind. If you believe such flattery, ultimately it will lead to self-deception. The Bible teaches, ". . . love does no harm to a neighbor . . .." (Romans 13:10) This is the Bible way and the happy way. Don't use your words to plot the downfall of another when your words are not based on reality (praise). To flatter another for their generosity in hopes to be given money is wrong.

PRAYER

*"Lord, help me not to use my power of speech
to manipulate or harm another. In Jesus' name. Amen."*

March 1

PROVERBS 1:20–21, 23

"Wisdom calls aloud outside; she raises her voice in the open squares.
She cries out in the chief concourses, at the openings
of the gates in the city she speaks her words
. . . turn at my rebuke; surely I will pour out my spirit on you;
I will make my words known to you."

WISDOM'S WAY

*I*t is today possible to reach nearly 250 countries and territories from almost any phone in America. Twenty nations can be direct-dialed without operator assistance. This number will double in five years.

Seventy percent of the long-distance-circuit miles in the Bell System are no longer telephone lines. Signals are relayed from city to city by a network of microwave towers.

Voices no longer travel through private circuits when you make a telephone call. They are chopped up, converted to digital pulses the computer can digest, and then squeezed through existing routes with thousands of other voice signals. At the other end, the computer separates all the pieces, puts them back together again, and out comes a voice. This is called "pulse-code modulation."

Communications made simple! In the days of Solomon, author of Proverbs, communication was made in a much simpler and natural way. Rather than digital pulses, it was the human voice; announcements were made at the social gatherings spots, crossroads, in the open squares, at the city gates. Because of the importance of the announcements, it was at these places where news was broadcast. Likewise, wisdom lifts her voice up to be heard in these locations. Because of wisdom's value, the announcement was made accessible to everyone; no one need be left out as our Proverb so well states: Wisdom is to reverence God (1:7), to learn His ways and to obey His commands. "Turn at my rebuke, surely I will pour out my spirit on you . . .." There is no need for anyone to be without wisdom—the wisdom that acknowledges our Creator, obeys that Creator and eventually be able to stand before that Creator.

PRAYER

"Lord, you've made Your voice clear.
May I now heed that voice. In Jesus' name. Amen."

Pastor Dan Butcher | 61

PROVERBS 2:10–12

"When wisdom enters your heart,
and knowledge is pleasant to your soul,
discretion will preserve you; understanding will keep you,
to deliver you from the way of evil ..."

THE SKILL OF LIVING

W isdom is that which enables us to use knowledge rightly. The Hebrew word for wisdom means "skill." The most common use of this word is in the book of Proverbs. According to Proverbs, wisdom is (skill) in daily living. True wisdom involves not only the intellect but moral uprightness, because a sinful lifestyle is ultimately self-destructive. Wisdom is exalted as the only path to a full and fruitful life (3:13–26). Proverbs Chapter 2 declares wisdom will give you discretion (the ability of behaving or speaking in such a way as to avoid offense) (v.11), and it will keep you from the way of evil and the man who speaks perverse thing (v.12), and it will deliver you from the immoral woman who flatters with her words. (v.16)

To be successful before God and man, you must be wise as well as informed.

⊱ PRAYER ⊰

"Lord, in all our knowledge, help us to be wise.
In Jesus' name. Amen."

PROVERBS 3:25–26

*"Do not be afraid of sudden terror, nor of trouble from the wicked
when it comes; for the Lord will be your confidence
and will keep your foot from being caught."*

PRESCRIPTION FOR FEAR

*I*t is reported that the newspaper counselor, Ann Landers, received an
average of 10,000 letters each month, and nearly all of them from
people burdened with problems. She was asked if there was any one
of them which predominated throughout the letters she received, and
her reply was that the one problem above all others seemed to be fear.

> *People are afraid of losing their health, their wealth,
> their loved ones. People are afraid of life itself.*
> *—The Bible Friend*

The essence of this section is that (v.22) wisdom will preserve
your life. For this reason, the righteous can be free of the anxiety that
plagues the wicked (vv.23–25). Verse 23 is a general promise: it is not
an absolute guarantee that the wise will never have occasion to stumble. Compared to the unwise, however, they will experience tranquility.

The climax of the text is the promise that God will be beside the
follower of wisdom (v.26). Proverbs never implies that people can be
safe through their own wisdom. "Common sense" and personal competence are soon exhausted if God's protection is missing.

Do not fear. Ultimately God is our refuge. ". . . The Lord is my rock
and my fortress and my deliverer . . . my shield and the horn of my
salvation, my stronghold. I will call upon the Lord, who is worthy to be
praised; so, shall I be saved from my enemies." (Psalm 18:2-3)

⚘ PRAYER ⚘

*"Lord, I can do everything possible to be prepared for sudden terror,
but ultimately my protection comes from You.
May never forget it. In Jesus' name. Amen."*

PROVERBS 4:24

*"Put away from you a deceitful mouth
and put perverse lips far from you."*

LIPS THAT YIELD

President Walter G. Clippinger of Otterbein College in Ohio enjoys the story of the fake blind man.

The pitiable creature, with dark glasses and his little tin cup was standing on the street corner, patiently waiting for some small contribution. A kindly man passed by and generously dropped a dime in the poor old fellow's cup. Then for some reason he turned around, and to his surprise, saw the blind man's glasses pushed up on his forehead and his eager eyes closely examining the recent gift.

"I thought you were a blind man," said the disgruntled donor.

"Oh, no," was the answer. "I am only substituting for the regular blind man today. I'm not really blind at all."

"Well, where is the regular blind man?" asked the other.

"Oh, he's gone to the movies; it's his afternoon off."

Deceit is defined as "a person who causes someone to believe something that is not true for the purpose of gaining a personal advantage." As Christians, we are not to deceive anyone with either our words or actions. We are not to seek an advantage. Whenever we want an advantage and feel we must deceive in order to gain it, it's a clear indication we are not trusting God for that need. Eventually, God will grant us what is good (cf. Matthew 7:11) "If you then, being evil, know how to give good gifts to your children, how much more will your Father who is in heaven give good things to those who ask Him?"

If we believe, then we can trust. If we trust, then we can leave off with deceit, for deceit is a perverse use of our lips.

⟿ PRAYER ⟾

*"Lord, help me with my lips, not to pervert their use by deceit.
In Jesus' name. Amen."*

PROVERBS 5:15

*"Drink water from your own cistern
and running water from your own well."*

UNTAINTED

Some years ago, the most married man in the world was found in Yugoslavia. It happened this way: A young woman confided to her girl cousin of her impending marriage to a man. The bridegroom was so shy and timid that he wanted to keep the marriage a secret. The cousin got curious. She got a glimpse of the bridegroom after the secret wedding and recognized him as her own husband. He had also married her secretly, claiming to be shy and timid.

That was only a beginning. A total of fifty women came forward and claimed that he had individually married them. In each case, he was the same bashful bridegroom. They called him Ivanhoe the Terrible, breaker of women's hearts. He was a traveling salesman, going from wife to wife by plane, supporting all fifty of them, with the explanation to each that his duties as a traveling salesman kept him away so much of the time.

They put him in jail, and he begged to stay there. He would rather be sent to prison than face those fifty wives.

I have a better idea; God's way is always the best way. Perhaps turning this "cad"(a man who behaves dishonorably toward women) over to his fifty wives would be a good idea after all.

Do not drink the dirty waters of adultery, instead "drink water from your own cistern, running water from your own well." Remain faithful to your spouse and avoid the heartache of adultery.

PRAYER

*"Lord, keep me faithful to You and my spouse,
though trials and years may dim my view,
faithfulness is always right before You.
In Jesus' name. Amen."*

March 6

PROVERBS 6:16–19

*"These six things the Lord hates
. . . one who sows discord among brethren."*

DOES A LOVING GOD HATE?

*D*uring the administration of Lincoln, a delegation from a western state called upon him with a written protest about a certain appointment. The paper had a list of specific objections against a Senator Baker, a long-time and beloved friend of the president. The objections were definite reflections on Baker's character.

Holding the paper in his hand, Lincoln asked with calm dignity: "This is my paper which you have given me?" When they assured him that it was, he asked further: "To do with as I please?" "Certainly, Mr. President," replied the spokesman.

Lincoln leaned over to the fireplace, laid the paper on the hot coals, turned to the group and said: "Good day, gentlemen."

Right! Many items of discord (a lack of agreement or harmony between people), are best burned. How we relish to hear the miss-deeds or short comings of another. Worse yet, we spread them around, however, God takes a deem view of any type of discord among brothers. He hates it! Gossip (a person who habitually reveals personal or sensational facts) is often the vehicle that produces discord. Such discord has the force of a Tornado, leaving in its wake destruction and misery, and a lack of agreement among family, church and community. Discord, given time, takes on its own life as it's passed from one individual to another, each adding their own comments, until finally it has taken on a life all its own, far removed from any truth it may have had originally.

Be sure of this, anyone who sow discord to you about another, will one day will be sowing discord about you to another.

✎ PRAYER ✐

*"Lord, remind us there are somethings that a loving God hates,
sowing discord is one of them. In Jesus' name. Amen."*

PROVERBS 7:1-2, 5

"My son, keep my words, and treasure my commands within you.
Keep my commands and live, and my law as the apple of your eye . . .
that they may keep you from the immoral woman,
from the seductress who flatters with her words."

PRONE TO WONDER

*F*rom London comes this report: Two women were talking at a fashionable London restaurant about their husbands. They showed each other photographs—and realized they were married to the same man.

Today the man—hotel night porter John Jones, 47—is in prison for five years. He was married before he met either of the two women.

The problem of immorality (see 2:16–19; 5:1–23; 6:20–35) and our current passage highlight the problem of adultery (sex with someone other than your spouse) and fornication (sex before marriage). There is a solution to immorality, keep God's commands . . . as the apple of your eye. People should treasure God's word as closely as you would treasure the pupil of your eye. If you do, ". . . they will keep you from the immoral woman, from the seductress who flatters with her words."7:5

Life is at its best when we do it God's way.

PRAYER

"Lord, I'm tempted to wonder, help me to value your Word
as the most prized possession I have. In Jesus' name. Amen."

PROVERBS 8:13

*"The fear of the Lord is to hate evil;
pride and arrogance and the evil way
and the perverse mouth I hate."*

A FEW THINGS TO HATE

In Shantung Compound, Langdon Gilkey defined sin as devotion to a finite interest; it is an overriding loyalty or concern for the self, its existence, and its prestige.

Pride, usually considered a virtue, is, under some circumstances, a basic form of sin. Dr. Karl Menninger, in *Whatever Became of Sin?* reminded us that vanity, egocentricity, arrogance, self-adoration, selfishness, and self-love are really synonyms for pride. Theologically, pride asserts itself into pride of power, knowledge, and virtue.

Writing in *Power, A New Social Analysis*, Bertrand Russell noted, "Every man would like to be God if it were possible; some few find it difficult to admit the impossibility."

How passing is this life, to live in pride (assumed superiority), arrogance (an exaggerated idea of one's importance) and a perverted (to turn away from what is right and good, corrupt) mouth is to waste your life. Also, we must be reminded that our reverence toward God displays itself in hating some items. We all know we are to love God and love our neighbor (Matthew 22:37–39), but our Proverb today instructs us to hate evil, pride, arrogance, and the perverse mouth.

So, here are some things we are to hate as a Christian, but first hate them in your own life if you have fallen into their snare before you turn your sights on others.

⟶ PRAYER ⟵

*"Lord, help me keep an eye on those things You hate,
and I should as well. In Jesus' name. Amen."*

PROVERBS 9:8

*"Do not correct a scoffer, lest he hate you;
rebuke a wise man, and he will love you."*

COUNSEL OR CONTEMPT

Sarah Dale Mannakee, who was born during the presidency of Ulysses S. Grant, and once taught where the Hatfield's and McCoy's feuded—Williamson, West Virginia—started painting seriously at age eighty-four, and had her first show when she was ninety-four. "I started out painting the things I knew and loved, like rivers, oceans, flowers , and hillsides." Some of her secrets for longevity included "stay busy, sleep well, eat well . . . and don't be a sourpuss!"

Good advice! A wise man (one who carefully considers consequences) will heed good health counsel; the scoffer (one who is disagreeable, treats something with contempt) will only hate you if you try to correct him. All Gehenna breaks out. A wise man is wise because he *loves* good advice. Sadly though, those who need it most are the last to heed it.

PRAYER

*"Lord, help me to heed wise counsel, not despise it.
In Jesus' name. Amen."*

PROVERBS 10:12

"Hatred stirs up strife, but love covers all sins."

A LITTLE HOUSE CLEANING

*Hating people is like burning down your own house
to get rid of a rat.—Harry Emerson Fosdick*

"I hate humanity. I am allergic to it. I see no one. I do not go out. I am disgusted with everything. Men are beasts, and even beasts don't behave like them."

Those are the words of actress Brigitte Bardot, sex symbol of the 1950s and 1960s. In those years, she made the headlines with her three marriages, a series of lovers, and "a sun-kissed life on the French Riviera." She planned to quit the movie world and retire to a farm.

Hate is an option. You can hate those who have done you wrong, whether imagined or real, but the reality is, over time, hate corrodes the soul: ". . . a little leaven leavens the whole lump," as Paul says (I Corinthian 5:6) You can't contain hate in one little area of your heart and not expect it to effect other areas. It will eventually permeate the soul like leaven does dough.

Do you need to forgive someone? When you forgive, you release your desire to punish them for their sin against you. God is no fool: "vengeance is Mine . . .." (Deuteronomy 32:35) God will take care of all injustice. Just remember, we have all sinned against God: ". . . for there is none righteous, no not one." (Romans 3:10) And if we fail to forgive others, God will not forgive us. (Matthew 6:14) "For if you forgive men their trespasses, your heavenly Father will also forgive you. But if you do not forgive men their trespasses, neither will your Father forgive your trespasses."

⁓ PRAYER ⁓

*"Father forgive us our trespasses as we forgive those
who trespass against us. Help me to believe this and to do it.
In Jesus' name. Amen."*

PROVERBS 11:3

*"The integrity of the upright will guide them,
but the perversity of the unfaithful will destroy them."*

CHOICES MADE SIMPLE

General William F. Dean was a prized prisoner of the Communists during the Korean struggle. One day, the General was advised that he had five minutes in which to write a letter to his family. It appeared to be the end. Calmly he accepted the order and proceeded to write. In the body of this now-historic letter appears a single line worthy of remembrance: "Tell Bill the word is integrity."

Integrity is your guiding light. Integrity has been defined as firm adherence to a code of morals, incorruptibility. I would often say to my son, "Whenever in doubt, do the next right thing." Never compromise the right thing, and that right thing is best defined by the Bible. The best way is always God's way.

Wondering what decision to make next? If you choose the side of righteousness, you'll never regret the choice. Integrity may not feel right; it may cost you, tire you, sometimes exasperate you. But you will eliminate the guilt and shame of perversity, which our Proverb teaches will eventually destroy you.

The choice is simple, and sometimes the simplest of choices is just plain doing the right thing; choose integrity and shield yourself against destruction.

PRAYER

*"Lord, remind me that integrity is the best of guides.
In Jesus' name. Amen."*

March 12

PROVERBS 12:14

*"A man will be satisfied with good by the fruit of his mouth,
and the recompense of a man's hand will be rendered to him."*

THE FRUIT OF MY MOUTH

In a certain pond on one of the farms in the East were two ducks and frog. Now these neighbors were the best of friends. All day long they used to play together. But as the hot summer days came, the pond began to dry up and soon there was such a little bit of water that they all realized that they would have to move. Now the ducks could easily fly to another place, but what about their friend the frog?

Finally, it was decided that they would put a stick in the bill of each duck, and then the frog would hang onto the stick with his mouth and they would fly him to another pond. And so, they did.

As they were flying, a farmer out in his field looked up and saw them and said, "Well, isn't that a clever idea! I wonder who thought of it!"

The frog said, "I did . . ."

Like our friend, it is best to keep a tight control over our mouth. James says it this way: ". . . let every man be swift to hear, slow to speak, slow to wrath . . .." (James 1:19) If you hope to be satisfied with "the fruit of your mouth," as today's Proverb teaches, watch when you speak, how you speak, and what you speak. The mouth is the hardest of habits to control, but if you control it properly, you can control any part of your body (James 3:2) ". . . If anyone does not stumble in word, he is a perfect (mature) man, able also to bridle the whole body."

So, what you say can bring you a wealth of fruit, just as a man's hard work brings him recompense.

PRAYER

*"Lord, remind me that what I say can reward me
just as much as a hard day's labor will.
In Jesus' name. Amen."*

March 13

PROVERBS 13:4

"The soul of a lazy man desires and has nothing;
but the soul of the diligent shall be made rich."

OH, LORD, BUT I'M TIRED

Even though over one-thousand new books are published every day—not counting pamphlets, booklets, and government reports—the Bible remains the world's bestseller. It has been translated into more languages and dialects than any other book. Yet, the Bible is not read as often or with as much understanding as its wide circulation might suggest.

The old expression, "Jack of all trades, but master of none," actually goes like this: "Jack of all trades, Master of one." We should be Master of at least one book in our lives—the Bible. As Sir Walter Scott well said, "There is only one Book." What keeps us from such mastery? Laziness! We have time for all the little time robbing tyrants in our lives, but the really important issues, we seem to abandon. Partially through a lack of priorities, partially through circumstances, but largely through laziness. After a difficult time at work, I always found myself fighting against my natural inclination for ease, repose, and slumber; all the while fighting the voice of the Holy Spirit urging me to read His word and pray.

Laziness capitalizes on our natural inclinations and often robs us of the riches that are ours—such as peace when trials are quickly upon us, wisdom during difficult decisions, and the moral strength to say "no" when we often say "yes." But above all, it robs us of God's favored presence, His communion with our soul, His sweet confidence that all is well between us and our God.

PRAYER

"Lord, I like my laziness, it's so warm and inviting,
but it robs me of Your presence and blessing.
Help me heed today's Proverb and be diligent
to mine the riches in Your Word.
In Jesus' name. Amen."

Pastor Dan Butcher | 73

PROVERBS 14:9

"Fools mock at sin, but among the upright there is favor."

ESSENTIAL PURPOSE

A flippant youth asked a preacher, "You say that unsaved people carry a weight of sin. I feel nothing. How heavy is sin? Is it ten pounds? Eighty pounds?" The preacher replied by asking the youth, "If you laid a four-hundred-pound weight on a corpse, would it feel the load?" The youth replied, "It would feel nothing, because it is dead." The preacher concluded, "That spirit, too, is indeed dead which feels no load of sin or is indifferent to its burden and flippant about its presence." The youth was silenced

Well spoken. People today mock (tease or laugh in a scornful manner) the idea of sin. Sin has been defined as an immoral act considered to be a transgression against a divine law. We sin when we use God's name in vain (Exodus 20:9), we sin when we murder, or when we neglect God, or dishonor our parents, or commit adultery, or steal (Exodus 20). To mock the reality of sin in our own lives is to fly in the face of the Bible, for it teaches ". . . for all have sinned and fall short of the glory of God." (Romans 3:23) It also denies the necessity for Christ's death (I Peter 3:18) "For Christ also suffered once for sins, the just for the unjust, that He might bring us to God . . .." For those who deny God, sin robs them of purpose, meaning, and life; for Jesus said, ". . . I have come to give you life, and that you may have it more abundantly (John 10:10). The reality of sin, even personal sin in each of our lives, is evident because so few people have a sense of peace and purpose in life. The effect of sin is to rob you of these.

∽ PRAYER ∾

"Lord, help me to never deny the reality of my own sin,
and its effect of robbing us of peace and purpose.
In Jesus' name. Amen."

PROVERBS 15:21

"Folly is joy to him who is destitute of discernment,
but a man of understanding walks uprightly."

JUDGE WELL

*O*ne of the strangest things *Believe-it-or-Not* Ripley told about was the woman in Genoa, Italy, called the "Doughnut Seller." For fifty-two years, Paisanan sold doughnuts on the streets until she had made enough money to hire a sculptor to create a beautiful statue of herself to be placed in the cemetery of Genoa. The statue was finished before her death, and she "spent the last three years of her life gazing at it."—Christian Victor

Folly has been defined as "lack of good sense." Now, to erect a statue of oneself, at great expense, and then to waste the remaining years of your life gazing on it, is a waste of a life.

Yet, in our day, people are just as foolish as they watch endless hours of TV, or play video games on their computer or Smart phone, when they could be investing their time in more worthwhile endeavors, such as helping the poor, getting an education, or volunteering. The problem lays with discernment: "the ability to judge well." Those who lack discernment, joy in the petty, worthless, or trivial. There are good books to read, places to visit, and lives you can impact for good, if you live with understanding. That starts with reverence for God and His ways. A little foolishness has its place, but not a prominent one.

⋅⁓ PRAYER ⁓⋅

"Lord, help me not to 'joy' in a lack of good sense,
but instead, to judge well my opportunities.
In Jesus' name. Amen."

PROVERBS 16:32

*"He who is slow to anger is better than the mighty,
and he who rules his spirit than he who takes a city."*

A FUSE TO SHORT

A college president not long ago made this arresting statement to a class of graduating seniors: "It gets easier and easier for man to dominate his universe . . . and harder for him to dominate himself." He went on to say, "It matters little what you learn or express if in the end you cannot find some ways of working things out with your neighbors." We cannot dominate the universe, but with God's help, we can dominate ourselves.—Mrs. A. E. Janzen

This speaks well with our Proverb. What does it really matter if you can take a city but have no control over your own temper. Eventually, the temper will dominate you, and your past conquests will pale in value when they recall your many outbursts, embarrassments, and unreasonable behavior.

If you want a sure-fire way to embarrass your entire family, lose your temper at a family gathering or public setting. After a while, your entire family will care less what you've accomplished. What they will remember about you is how you displayed grace and patience under pressure. The person who does this continually will not be forgotten. Why? Because patience is so personal. We all need it!

∽ PRAYER ∝

*"Lord, help me to have a longer fuse than what I have now,
and help me to remember how people love to be shown patience.
In Jesus' name. Amen."*

PROVERBS 17:14

*"The beginning of strife is like releasing water;
therefore, stop contention before a quarrel starts."*

THIS DOES NOT HAVE TO END POORLY

An old writer tells of two brothers who went out to take a walk in the night, and one of them looked up to the sky and said, "I wish I had a pasture-field as large as the night heavens." And the other brother looked up into the sky, and said, "I wish I had as many oxen as there are stars in the sky."

"Well," said the first, "how would you feed so many oxen?" Said the second, "I would turn them into your pasture."

"What! whether I permitted it or not?"

"Yes, whether you permitted it or not."

And there arose a quarrel; and when the quarrel ended, one had slain the other.—Walter Baxendale

Silly, most certainly, but many fights with others end up just as deadly. The cure is to stop the contention before an ugly argument breaks out. If a disagreement breaks out, and who is there that has not been in one, it takes only a few moments before you can see that this will end poorly. The wise person will leave off the contention early on. He knows this will lead to nothing but bitterness, broken relations, and feelings of guilt.

Put on the brakes when you see the stop light. If you do not, you're only heading for catastrophe.

⇁ PRAYER ↽

*"Lord, keep me from arguing over the trivial,
and remind me that most of it is trivial.
In Jesus' name. Amen."*

PROVERBS 18:19

"A brother offended is harder to win than a strong city,
and contentions are like the bars of a castle."

DON'T THROW ROCKS
IF YOU LIVE IN A GLASS HOUSE

The Monatsschloos, a vast palatial edifice which still towers above the city of Salzburg, Austria, was a birthday offering to a fair lady. The giver was the mighty Count of Hohenems, ruler of Salzburg from 1612 to 1619. The recipient was the beauteous Barbara Mabon. The promise made in a moment of tenderness was soon forgotten. When Barbara's birthday was only four weeks away, the count suddenly remembered his pledge. It was not too late. He summoned his subjects and eloquently described his predicament. He called on them to help him. And they did not fail him.

Several thousand mighty masons, bricklayers, and carpenters went to work to redeem their prince's word. They labored night and day, in relays, without any appreciable rest or pay and completed the stronghold just in time for Barbara's natal anniversary. It is an all-time speed record.

What a wonder! Still yet, it is easier to build a castle in four weeks to keep your promise than it is to win an offended brother. I am amazed when people, even Christians, can hold a grudge or an offense for years and even for a lifetime. They will not call, speak, or communicate because of some offense they experienced when they were siblings or adults. Good grief, how about a forgiving heart? Christ taught if you do not forgive, you will not be forgiven. "So My heavenly Father also will do to you if each of you, from his heart, does not forgive his brother his trespasses.")Matthew 18:35)

So, who do you need to forgive? It's time to let that go, before there is no more time for you, and you find yourself standing before God.

⟨ PRAYER ⟩

"Lord, forgive us our trespasses as we forgive
those who trespass against us. In Jesus' name. Amen."

March 19

*"What is desired in a man is kindness,
and a poor man is better than a liar."*

HEART ISSUES

*L*ord Palmerston, Queen Victoria's Prime Minister, was crossing Westminster Bridge when a little girl ahead dropped a jug of milk. The jug broke into fragments, and she dissolved into tears. Palmerston having no money with him dried her eyes by telling her that if she came to the same spot next day at that hour he would pay for both jug and milk. The following morning, during a cabinet meeting, he suddenly remembered his promise to the little girl, left the bewildered ministers, dashed across the bridge, popped half a crown into the waiting child's hand and hurried back.—*All Nations Missionary Review*

Kindness is something we can all afford. It does not require money, though money can be used, it does not require a degree, or rank, or culture, but it does require a kind heart. You can be poor and still show kindness, but if you are rich and a liar, you will not enjoy God's favor. Really in the end, kindness does not compare to the joy we receive when we are kind. God sees the world so differently than we do. He'd rather you be kind than rich, poor than a liar. It is high time we start seeing life as God does.

PRAYER

*"Lord, help me to see life as You do,
and to value what You value: kindness and honesty.
In Jesus' name. Amen."*

PROVERBS 20:2

*"The wrath of a king is like the roaring of a lion;
whoever provokes him to anger sins against his own life."*

DON'T GET IN THE CAGE WITH A LION

French aristocrat, Baron Richard D'Arcy, kept a strange pet in his home: a two-year-old lion. One night, the baron tried to make his pet enter the bathroom where it usually spent the night, but it refused to go and leaped on its master. In a matter of minutes, the lion had clawed the baron to death. Later the police killed the beast with sub machine-gun fire.

It's sad that the lion had to die, but Baron D'Arcy should have known better. This illustrates well the Proverb for today: do not anger those who are more powerful than yourself. The king is one example. Perhaps in our day, it would be our supervisor, policeman, or governing officials. People are not all that forgiving, and if you provoke your boss, for instance, they will be sure to pay you back. So, if you must disagree with those in authority, do it in an agreeable way, or you will be sure to pay, and pay you will.

Do not poke at the lion; he can be most disagreeable.

⟶ PRAYER ⟵

*"Lord, for those of us who are slow learners,
remind us that provoking the lion (boss, official, policeman, etc.)
is going to turn out badly for us.
In Jesus' name. Amen."*

PROVERBS 21:30–31

*"There is no wisdom or understanding or counsel against the Lord,
the horse is prepared for the day of battle, but deliverance is of the Lord."*

NOT MY PREFERENCE

"*M*odern physics faces an antimony in its study of light. There is cogent evidence to show that light consists of waves and equally cogent evidence to show that it consists of particles. It is not apparent how light can be both waves and particles, but the evidence is there, and so neither view can be ruled out in favor of the other. The two seemingly incompatible positions must be held together, and both must be treated as true . . .."[1]

It is possible in this world for a free man to make preparations for an event, as our Proverb states, guided by wisdom, understanding, and counsel; yet all the while the final outcome is not based on those preparation but on God's sovereign choices. This is baffling in one regard, and conundrum (a confusing and difficult problem or question). On the other hand, it is comforting. How can man be free to choose and be held accountable for choices, yet God overrules for His own purposes? But in comforting, we can learn to trust God for good and noble efforts that go either unrewarded, unrecognized, or unsuccessful. It is better to trust God with our plans while we strive to do good, even when it appears no good has come out of it.

PRAYER

*"Lord, You're ultimately in control.
I trust You for outcomes, though they may not be my preference.
In Jesus' name. Amen."*

March 22

PROVERBS 22:5

*"Thorns and snares are in the way of the perverse;
he who guards his soul will be far from them."*

ON GUARD

*P*erversity has been defined as "a deliberate desire to behave in an unreasonable or unacceptable way; the quality of being contrary to accepted standards or practice."

A man who steals is perverse; a man or woman who live together without being married is perverse; a man who bears a false witness against his neighbor is perverse. All these, and many more, are unacceptable and unreasonable, at least to the Bible. Our culture has changed, but the Bible has not. Outdated, some shout from the roof tops, but nature's design well illustrates the Bible's standard is best. I remember reading in the newspaper when AIDS first broke out among society, that the best safeguard against the disease was not to use intravenous drugs with dirty needles and to have only one sex partner. Multiple sex partners, especially among the homosexual, increased the spread of the virus. Heterosexual partners and monogamy for life is the Biblical standard. So, perversity as defined by the Bible, is the reasonable standard, and to live contrary to it invites a whole host of "thorns and snares," into your life: disease, heartbreak, and futility.

Guard your soul against perversity, it will improve your health and bring peace to your soul.

⟶ PRAYER ⟵

*"Lord, keep me reasonable and acceptable in Your sight,
and steer me away from the 'thorns and snares' in this life.
In Jesus' name. Amen.*

PROVERBS 23:22

*"Listen to your father who begot you,
and do not despise your mother when she is old."*

YOUR BEST FUTURE

*T*he future destiny of a child is the work of a mother.—Napoleon Bonaparte

Doctor Charles Parkhurst, distinguished preacher and reformer from New York, in an address in which he dealt with his early religious life, related how he had often heard his father pray in the church, at the family altar, and at the family table. But it was only when he heard him praying aloud on his knees in the barn that he knew the reality of prayer and the deep reality of the religious life.—C. E. Macartney

So, there you have it. Praying parents give the best counsel, the best example. Listen, my friend, to their example. Spend time yourself on your knees before God. It will purify your soul, steel your resolve, and grant you the wisdom to face a sometimes hostile and hazardous world. Call often on them for their experience, for when you listen to your parents, most often you are listening to the voice of God.

⟨ ∾ PRAYER ∾ ⟩

*"Lord, it's hard to slow down and listen,
but may we be still enough to listen to the counsel of our parents.
In Jesus' name. Amen."*

PROVERBS 24:17–18

"Do not rejoice when your enemy falls,
and do not let your heart be glad when he stumbles,
lest the Lord see it, and it displease Him,
and he turn away His wrath from him."

TURN ABOUT IS FAIR PLAY?

When World War I broke out, the War Ministry in London dispatched a coded message to one of the British outposts in the inaccessible areas of Africa. The message read: "War declared. Arrest all enemy aliens in your district."

The War Ministry received his prompt reply: "Have arrested ten Germans, six Belgians, four Frenchman, two Italians, three Austrians, and an American. Please advise immediately who we're at war with."

We get confused as to who the real enemy is. We have our own personal list. "Lord, I sure hope you see fit to break his leg or at least chip his tooth in a fall. Don't kill him Lord; just make him suffer for a while." However, God's perspective is so different than ours. He says to "love our enemies, bless those who curse you, do good to those who hate you . . .." (cf. Matthew 5:44) We're not even to rejoice over the fall of an enemy, lest God turn away His wrath. The judgment of God is a last resource. He prefers mercy over judgment. (cf. Hosea 6:6 and Matthew 9:13) However, we prefer that our enemies are judged first, and Your mercy is saved for us.

Do not rejoice over the downfall of an enemy, or even someone who mildly irritates you. Remember, our enemies are not necessarily God's enemies. God probably has a greater good in mind for them.

⌒☙⌒ PRAYER ❧⌒

"Lord, I have my enemies. Help me to remember
there was a time when I was Your enemy,
lost in my rebellion and pride.
In Jesus' name. Amen."

PROVERB 25:24

*"It is better to dwell in a corner of a housetop,
than in a house shared with a contentious woman."*

MARITAL COMBAT

Chauncey M. Depew had an old friend at Peekskill who, after courting the same woman for twenty years, married her. "Josephus," said Chauncey, "why did you not marry that splendid woman long before now; why did you wait all these years?"

"Chauncey," explained the other, "I waited until she talked herself out. You see, I wanted a quiet married life."—Maxwell Droke

Contentious has been defined as causing, or likely to cause, an argument. Some things are best left alone. However, there are those, in this case women, who cannot. They will argue over the slightest provocation, most of which are unnecessary. They seem to lack the capacity to be tolerant (accept or endure something one does not agree with). Just because you do not agree, does not mean you have to be disagreeable. There are subjects that disagreeing over is necessary, but there are some women who cannot make that distinction. Everything they do not agree with they argue over, and argue, and argue. Their marriage is a constant combat zone. What is needed is good, old tolerance, prayer, and a gentle and quiet spirit, which is highly honored in God's eyes. (cf. I Peter 3:3,4) "Do not let your adornment be merely outward-arranging the hair, wearing gold, or putting on fine apparel—rather let it be the hidden person of the heart, with the incorruptible beauty of a gentle and quiet spirit, which is very precious in the sigh of God."

PRAYER

*"Lord, for all of us, we need a healthy dose of tolerance,
gentleness, and a quiet spirit.
In Jesus' name. Amen."*

PROVERBS 26:2

"Like a flitting sparrow, like a flying swallow,
so a curse without cause shall not alight."

HERE TODAY GONE TOMORROW

*A*n undeserved comment or attitude about another will not stay
long enough to have a penalty attached to it. How we worry
about what others think or say about us, truth will prevail, lies and
exaggeration will fall away like the flight of the flitting sparrow. The
flitting (lasting for a very short time) sparrow will be on the ground
but for a moment and then off again to another spot, only to be there
for another short moment. So, stop worrying about what is said against
you or about you. Lies have a short shelf-life. Instead, pray and trust
God (cf. Proverbs 3:5,6).

✎ PRAYER ✎

"Lord, I worry too much about
what's here today and gone tomorrow.
Help me to trust You about my reputation.
In Jesus' name. Amen."

PROVERBS 27:8

"Like a bird that wanders from its nest,
is a man who wanders from his place."

TO WANDER IS TO JEOPARDIZE

*T*his verse may speak against a person abandoning his responsibilities at home along with its comforts. Just as a bird wandering from its nest too early or too far brings hardship on itself, so a young person leaving home too soon may find himself unable to care for himself (e.g., the prodigal son, Luke 15:11–32).

Do not grow weary of one's own home with its duties and routines! If you have a wandering spirit and charge off into some distant adventure, forsaking responsibilities too young, you set yourself up for danger. Your expectations will not be met. The Prodigal Son of Luke 15:11–24 found out the hard way that his youthful energy and dreams were not at all met. If you're familiar with the story, the young man demanded his inheritance early on, went to a distant country and squandered his inheritance on wine, women, and song. But things changed, and indeed they did, for he found himself, lonely, destitute and penniless. Home didn't look so bad then. Fortunately, he returned to his father, who in this parable represents God, and was warmly and lovingly welcomed back. As Christ describes in verse 24, "for this son was dead and is alive again; he was lost and is found. And they began to be merry."

Home is eventually left by adults of mature mind, but to leave as a youth or without preparation can be disastrous.

⇜ PRAYER ⇝

"Lord, help be to stay put and stay at it
until I am mature enough to move on.
In Jesus' name. Amen."

PROVERBS 28:9

*"One who turns away his ear from hearing the law,
even his prayer is an abomination."*

I'LL GET AROUND TO IT

There is a form of deafness known to physicians in which the person affected is able to hear everything except words. In such a case, the ear, as an apparatus for mere hearing, may be so perfect that the tick of a watch or the song of a bird is really appreciated. But owing to a local injury deeper than the ear, for it is in the brain itself, all spoken words of his mother tongue are as unintelligible to the sufferer as those of a foreign language.

Give him a book and he may read as understandingly as ever, but every word addressed to him through his ear reaches his consciousness only as a sound, not as a word.—W. H. Thompson

I guess God has a "form" of deafness. When the unrighteous, or wicked, or otherwise godless man finally calls on God for help or for a petition, God does not hear. I have repeatedly reminded my audience, "God is no fool." Those who spurn God's law through disbelief will find God terribly distant when their hour of crisis comes. Proverbs 15:8: "The sacrifice of the wicked is an abomination to the Lord."

The good news is God will hear your cry of repentance. Call on God for salvation now, while God still hears (II Corinthians 6:2) ". . . Behold, now is the accepted time; behold, now is the day of salvation." That way, when you cry to Him as a son, He'll hear you.

⮞ PRAYER ⮜

*"Lord, remind me gently that
You stretch out Your kind hand
to me daily for salvation.
May I never reject it,
believing someday I'll get right with you.
In Jesus' name. Amen."*

PROVERBS 29:20

"Do you see a man hasty in his words?
There is more hope for a fool than for him."

THE DISCIPLINE THAT DELIVERS

The dull, stupid man may be instructed and guided and made to listen to reason; the hasty and ill-advised speaker consults no one, takes no thought before he speaks, nor reflects on the effect of his words; such a man it is almost impossible to reform.

Calvin Coolidge wisely expressed it: "One of the first lessons a president has to learn is that every word he says weighs a ton."

What is the solution to such a tragic disposition? James offers this: "So then, my beloved brethren, let every man be swift to hear, slow to speak, slow to wrath; for the wrath of man does not produce the righteousness of God." (James 1:19)

Swift, slow, and slower. Listen more, speak less, and be angered even less than that. What a discipline it is to follow James' sage advice, but the benefits will reward you richly.

PRAYER

"Lord, help me to be quick to hear and slow to speak
though I have a propensity to reverse the order.
In Jesus' name. Amen."

PROVERBS 30:33

"For as the churning of milk produces butter,
and wringing the nose produces blood,
so the forcing of wrath produces strife."

LOOKING FOR A FIGHT

This Proverb lists three activities that bring a result: "churning of milk produces butter," "wringing the nose produces blood," and the third result, anger will eventually bring strife (angry disagreement over fundamental issues). If you have stored up anger in your soul, it will eventually show itself in a fight, and you will be the one to pick it.

They say in Malabar, "Anger is a stone cast into a wasp's nest."—Septuagint. Why would anyone want to cast a rock into a wasp's nest? For the same reason why people pick a fight—because they want to. Their anger has finally boiled over. They have been simmering for a while, now it's boiled over.

The best way to diffuse anger is to cast your care on the Lord. "Casting all your care upon Him, for the He cares for you." (I Peter 5:7) Talk to God about what's angering you, and if you don't have time to pray, remember this, swallowing angry words before you say them is better than having to eat them afterwards.

PRAYER

"Lord, remind me when I'm in a disagreement to 'keep cool;
anger is not an argument.'—Daniel Webster
In Jesus' name. Amen."

PROVERBS 31:11–12

*"The heart of her husband safely trusts her;
so he will have no lack of gain.
She does him good and not evil all the days of her life."*

SHE IS A PERPETUAL SPRING

"The heart of her husband trusts in her." You can trust her faithfulness to your marriage vows. She is not flirtatious or immodest. When you go out of town, you do not have to worry that she will be with another man (7:19). You can trust her with your reputation. She will bear your name with dignity. She will not gossip or reveal your secrets to others. You can trust her with your money (and your credit cards). She will not spend you into debt. You can trust her oversight of your children and household.

A woman like this has her own beauty, as this Proverb also teaches in verse 30: "Charm is deceitful and beauty is passing, but a woman who fears the Lord, she shall be praised." A plain-looking woman who honors God has an inner beauty that overshadows her looks. Oh, how happy (blessed) is the man who has a woman like this; "she does him good and not evil all the days of her life." (v.12) Charm is deceitful (it has other motives) and beauty is passing, for sure, but a woman like this will be a perpetual spring of joy to her husband long after better looking women have lost their beauty. Hopefully, the man she is married to is worthy of her.

PRAYER

*"Lord, we stand in awe of Your word,
it is truly a lamp to our feet and a light to our path.
Help us to walk in its light. In Jesus' name. Amen."*

April 1

PROVERBS 1:19

"So are the ways of everyone who is greedy for gain;
it takes away the life of its owners."

HOW TO AMBUSH YOURSELF

*A*n eccentric adventurer named Harry Lasseter went to Sydney, Australia in 1931, cornered three promoters and told them a fantastic tale that so fired their imaginations that it never occurred to them that the man might be unbalanced, dreaming, or just lying to get a job. He stated that, as a lone prospector in the barren back country thirty years before, he had discovered a chain of rocks that he was certain contained at least $5,000,000,000 worth of gold.

Believing him, the promoters organized an expedition and, led by Lasseter, set out to claim the fabulous reef. As he failed to find it after a search of many months, the leaders ordered their party to return home, having realized that the reef existed only in the man's imagination. Although Lasseter partly admitted it, he went on alone—and died of thirst. To stop others from making the same mistake, the hoax was given considerable publicity. Yet, within the next few years, ten other expeditions not only went out to find this reef but got lost and their rescues cost the Australian government approximately $2,000,000.

Proverbs 13:21 says "Evil pursues sinners . . ." To be greedy for gain is a sure-fire way to entangle yourself in evil. The essence of today's Proverb is well expressed in 1 Timothy 6:10: "For the love of money is the root of all evil; which while some coveted after, they have erred from the faith, and pierced themselves through with many sorrows."

Greed (an intense and selfish desire for something, especially wealth, power, etc.), is the way of the wicked. (Psalm 9:16) "The wicked is snared in the work of his own hands."

➤ PRAYER ➤

"Lord, protect me against greed,
lest I find myself pursuing 'many sorrows.'
In Jesus' name. Amen."

PROVERBS 2:7

"He is a shield to those who walk uprightly."

SHIELDED

The tragedy of Watergate for the whole country is that people at the heart of our government yielded to the anxiety that whispers so convincingly in all our hearts that achievement is more important than character. God help us out of this wreckage to learn anew that the highest value and most enduring power in human enterprise is character.

If you want God's protective power, His delivering power, His intervening power, then walk uprightly. Set aside your earthly accomplishments, privilege, power, and esteem; and instead walk in the shadow of God Almighty. He will then give you His protective shield. Don't sacrifice your character to gain man's passing applause and in consequence lose the shield of God's protection.

PRAYER

"Lord, I take You as my protective shield,
and give my allegiance to an upright life.
In Jesus' name. Amen."

PROVERBS 3:27

*"Do not withhold good from those to whom it is due,
when it is in the power of your hand to do so."*

OUR GOOD OBLIGATIONS

Sunday, 8:15 pm. A junior at the University of Miami walked into the dingy third-floor office of "Universal International Term papers Limited, Inc." He scribbled out his order and handed it to the clerk. "I'm sorry," she said. "We don't have that paper in stock. We'll have to order it." The clerk dialed the firm's main office in Boston and then attached the telephone receiver to a copying machine. A few minutes later, page after page of an impressively researched paper, transmitted from Boston, rolled off the copier.—*Time*

People deserve honesty. Our Proverb teaches that all appropriate obligations are our debts. Most of all, we are to "Owe no one anything except to love one another, for he who loves another has fulfilled the law." (Romans 13:8)

Is it time to fulfill an obligation of good that you have been meaning to but haven't had the time? Take the time now to make that phone call, restore that money, or offer that apology, etc.

The fulfillment to love our neighbor in deed, not just in word, fulfills all good to whom it is due.

⟶ PRAYER ⟵

*"Lord, help me never to withhold good from the deserving.
In Jesus' name. Amen."*

PROVERBS 4:7–8

"Wisdom is the principal thing; therefore, get wisdom . . .
Exalt her, and she will promote you;
she will bring you honor, when you embrace her."

THE PRINCIPAL PURSUIT

*P*roverbs defines wisdom as originating in the "fear of God." (Proverbs 1:7) True wisdom involves not only intelligence but also moral integrity (moral righteousness). To acknowledge God's existence and to live this life in obedience to His Word, may sound traditional and outdated, but the fruit of such a life is "peace and joy," which many God-denying intellectuals lack. They also lack purposeful living, which in the end, leads to a lot of drinking, disillusionment, and bitterness.

Wisdom, however, will do the following for you:

- She will preserve and keep you. (v.6)
- She will honor you. (v.8-9)
- She will extend your life. (v.10)
- You will not stumble in your decision. (v.12)
- She is your life. (v.13)

So, pursue wisdom (reverence and holy living) and you will enjoy this life to its fullest and will be welcomed in the next.

PRAYER

"Lord, remind me that many of my pursuits
are like children grasping after bubbles:
shinning, beautiful, but oh so temporary;
that true life has always been and will always be in You.
In Jesus' name. Amen."

PROVERBS 5:7–8

*"Therefore, hear me now, my children,
and do not depart from the words of my mouth.
Remove your way far from her,
and do not go near the door of her house."*

DO NOT APPROACH

*D*read this sin, for it certainly will be your ruin. This caution is introduced with a solemn preface: "Hear me now therefore, O you children!" Whoever you are that read or hear these lines, take notice of what I say.

A Greek student in Athens, Greece, was sentenced to eight months imprisonment on charges of marrying two women within 48 hours. He appealed the sentence and was set free pending a new trial. The court heard that Petros Novaras, 29, married Vassiliki Chioti on January 24, 1971, in the central Greek town of Lamia, and took off in his car for a honeymoon. After an engine trouble, he sent his wife down to Athens on a bus. In the meantime, he went to a suburb in Athens and married a 29-year-old lass, the court heard. He then continued his honeymoon with his second wife. At the court, the accused testified: "Both families were putting unbearable pressure on me. So I decided to take them both so as not to hurt anybody's feelings."

"Warning, warning, warning, Will Robinson," so speaks the robot on the sci-fi series, *Lost in Space*. Our Proverb today fervently warns us to stay clear of tempting situations; ". . . remove your way far from her." (v.8) If you hope to be kept from harm, stay out of harm's way. Passion often assaults good reason and good morals, so determine now to take the long way home and stay out of reach of this type of woman, if not, she'll be the ruin of you.

∾ PRAYER ∾

*"Lord, this concept is so simple, yet so tempting;
may our shoes never trespass into this forbidden land.
In Jesus' name. Amen."*

April 6

PROVERBS 6:1–5

"My son, if you become surety for your friend,
if you have shaken hands in pledge for a stranger . . .
deliver yourself like a gazelle from the hand of the hunter,
and like a bird from the hand of the Fowler."

ASSUMPTION OF RESPONSIBILITIES

During the early days of his career, when funds were low, Sherwood Anderson's publisher thought to encourage him by sending him each Friday a check big enough to meet his week's expenses. Anderson stood it for three weeks and then brought the newest check, unopened, back to the publisher's office. "It's no use," he said. "I find it impossible to write with security staring me in the face."—*Boston Globe*

At first glance this passage would seem to say no more than that one should not cosign a note or, if one has already made that mistake, should get out of the arrangement as quickly as possible. While the text does say at least this much, it also implies that no one should get into legal entanglements and indebtedness in which circumstances are out of one's control. This is certainly the case where giving security for another is concerned. In this culture and time, seizure of assets and home and even the selling of the debtor into slavery were common penalties for failure to make payment (Matthew 18:25), and the cosigner could well have met the same fate.

⁓ PRAYER ⁓

Lord, gently remind me that You are my best security,
financially and spiritually.
In Jesus' name. Amen."

Pastor Dan Butcher | 97

PROVERBS 7:27

"Her house is the way to hell,
descending to the chambers of death."

A LITTLE HEAVEN OR A LOT OF HELL

Some years ago, the most married man in the world was found in Yugoslavia. It happened this way: A young woman confided to her girl cousin of her impending marriage to a man. The bridegroom was so shy and timid that he wanted to keep the marriage a secret. The cousin got curious. She got a glimpse of the bridegroom after the secret wedding and recognized him as her own husband. He had also married her secretly, claiming to be shy and timid.

That was only a beginning. A total of fifty women came forward and claimed that he had individually married them. In each case, he was the same bashful bridegroom. They called him Ivanhoe the Terrible, breaker of women's hearts. He was a traveling salesman, going from wife to wife by plane, supporting all fifty of them, with the explanation to each that his duties as a traveling salesman kept him away so much of the time.

They put him in jail, and he begged to stay there. He'd rather be sent to prison than face those fifty wives.

Amazing! I guess this guy is never satisfied! Our Proverb describes the adulterer as one who takes a fast track to "hell," ". . . descending to the chambers of death." Like the guy above, keeping fifty women happy and content would be a form of "hell" here on earth in itself.

The answer to this kind of "purgator" is found at the beginning of the Chapter: "My son, keep my words, and treasure my commands within you. Keep my commands and live . . ." Proverbs 7:1–2a) Anyone who sets their heart on that will experience a little of "heaven" on earth, rather than the unhappy fellow in our illustration.

PRAYER

"Lord, let me never forget that man's thoughts
and ways often create their own form of hell,
right in their own backyard. In Jesus' name. Amen."

PROVERBS 8:12

"I, wisdom, dwell with prudence,
and find out knowledge and discretion."

WELL CONSIDERED

*T*he word translated "prudence" may be used in a bad sense ("craftiness"—Exodus 21:14; Joshua 9:4), but in Proverbs it is used in a good sense for "sensible behavior." (Proverbs 1:4; 8:5) The word rendered "discretion" can also mean "evil plans," but in Proverbs it often refers to careful behavior that arises from clear thinking.[1] Wisdom teaches how to live a discreet and careful life as opposed to a reckless one.

Careful and thought-out plans are always a benefit. Today's Proverb exhorts the reader to think carefully about wisdom and its characteristics. What will destroy wisdom is impatience. When we become impatient, we do not clearly think through consequences (prudence), we disregard the facts (knowledge), and we shun speaking in a way that avoids offense (discretion).

So, perhaps a couple of life changes are warranted in your future?

PRAYER

"Lord, may my constant companions be
prudence, facts and discretion.
In Jesus' name. Amen."

April 9

PROVERBS 9:7

*"He who corrects a scoffer gets shame for himself,
and he who rebukes a wicked man only harms himself."*

FRIEND OR FOE

*B*efore I went to college, I worked with a man who knew more Bible facts than many preachers. Yet he claimed to be an atheist. He studied the Bible only to argue about it and to try to refute it. God holds such persons responsible for knowledge about which they do nothing.

The warning against trying to instruct mockers (vv.7–9) is characteristic of Proverbs. Even as it urges the young man to faithfulness and prudence, it always recognizes that there are some who will never listen.

Jesus says it this way: "Do not give what is holy to the dogs; nor cast your pearls before swine, lest they trample them under their feet, and turn and tear you in pieces." (Matthew 7:6) Dogs and swine refer to people who are enemies of the gospel, just not unbelievers, such enemies are to be left alone. One example of this was Herod Antipas, governor of Jerusalem. He had heard John the Baptist gladly (Mark 6:20), but then later had him beheaded. (Matthew 14:1–12) When Jesus stood before Herod, He said nothing. (Luke 23:8,9) Herod had become a "dog"or a "pig," spiritually.

⇝ PRAYER ⇜

*"Lord, help me not to scoff at an appropriate rebuke,
lest I find myself in the company of the wicked.
In Jesus' name. Amen."*

PROVERBS 10:3

"The Lord will not allow the righteous soul to famish,
but He casts away the desire of the wicked."

RIGHT THIS MOMENT?

When you have nothing left but God, then for the first time you become aware that God is enough.—Maude Royden

Psalm 37:17 says it this way: "For the arms of the wicked shall be broken, but the Lord upholds the righteous." There are times or periods in our lives when all seems lost. Economic hardships, estranged relationships, and more questions for God than answers from Him.

Our Proverb today teaches that even during the heartache, we are not neglected, though it feels like it. Promises made are promises kept. God does reward the righteous and judge the wicked. We may not be experiencing God's provisions right now or seeing with glee the wicked judged this instant, however, things usually do not stay as they are right now. God's delays are not denials. Keep trusting, keeping living a righteous life (do not mock God by asking for his provisions while denying his laws), and you'll see the day when God provides as promised and judges as warned.

⌇ PRAYER ⌇

"Lord, help me not to make the mistake
that my timing is Your timing.
In Jesus' name. Amen."

PROVERBS 11:22

*"A ring of gold in a swine's snout,
so is a lovely woman who lacks discretion."*

A PIG'S NOSE

*T*he humor of this Proverb is obvious. The point of the comparison is that in both cases beauty is in an inappropriate place. Note that the woman has abandoned discretion; an immoral way of life is implied.

A hog would be less disgusting with a ring in its nose than a beautiful woman with corrupt morals. As a pig roots in the dunghill, the beautiful woman cast aside modesty, discretion, and good moral choices.

Beauty in our culture and age is so prized that lax morals are often of little consequence. So, we continue to worship the created and ignore the Creator, all the while wondering why there is no lasting meaning in our lives.

PRAYER

*"Lord, may we not fill our lives with the superficial
and ignore Jesus, the real 'bread of life.'
In Jesus' name. Amen."*

April 12

PROVERBS 12:15

*"The way of a fool is right in his own eyes,
but he who heeds counsel is wise."*

TO HEED OR NOT TO HEED?

Billy Graham, evangelist, speaking in Madison Square Garden, offered parents six suggestions on how to curb juvenile delinquency: 1. Take time with your children, 2. Set your children a good example, 3. Give your children ideals for living, 4. Have a lot of activities planned, 5. Discipline your children, 6. Teach them about God.—*United Press*

Sound advice from the world's foremost evangelist. However, there are those who see themselves wiser who would downplay the idea of teaching children about God. They espouse the idea that when children are old enough, they should be able to choose for themselves about religion. There is a subtle hypocrisy in this. These same parents will not let their children decided what food to eat, or whether they'll attend school, or when they'll take a bath. The good Lord has given the parents these responsibilities and for good reason. Parent's know better! Or at least they should.

The wise of heart will heed Reverend Graham's advice and be quick to teach their children about God. Take them to Sunday School at a Bible believing Church, and get them involved in the life of the church itself. You have them for such a short time, and then they will be on their own making decisions for themselves. Be sure to heed this wise counsel. Do not be wise in your own eyes as to imagine that you or your children don't need God or His Word (Bible).

PRAYER

*"Lord. help us all to seek wise counsel,
and to recognize it when we see it. In Jesus' name. Amen."*

PROVERBS 13:3

"Whoever guards his mouth preserves his life;
he who opens wide his lips comes to ruin."

GUARD THE LIPS

Guard your words, enjoy your life. If there is one asset successful people have, it's they've learned long ago to keep their thoughts to themselves. Some people want genuine and profitable counsel, but not all. If it is your boss, family, or friend, choose your words carefully. Soft words are preferred when correcting; harsh words will get you escorted to your car by security or divorced, if there are enough of them. Encouraging words are best of all; use them often. Avoid sarcasm, which is a clever cloak for anger.

In summary, "be quick to hear, slow to speak and slow to anger." (James 1:19)

⟶ PRAYER ⟵

"Lord, help me to keep a guard on my life,
and may he never go off duty. In Jesus' name. Amen."

April 14

PROVERBS 14:4

"Where no oxen are, the trough is clean;
but much increase comes by the strength of an ox."

THE MINOR VS THE MAJOR

*I*n the absence of oxen, the feed-trough is clean (a minor advantage); but where there are oxen, despite the messy feed-trough, there is a greater harvest (a major advantage).

Life is such that we sometimes must give up something for the greater gain. Today's Proverb well describes the strength of the oxen and its benefit (an abundant harvest) comes with having to feed, shelter, and clean up after them. This is a principle of life. So, expect it! Also, it is best to stop complaining about it; it is not going away soon. One other thought: the benefits that comes with change, the dirty and the unfamiliar, often last much longer and are much more of a benefit than the shorter lapsed time of having to deal with the uncomfortable side of life.

~ PRAYER ~

"Lord, I hate messes: the dirty, the uncomfortable feeling
of the new. But remind me these circumstances often carry a far
greater benefit than a messy trough to clean.
In Jesus' name. Amen."

April 15

PROVERBS 15:13

*"A merry heart makes a cheerful countenance,
but by sorrow of the heart the spirit is broken."*

WHAT A SMILE CREATES

*It costs nothing but creates much.
It enriches those who receive it
Without impoverishing those who give it.
It happens in a flash, and the memory of it sometimes lasts forever.
None are so rich that they can get along without it,
And none so poor but are richer for its benefits.
It fosters good will in a business,
It creates happiness in the home,
And is the countersign of friends.
It is rest to the weary,
Daylight to the discouraged,
Sunshine to the sad,
And nature's best antidote for trouble.*
—Henry H. Evansen

A merry heart, often expressed in a smile, is good medicine. A smile creates an atmosphere that is loving, receiving, and encouraging. One of the best ways to keep a "merry heart," is to be thankful. It's hard to be down or depressed when you are thanking God for everyday benefits you enjoy but have grown used to. The purr of a cat, the shelter of a home, or the anticipation of reading a good book. All these warrant a "Thank you, Lord." But most of all, thanks to God who has not dealt with us according to our sins. "He has not dealt with us according to our sins, nor punished us according to our iniquities. For as the heavens are high above the earth, so great is His mercy toward those who fear Him; as far as the east is from the west, so far has He removed our transgression from us." (Psalm 103:10-11) Now that should give us "a merry heart," ushering in a "cheerful countenance (a smile)."

⟶ PRAYER ⟵

"Lord, keep me from carrying my own sorrow, but to cast them on You in exchange for a smile. In Jesus' name. Amen."

PROVERBS 16:33

"The lot is cast into the lap,
but its every decision is from the Lord."

MOMENT TO MOMENT ADJUSTMENTS

The Ben Lancer, the first "dynamically positioned" oil-and-gas drilling ship built in Britain was launched on Scotland's River Clyde. The vessel could drill in a fixed position without being anchored in the conventional manner. Dynamic positioning is the computer-controlled process which involves automatic checking of the ships at one-second interval and adjusting it by making minute corrections in the propeller pitch settings.

If man can design a ship that makes moment by moment adjustments and corrections to the propeller, surely God is able to make such adjustments in our lives, if we seek His counsel.

The events in our lives, those that we take rather casually, are ordered by God. We have our part, then the divine steps in, the hand is unseen, and the voice is unheard, but we are not the crafters of our own fate as we may suspect. Lot casting was a way to determine the mind and will of God, particularly in the Old Testament. (I Samuel 14:41) Now that the Holy Spirit dwells in the heart of every true believer, the Holy Spirit guides his willing children.

Trust God for the circumstances that may cause you confusion and pain. God is able to bring good out of bad, "For we know that those who love God all things work together for good . . .." (Romans 8:28a)

∼ PRAYER ∼

"Lord, help me to stop worrying that all things depend on me,
but instead trust Your guiding hand. In Jesus' name. Amen."

PROVERBS 17:9

*"Whoever covers an offense seeks love,
but he who repeats a matter separates close friends."*

THE SOUL'S SCIENCE

*O*nce President Lincoln was asked how he was going to treat the rebellious Southerners when they had finally been defeated and returned to the Union of the United States. The questioner expected that Lincoln would take a dire vengeance, but he answered, "I will treat them as if they had never been away."[2]

When you forgive someone, you are surrendering your right to hurt them back for hurting you. Forgiveness is the oil that makes the wheels of life turn. If you want a smooth ride and the most enjoyable this side of heaven, *forgive*. If you want your life to grind to a halt, keep bringing up past offenses. It has been well said that an unforgiving heart is like drinking poison and expecting it to kill someone else.

So, who do you need to forgive? Who needs your covering of love? Do it today! Kneel in prayer and ask God to forgive you and then ask Him for His help in forgiving your offender.

⤙ PRAYER ⤚

*"Lord, help me to cover, not to repeat.
In Jesus' name. Amen."*

2. William Barclay, The Gospel of Luke

PROVERBS 18:6

*"A fool's lips enter into contention,
and his mouth calls for blows."*

THOSE ARE FIGHTING WORDS

A congregation of the Church of God in Christ in Wichita, Kansas, asked a court to stop four of the members from disrupting services. Bishop Graze Kinard said the four had run through the sanctuary moaning and shouting while he tried to conduct services.

He alleged that they shut the pastor's Bible while he was preaching, took away the pastor's microphone, hit him over the head, and pinned down the pianist's arms. Police had to step in several times, and the congregation dwindled from six-hundred to fifty because of the trouble, complained the bishop. The trouble apparently stemmed from a battle over control of the church, said police.—*Christianity Today*

Shameful! If a church is not following your leadership, it is best you serve elsewhere. Why is it a person feels compelled to argue minor points? Why not listen, smile, and keep your own thoughts to yourself? Any fool will argue, and most fools do. There are times when it is best to respond, a gentle tongue carries the argument, and it usually only needs to be said once.

PRAYER

*"Lord, keep me from playing the fool by arguing over the minor
as though it was a major. In Jesus' name. Amen."*

PROVERBS 19:1

*"Better is the poor who walks in his integrity
than one who is perverse in his lips and is a fool."*

CHARACTER OVER CASH

The tragedy of Watergate for the whole country was that people at the heart of our government yielded to the anxiety that whispered so convincingly in all our hearts that achievement is more important than character. God help us out of this wreckage to learn anew that the highest value and most enduring power in human enterprise is character.

Basically, it is better in the eyes of God to be poor than perverse. The poor man who lives a guileless, innocent life, content with his lot, and using no wrong means to improve his fortunes, is happier and better than the rich man who is hypocritical in his words and deceives others, and has won his wealth by such means, thus proving himself to be a fool, a morally bad man.

If you are interested in doing it God's way, choose rather to lose money by righteous living than to gain it by a perverse lifestyle.

PRAYER

*"Lord, help us to choose a holy character
over an unholy career. In Jesus' name. Amen."*

PROVERBS 20:24

"A man's steps are of the Lord;
how then can a man understand his own way?

"With thoughtless and impatient hands,
we tangle up the plans the Lord has wrought.
And when we cry in pain, He saith,
"Be quiet, dear, while I untie the knot."
—Author Unknown

PEACE

Today's Proverb teaches that God directs a man's steps. Even if that man falls, the Lord upholds him. "The steps of a good man are ordered by the Lord, and He delights in his way. Though he falls, he shall not be utterly cast down; for the Lord upholds him with His hand." God directs our decisions, and though He does not participate in our self-willed sin, He keeps His hand on us, bringing to completion His will for us. We feverishly make our plans, then worry, and then plan some more; but the Lord's pre-determined path for us will stand. "There are many plans in a man's heart, nevertheless the Lord's counsel—that will stand." (Proverbs 19:21) So, stop trying to figure out every disappointment and failure. Stop with the "what ifs." Put your mind at ease and trust God, finally! God has it under control. Concentrate on being obedient to His Word, and the rest will fall into place as God directs.

PRAYER

"Lord, when will I learn that You have this under control?
Help me to trust You with what I cannot understand,
agree to, or change, and enjoy my life as You have determined.
In Jesus' name. Amen."

PROVERBS 21:3

*"To do righteousness and justice
is more acceptable to the Lord than sacrifice."*

*The measure of a man's real character is what he would do,
if he knew he would never be found out.*—Macaulay

*God prefers people's obedience—
their doing what is right in their daily living (cf. v.7)
and justice—over their occasional sacrifice.*

JUST OR UNJUST?

"With what shall I come before the Lord, and bow myself before the High God? Shall I come before Him with burnt offerings, with calves a year old? (v.6) Will the Lord be pleased with thousands of rams, ten thousand rivers of oil? Shall I give my firstborn for my transgression, the fruit of my body for the sin of my soul? (v.7) He has shown you, O man, what is good; And what does the Lord require of you? But to do justly, to love mercy, and to walk humbly with your God." (v.8)

So simple. God sees and God hears. Always do the next right thing before God, as God defines it, and you will be pleasing in His eyes. Do not think that an occasional monetary gift to charity, or occasional service (volunteering at the homeless shelter during the holidays) will be well received by God when the remainder of your life is unjust and unrighteous. So, simple! But so just.

∽ PRAYER ✎

*"Lord, remind me You want my heart,
not just occasional helping hand.
In Jesus' name. Amen."*

PROVERBS 22:6

*"Train up a child in the way he should go,
and when he is old, he will not depart from it."*

AS THE TWIG IS BENT

*I*t is generally true that most children who are brought up in Christian homes, under the influence of godly parents who teach and live God's standards, follow that training. There are exceptions, but as a general principle, and Proverbs are general principles, *not* guarantees, children raised in a loving and godly environment, return to that training.

So, don't give up; keep striving, keep praying, and stay in the Word. The Lord will fill the gaps.

PRAYER

*"Lord, remind us parents of the old but true saying,
'Just as the twig is bent, the tree's inclined.'
In Jesus' name. Amen."*

PROVERBS 23:17

*"Do not let your heart envy sinners
but be zealous for the fear of the Lord all day;
for surely there is a hereafter, and your hope will not be cut off."*

CONSIDER THE END

Never envy the prosperous who are corrupt; those who seem to have it so easy: money, health, talented children, favorable circumstances. What happens to them in the hereafter? Condemnation; and rightfully so. They cheated others, they defamed, mocked, laughed at, and abused the good, the poor. They neglected God with the thought that God will see it their way when they die. They deserve their judgment; they worked for it. The end will not shape up well for them. Instead, for the rest of us, be zealous for God. Your hope will not be in vain. The hour is coming when you will be justly rewarded.

PRAYER

*"Lord, remind us when we get to feeling sorry for ourselves
that the prosperity of the wicked will be short-lived.
In Jesus' name. Amen."*

April 24

PROVERBS 24:12

"If you say, 'Surely, we did not know this,'
does not He who weighs the hearts consider it?
And will He not render to each man according to his deeds?"

A LITTLE OR A LOT

A brisk little lady inquired at a travel bureau about a certain European tour. The agent mentioned that this particular tour included the Passion Play at Oberammergau. The woman drew herself up to her full five-feet-one and replied icily, "I'm sick and tired of all this sex stuff—and I'm surprised at you!" Then she stormed out.—Vancouver, B. C. *Sun*

Yes sir, ignorance in action is quite a sight. So, how does God respond to us when we do not know His Word and yet live in direct violation to it? Our Proverb today states He will judge us based on our works. If you really want to see what an individual believes, watch what he does. Those who believe in diet and exercise, *diet and exercise*. Those who believe in social activism, *actually get out and are socially active*. Those who believe in God, yet are ignorant, obey what they know, and God will hold them accountable for what they do. There are those who are well acquainted with the Bible, but do not show any good works. Conversely, there are those who know very little about God but are strict to obey what they do know.

To believe and do is huge in the Bible, even if it's based on little knowledge or volumes of knowledge. The solution is to get to know God intimately through the Bible and His Son, Jesus Christ, and then to obey. Now that you know this, be sure to act.

PRAYER

"Lord, help us to know You intimately through faith
in the living Word, Jesus Christ
and through the written Word, the Bible.
In Jesus' name. Amen."

PROVERBS 25:28

*"Whoever has no rule over his own spirit
is like a city broken down, without walls."*

WISE SELF-CONTROL

*J*udge John A. Weeks spotted a man sitting in the rear of his Minneapolis courtroom wearing a hat. Disturbed by this disregard for courtroom decorum, he ordered the man to leave. Then the clerk called for the burglary case of George A. Rogde, who had been freed on bond. Rogde did not come forward. "Your honor," said the prosecuting attorney, "that is the man you ordered from the courtroom." Police are still looking for Rogde.—*Minneapolis Tribune*

Watch your appetites and emotions! If you can't control them, your goose is cooked. Like an unwalled city is easily taken, you too will fall to the next evil thought, the next evil impulse, the next evil endeavor. You will be outmaneuvered every time by the adversary who is able to keep his emotions in check. Focus on yielding to the Holy Spirit, and He will enable you to reign in your emotions and passions.

⟿ PRAYER ⟾

*"Lord, I need Your help desperately.
Keep me from tearing down the walls of my defense
by an unbridled emotion or passion. In Jesus' name. Amen."*

PROVERBS 26:11

*"As a dog returns to his own vomit,
so a fool repeats his folly."*

A ROUND TRIP TICKET

A little lad of six was invited to lunch in a neighbor's home. When all were seated at the table, the food was served. The little boy was puzzled and with the forthright frankness of a child, asked the host: "Don't you say any prayer before you eat?" The host was highly embarrassed over the boy's blunt inquiry and mumbled, "No, we don't take time for that." The lad was silent for a time, then said, "You're just like my dog. You start right in."—Al Bryant

It is possible to be just like a dog in other ways, too. Today's Proverb, though disgusting, well illustrates the fool who does not learn from his mistakes. There are many, who after a brief period of reformation, or sobriety, or being clean, return to their former destructive ways. Jesus warns a man he just healed not to return to his former evil ways. "Afterward Jesus found him in the temple, and said to him, 'See, you have been made well. Sin no more, lest a worse thing come upon you.'" (John 5:12)

What are you being tempted to do, again? Is it lying, stealing, drinking, drugs, etc.? Do you remember how sick you were in the first place, which prompted you to stop? Do not return to the vomit! Vomit is vomit; it will only make you sick again.

PRAYER

*"Lord, help me not to return to my former vomit,
which so disgusted me in the first place. In Jesus' name. Amen"*

PROVERBS 27:7

*"A satisfied soul loathes the honeycomb,
but to a hungry soul every bitter thing is sweet."*

HUNGER IS THE BEST COOK

In England, *The Forsyte Saga* TV series was so popular that ministers changed the hours of Sunday evening services because they conflicted with the program. One man, whose home was flooded with seven feet of water, refused to come to the window to be rescued by a helicopter because he was watching an episode.—*The New York Times*

Our Proverb has multiple applications, but I apply it to the hungering soul who has so little spiritually, that once he finds the Savior, he has found his life. He is now satisfied, though tempted with the world's honeycomb, he knows there is no other true peace. Conversely, those starving souls seeking some solace from life's harshness, feed on every little philosophy and scheme that comes their way only to experience the bitterness of emptiness and broken promises.

⟿ PRAYER ⟾

*"Lord, help me not to mistake bitterness for blessing,
a satisfied soul for scraps. In Jesus' name. Amen."*

PROVERBS 28:13

"He who covers his sins will not prosper,
but whoever confesses and forsakes them will have mercy."

CONFESSING OVER CONCEALING

You can never repent too soon because you never know how late it is.—Fuller

Concealing your sin will not deliver you from God's wrath. "When I kept silent, my bones grew old, through my groaning all day long. For day and night Your hand was heavy upon me."

We must be willing to acknowledge our wrong! Some would say *that* is wrong. Today's philosophy is to "deny, deny, and deny again." When a patient conceals his sickness, he cannot expect to get well. When we fail to acknowledge our sin to God and to those we have sinned against, we cannot expect God's favor.

However, God prefers mercy over judgment. "Return, backsliding Israel," says the Lord. "I will not cause My anger to fall on you for I am merciful," says the Lord; "I will not remain angry forever. (Jeremiah 3:12) ". . . He does not retain His anger forever, because He delights in mercy." (Micah 7:18)

Acknowledge your wrong. God waits on you, and then make it right with those you have transgressed. You will be surprised by mercy, both from God and man.

PRAYER

"Lord, help me not to be so proud as to hide my sin,
but so wise as to forsake them. In Jesus' name. Amen."

PROVERBS 29:11

"A fool vents all his feelings, but a wise man holds them back."

DON'T LOSE COMMAND

A college president not long ago made this arresting statement to a class of graduating seniors: "It gets easier and easier for man to dominate his universe . . . and harder for him to dominate himself." He went on to say, "It matters little what you learn or express if in the end you cannot find some ways of working things out with your neighbors." We cannot dominate the universe, but with God's help, we can dominate ourselves.—Mrs. A. E. Janzen

If you don't conquer your temper, it will eventually ruin you. Lives have been lost, careers ruined, and marriages crippled when we speak and act in anger. "He who is slow to anger is better than the mighty, and he who rules his spirit than he who takes a city." (Proverbs 16:32) It is a sign of weakness to lose your temper, and people tend to remember weaknesses. I say respectfully, when anger enters the front door, wisdom quickly exists out the back. So, take time for a second thought; it just may very well move you from being a fool to a man of great understanding. "He who is slow to wrath has great understanding, but he who is impulsive exalts folly." (Proverbs 14:29)

⸱⸰⸱ PRAYER ⸰⸱

"Lord, You know how quick I pull the trigger on anger.
Help me, Jesus, to command it, rather it command me.
In Jesus' name, Amen."

April 30

PROVERBS 30:5-6

*"Every word of God is pure; He is a shield to those
who put their trust in Him. Do not add to His words,
lest He rebuke you, and you be found a liar."*

SHIELDED

*"And so, I thought, the Anvil of God's Word
For ages skeptic blows have beat upon;
Yet, though the noise of falling blows was heard,
The Anvil is unharmed, the hammers gone."*

—John Clifford

*I*n the real world of experience, people have found the Bible to stand. It stands in birth; it stands in life, and it stands in the end. There is no corruption, no mixture of error and truth, no speculation, no imagined encounters, no contemporary philosophy; it is just pure (not mixed with any other material). "The words of the Lord are pure words, like silver tried in a furnace of earth, purified seven times." (Psalm 12:6) "Your word is very pure; therefore, your servant loves it." (Psalm 119:40) Therefore, God becomes your shield when you place yourself under the protection of His Word.

Do not add to it; it is perfect. It needs no additions. "Whatever I command you, be careful to observe it; you shall not add to it nor take away from it." (Deuteronomy 12:32)

The mind of God is gained by careful reading, trusting what you have read, and then experiencing God as he keeps His word to you.

PRAYER

*"Lord, Your Word is my shield. May I never be so wise
as to add to it and be found out to be a liar.
In Jesus' name. Amen."*

May 1

PROVERBS 1:24–27

"Because I have called and you refused,
I have stretched out my hand and no one regarded . . .
I will laugh at your calamity;
I will mock when your terror comes like a storm . . ."

OFFER WITHDRAWN

A friend of mine has spent his life in evangelism. Many years ago, he told me that, having preached in revivals all over the world, he found the most difficult place for evangelism was in a fertile valley of Southern California. People living there had come from such places as Arkansas, Oklahoma, and Texas with all their earthly goods stacked on old, worn-out automobiles. Now they owned productive farms, lived in fine debt-free homes, and enjoyed all the creature comforts they desired. This friend said when he talked to them about heaven many replied, "Heaven? Southern California is good enough for me."[3]

Trust me, Southern California is not Heaven. To be casual about the offer of unearned forgiveness through Christ is to invite the mocking laugh of God! God has stretched out His hands, but many have refused. They regard the message of Jesus as superstition, a child's story, or only for the weak of mind. Our Proverb teaches if you reject God's offer long enough, the offer will be withdrawn! Jesus Himself said, "For everyone practicing evil hates the light and does not come to the light, lest his deeds should be exposed." (John 3:20) We have God's offer of love in this life and His judgment in the next!

God is stretching out His hands to you through Jesus Christ. If you come to Him, He will rejoice over you and you'll hear no laughter.

✎ PRAYER ✎

"Lord, may I always reach for Your outstretched hands.
In Jesus' name. Amen."

3. Hobbs, H. H. (1990). *My favorite Illustrations* (p. 148). Nashville, TN: Broadman Press.

May 2

"My son, if you receive my words,
and treasure my commands within you,
so that you incline your ear to wisdom, apply your heart . . .
then you will understand righteousness and justice,
equity and every good path."

SUREFOOTED CHOICES

When he was 24 years old, Abraham Lincoln served as the post-master of New Salem, Illinois, for which he was paid an annual salary of $55.70. Even then, 24 years before he entered the White House, the rail-splitter was showing the character that earned him the title of "Honest Abe."

The New Salem post office was closed in 1836, but it was several years before an agent arrived from Washington to settle accounts with ex-postmaster Lincoln, who was a struggling lawyer not doing too well The agent informed him that there was $17 due the government. Lincoln crossed the room, opened an old trunk, and took out a yellowed cotton rag bound with string. Untying it, he spread out the cloth, and there was the $17. He had been holding it untouched for all the years. "I never use any man's money but my own," he said.

Honest Abe had it right! He knew the best path. Our Proverb teaches that those who receive God's words, treasure them, and incline their ear to their wisdom, will by constant exposure to God's voice know what is the best path to take in life. (v.9)

All paths of duty before God and man will be directed by God's wisdom. This involves sacrifice and a constant conviction that true wisdom in this life stems from God. God gives wisdom for life's paths. (v.6) "For the Lord gives wisdom . . ." (skill in successfully living), and wisdom always pleases God, and to please God is always your best good.

PRAYER

"Lord, may we treasure Your Wisdom throughout our day
as we face many, many paths to walk. In Jesus' name. Amen."

PROVERBS 3:34

"Surely He scorns the scornful but gives grace to the humble."

THE FAVOR OF THE HUMBLE

*H*ave you ever thought of it, that only the smaller birds sing? You never heard a note from the eagle in all your life, nor from the turkey, nor from the ostrich. But you have heard from the canary, the wren, and the lark. The sweetest music comes from those Christians who are small in their own estimation and before the Lord.—*Watchman-Examiner*

Our Proverb warns us against being so proud as to scorn God (to feel or believe that someone or something is worthless). To do so is to place yourself in the position of being scorned by God Himself! Paul put it this way, "Be not deceived, God is not mocked; for whatever a man sows, that he will also reap." (Galatians 6:7) So, if you keep up your rants, your mocking, your high-handed derision, one day you'll reap what you've sown and stand before this God, whom you affirm does not exist, and it will be your turn to be scorned!

However, God prefers mercy over judgment. (James 2:13) So, the humble (having a low estimate of one's own importance) will receive God's Word. Why? because he does not see himself as so important, so smart, so experienced, as to fly in the face of what the Bible teaches.

✎ PRAYER ✎

"Lord, You have said it so well:
'With the pure, You will show Yourself pure;
and with the devious, You will show Yourself shrewd.' (Psalm18:26)
In Jesus' name. Amen."

PROVERBS 4:20–22

"My son, give attention to my words;
incline your ear to my sayings . . .
for they are life to those who find them . . ."

A SOLID OAK COFFIN

A ninety-two-year-old man in Stanstead Abbots, England, is the proud possessor of a solid oak coffin, which he purchased thirty-three years ago for $100.

Every day since then he has visited the shed in which he keeps the coffin to give it a polishing. If he feels drowsy, he crawls into it and takes a nap. After doing this for thirty-three years, he is satisfied that his long rest will be comfortable for his body. "I'm making sure I go out respectable—with an oak coffin that has solid brass handles and everything!"

Everything was prepared for this man's body and its final resting place, but Proverbs puts the emphasis not on the body *but on our soul*. If you prepare your soul by giving strict attention to God's Word, incline your ear to His sayings, then you will find Life.

Stay true to wisdom. The eyes are to stay fixed on right teaching (vv.21, 25) as the feet are to stay in the right path. (vv.26–27) The mouth and lips must shun using twisted words. (v.24) Above all, the heart must be guarded by sound doctrine. (vv.21, 23) If the son listens to his father, the whole body will be healthy. (v.22)

PRAYER

"Lord, keep us from chasing what will be lost,
so that we might gain what will never be lost.
In Jesus' name. Amen."

PROVERBS 5:22

*"His own iniquities entrap the wicked man,
and he is caught in the cords of his sin."*

DON'T THROW FREEDOM AWAY

*H*igh atop the United States Capitol dome in Washington stands the statue of the stately "Freedom Lady," almost 20-feet high. The sculptured Freedom Lady was brought from Rome during a fierce storm, and the captain ordered some cargo thrown overboard. The sailors wanted to include the heavy statue, but the captain refused, shouting above the wind, "No! Never! We'll flounder before we throw "Freedom" away."—James C. Helley

Sin will throw your freedom away. In the above Proverb, the Hebrew word for "entrap" is a term used to catch an animal in a snare or net. Likewise, whenever we transgress God's law (lie, cheat, fornicate, cuss, etc.), the unanticipated result is to be ensnared. It is not an immediate act, but a process that slowly weaves its cords around us. Unfortunately, bondage ends up being "hell" for the enslaved.

However, Christ brings freedom. Jesus said, "Most assuredly, I say to you, whoever commits sin is a slave of sin . . . Therefore, if the Son makes you free, you shall be free indeed." (John 8:34, 36)

Trust Christ as your Savior from sin, and then live for Him as your Lord.

⟶ PRAYER ⟵

*"Lord, keep me from the cords of sin,
enable me to live in the freedom of Christ.
In Jesus' name. Amen."*

PROVERBS 6:23

"For the commandment is a lamp, and the law a light;
reproofs of instruction are the way of life . . ."

186,000 MILES A SECOND

*E*instein said that the reason he could construct the theory of relativity was because there is one thing in the world that is unchangeable. That one thing—the speed of light—is the only constant in this physical, material universe.

Light travels at the rate of one-hundred-eighty-six thousand miles per second—seven times around the world at the tick of a clock.

There is another constant in life—reproof. To reprove someone is to "express blame or disapproval for something said or done." For example—children. Their lives are constantly being reproved. From not sticking their fingers in an electrical socket to stop hitting their little sister. Today's Proverb goes one step further. Reproofs "are the way of life." Adults need reproof, so God, in His wisdom, has given us a lamp—His Word. God's law is a light, so do not fear reproofs. When someone expresses their legitimate disapproval for what you have done, receive it! That is life! Especially if it is true. Especially if it is God. When God says do not take His name in vain (cf. Exodus 20:7), embrace it—it's life-giving. If you are a slob and do not clean up after yourself, receive the blame and make the changes. It will only make your life better. Of course, some people like walking on their clothes; because they're lying on the floor, it makes them feel at home!

PRAYER

"Lord, help me not to fear disapproval, some of which I need.
Help me to embrace the commands of God
that steer me toward the light. In Jesus' name. Amen."

PROVERBS 7:10–15

*"And there a woman met him,
with the attire of a harlot,
and a crafty heart.*

ANATOMY OF A BAD CHOICE

From Bologna, Italy, a prostitute, stripped of her driving license after being caught plying her trade in her car, could have the license back, a local judge ruled.

The prostitute's lawyer had objected to the reason given by a policeman for taking the license away: "She is leading a scandalous life."

Defense lawyer Salvatore d' Errico argued that one could "drive a car carefully and at the same time lead a scandalous life."

There is no car needed for today's Proverb. Solomon tells the story of young man who was ruined by an adulterous woman.

What was he like?

He was a young man void of understanding. (v.7)

He was idle, "passing along the street." (v.8)

He placed himself near her home. (v.8)

He hid under the cover of darkness, "in the black and dark night." (v.9)

What was she like?

She was married. (v.19)

She dressed like a harlot. (v.10)

She was crafty. (v.10)

She was loud and rebellious. (v.11)

She was here and there and everywhere except where she should be. (v.11b,12)

Solution: "The fear of the Lord will keep you far from her embrace." (Proverbs 1:7)

⟶ PRAYER ⟵

*"Lord, the agents of Hell are still playing this same card.
Help us be wise and pure. In Jesus' name. Amen."*

May 8

PROVERBS 8:19

*"My fruit is better than gold, yes, than fine gold,
and my revenue than choice silver."*

WISDOM'S REVENUE

The US Census Bureau gave the following figures:

In 1920: 1 divorce for every 7 marriages
In 1940: 1 divorce for every 6 marriages
In 1960: 1 divorce for every 4 marriages
In 1972: 1 divorce for every 3 marriages

In 1977, 2,176,000 marriage licenses were issued in the United States—and 1,090,000 divorces were granted. A ratio now of 1 to 2!

More frightening, it was estimated that as early as 1990, divorces would outnumber marriages.

These are old statistics. What these marriages needed was a healthy dose of God's wisdom.

Wisdom involves not only intelligence but also moral integrity. (vv.7–9) Ultimately, a sinful lifestyle is self-destructive. Consider the current divorce rate. Divorce scars all those involved in it, and it's not uncommon that those scars last a lifetime; not to consider the cost. So, it's no exaggeration that God's wisdom ". . . is better than gold, and my revenue than choice silver." (v.19) If God's wisdom had ruled the day, many of these divorces could have been avoided. Jesus put it this way: "So then, they are no longer two but one flesh. Therefore, what God has joined, let not man separate." (Matthew 19:6)

PRAYER

*"Lord, may I never believe that I'm wiser than You.
Help me to always live in the shadow of Your wisdom.
In Jesus' name. Amen."*

May 9

PROVERBS 9:10–11

*"The fear of the Lord is the beginning of wisdom,
and the knowledge of the Holy One is understanding.
For by me your days will be multiplied,
and years of life will be added to you."*

THE JOHN LENNON BOAST

John Lennon, 26, a member of the British rock 'n roll quartet, the Beatles, told a London reporter, "Christianity will go. It will vanish and shrink. I need not argue about that; I'm right and I will be proved right. We're more popular than Jesus now . . .."—*Christianity Today*

As you may know, John Lennon was fatally shot in the archway of the Dakota Apartments, his residence in New York City, on December 8, 1980.

The Beatles have been disbanded for years, and John Lennon's boast ended poorly for him. God usually does not deal with blasphemy so severely. He prefers mercy over justice. (cf. James 2:13) But some boasts directly challenge God.

"Forsake foolishness and live, and go in the way of understanding." (v.6) It is foolish to challenge God. So, reverence Him, and treat His Word with respect. Then you will have the wisdom to see life as it is—a direct creation of God Almighty, and you'll have the understanding to enjoy it for many years to come.

❧ PRAYER ❧

*"Merciful and kind Lord, help me to be humble enough
to see my place, and wise enough not to stay there.
In Jesus' name. Amen."*

PROVERBS 10:9

*"He who walks with integrity walks securely,
but he who perverts his ways will become known."*

THE SECURITY OF THE RIGHTEOUS

A Washington merchant had gone Lincoln one better with this
sign in his shop window: "You can fool some of the people
some of the time, and, generally speaking, that's enough to allow
for profit."

For some, a profit, regardless of how it is made, is all that matters. Today's Proverb teaches us that a life of good moral choices
will secure your way. "Then you will walk safely in your way, and
your foot will not stumble." (Proverbs 3:23) However, if you are
deceitful and twist justice, you will eventually be had, or as some
say "busted."

Christ exhorts his apostles to be harmless, without injury to
moral standards. "Behold, I send you out as sheep amid wolves.
Therefore, be wise as serpents and harmless as doves." (Matthew
10:16)

A good moral lifestyle does have its sacrifices, but it has a plus
side as well. Isaiah 32:17 declares, "The work of righteousness will
be peace, and the effect of righteousness, quietness and assurance
forever." Peace stems from righteous living, which greatly aides a
good night's sleep. For others, however, they look one way and row
another. There is always the nagging, insecure feeling that you're
about to be caught for their wrong. Try sleeping on that thought.

PRAYER

*"Lord, may I find my security in Your secure ways.
In Jesus' name. Amen."*

PROVERBS 11:17

"The merciful man does good for his own soul,
but he who is cruel troubles his own flesh."

MISERY VS MERCY

*I*t is our misery that calls forth God's mercy. A parent well knows this. When a child is crying due to a severe cold, a sore throat, runny nose, and all he can do is put his arms around your neck and cry, what type of feeling does this evoke? Pity, mercy; so you reach out and try to relieve her child's pain. His misery calls on your mercy. Likewise, God will bless your soul every time you relieve the misery of another.[1] It does a soul good, as our Proverb teaches.

However, there are those who are otherwise persuaded. These types of people can be cruel (willfully causing pain or suffering to others), kicking a starving cat away, or saying a cruel word. They trouble their own self. Strange thing though, these types are the first to beg for mercy when suddenly they find themselves beyond the reach of helping themselves.

Relish in God's mercy to us through Jesus Christ. "For He made Him who knew no sin to be sin for us, that we might become the righteousness of God in Him." (2 Corinthians 5:21) And don't forget to extend mercy when called upon to do so, for the night is coming for all of us to face the justice of God.

PRAYER

"Lord, remind us that when we show mercy,
we receive Your mercy. In Jesus' name. Amen."

PROVERBS 12:22

*"Lying lips are an abomination to the Lord,
but those who deal truthfully are His delight."*

LIARS AND LOVERS OF LIES

*D*uring the 1983 National Spelling Bee held in Washington, DC, thirteen-year-old Andrew Flosdorf of Fonda, New York, eliminated himself from the contest when he informed the judges he had misspelled "echolalia." The judges had failed to catch the error. When questioned as to why he turned himself in, he straightforwardly replied, "I didn't want to feel like a slime."

Do you want to feel like a slime? Do not lie! Do you want God Almighty to delight in you? Tell the truth!

The word abomination means, "something that causes disgust or hatred." Frankly, I do not want my behavior to be on God's "disgust" list. The habit of lying is just that—a habit. Some have lied for so long, it is second nature to them. Don't like the way a circumstance is shaping up? Lie. Don't want to feel bad? Lie. Don't want to look bad or be embarrassed? Lie. Liars are usually caught. The timing may be delayed, the temporary reprieve satisfying, but payday is just around the corner. Revelation 22:15 teaches that liars will miss heaven. "But outside (of heaven) are dogs (scoundrels) and sorcerers and sexually immoral and murderers and idolaters, and whoever loves and practices a lie."

～ PRAYER ～

*"Lord, may I always be Your delight.
Help me to be perfectly honest. In Jesus' name. Amen."*

May 13

PROVERBS 13:12

*"Hope deferred makes the heart sick,
but when the desire comes, it is a tree of life."*

SWEET TO THE SOUL

*D*uring World War II, a pharmacist's mate, Wheeler B. Lipes, Jr., performed a lifesaving appendectomy on Seaman Darrell Dean Rector aboard the submarine, *Sea Dragon*. Maneuvering behind enemy lines in the Pacific, the closest thing to a doctor on board was pharmacist's mate Lipes, a lab technician by training, who had witnessed an appendectomy.

Facing certain death if not operated upon, Rector agreed to Lipes correcting the situation. Without surgical instruments, Lipes used a knife blade for a scalpel, a tea strainer to administer ether, and spoons from the galley to keep the incision open during surgery. The crude tools were sterilized with alcohol from a torpedo.

Surgery was performed in the officers' quarters on September 11, 1942; the first appendectomy aboard a submerged submarine. Rector resumed his responsibilities in thirteen days.[4]

Everyone celebrates when a long-cherished hope is accomplished. Especially if it's a matter of life or death. However, God calls upon us to "depart from evil." An excellent example is drinking. Many desire to become sober one day, but they are unwilling to stop drinking in the moment. No "tree of life" for them. God will not bless if a person remains in their self-manufactured sin.

The science is simple; stay true to God and God's Word, and your desires will blossom into a "tree of life."

∙∽ PRAYER ∼∙

*"Lord, grant us the grace to continue toward our desires,
even if we don't always get what we hope for. In Jesus' name. Amen."*

---

4. Jones, G. C. (1986). *1000 illustrations for Preaching and Teaching* (p. 83). Nashville, TN: Broadman & Holman Publishers.

PROVERBS 14:30

"A sound heart is life to the body,
but envy is rottenness to the bones."

THE GRINCH

O ne of Dr. Seuss' children's book creatures is "Grinch," who is a creature who can't bear the sight of anyone enjoying himself without getting so mad it bites itself.[1]

It is a well-known fact that a person's emotional state affects his physical health. The Bible has taught this for centuries. "A merry heart does good, like medicine, but a broken spirit dries the bones." (Proverbs 17:22) "The light of the eyes rejoices the heart, and a good report makes the bones healthy." (Proverbs 15:30)

Conversely, envy (a feeling of discontentment aroused by someone else's possessions, qualities, or luck) will physically make you sick, and eventually lead you to hating life, always wanting what you do not have. It is a constant starving of the soul which is never satisfied; eaten alive from the inside.

Like Dr. Seuss' "Grinch," we tend to bite our own soul whenever we discontent ourselves over others success or good luck. Stop the carnage. God has other food for us to feed on, such as his favor. "For You, O Lord, will bless the right, with favor You will surround him as with a shield." (Psalm 5:12)

⸙ PRAYER ⸙

"Lord, may I never devour myself with envy,
while You are holding out Your hand of favor.
In Jesus' name. Amen."

May 15

PROVERBS 15:15

"All the days of the afflicted are evil,
but he who is of a merry heart has a continual feast."

NO ICE CREAM FOR YOU

Richfield, Utah (UPI)—Prisoners in the Sevier county jail are already complaining about the new $200,000 facility because it does not have any windows.

The 19 inmates, who moved into the new jail said they now cannot yell to the owner of Craig's Ice Cream shop across the street to get ice cream cones delivered to their cells.[1]

In the above story, the afflicted are evil! They deserve their prison sentence. No ice cream for them! However, in today's Proverb, the afflicted are the poor, the oppressed; they are in their misery due to the circumstances of life.

In contrast, Solomon pitches the idea that those who a have a merry heart will continually enjoy life even though they too have adverse circumstances. Yes, your life may be legitimately adverse and unjust, but a continual outlook of gloom will only make it worse. All your days will be miserable, plus it will not change your immediate circumstances.

So, pull the weed of complaint, woe, and start thanking God for the little things (my car started this morning) and the big (God loves me though sometimes I fail Him), and you'll reap a harvest of continual feasting. "Rejoice always, pray without ceasing, in everything give thanks; for this is the will of God in Christ Jesus for you." (I Thessalonians 5:16, 17)

⟶ PRAYER ⟵

"Lord, help me keep a merry heart,
that I might enjoy Your continual goodness throughout my life.
In Jesus' name. Amen."

PROVERBS 16:9

"A man's heart plans his way, but the Lord directs his steps."

MAN PROPOSES, GOD DISPOSES

A young reporter called on Mark Twain to interview him. He found the writer comfortably ensconced in bed, reading. The reporter asked Mark for the story of his life.

"Well," drawled Mark, "in the days of George III, when I was a young man, I used to . . ."

"Pardon me," interrupted the young man, "I know that you are no spring chicken, but you couldn't possibly have been living in the time of George III."

"Fine, my boy," exclaimed Mark. "I heartily congratulate you. You are the first and only reporter I have ever met who corrected a mistake before it appeared in print.[1]

Even the noted Mark Twain was re-directed as he spoke. Solomon teaches that God directs our steps, even though we think they are entirely our own way. "The lot is cast into the lap, but its every decision is from the Lord." (v.33) We tend to believe because we cannot see God rolling aside the clouds and dynamically stepping into view, that He doesn't orchestrate the affairs of our life. Yet, our Proverb makes it clear that the Lord "directs his steps," (v.9) even when that man "plans his way." What we may see as coincidence is just God's way of remaining anonymous in our lives. The majesty of Almighty God can divinely balance the scales between man's free choices and His pre-determined plans.

So, stop fretting over "spilt milk," past mistakes, and regrets. Trust that God will work for the Bible says in Romans 8:28, "and we know that all things work together for good to those who love God . . .." God can take our sin and bring good out of it while not condoning that sin.

⟶ PRAYER ⟵

"Lord, remind me that as I make my plans,
You're looking over my shoulder. In Jesus' name. Amen."

PROVERBS 17:27

*"He who has knowledge spares his words,
and a man of understanding is of a calm spirit."*

30,000 TEETH

A snail is a very interesting creature. Naturalists tell us that it has teeth on its tongue! A scientist examining one such organ under his microscope counted as many as 30,000. The snail keeps its toothy little tool rolled up like a ribbon, until it is needed; then it thrusts out this sharp appendage and, although its teeth are very small, it saws through the toughest leaves and stems with comparative ease.[1]

Who would imagine that snails have teeth? This little ribbon-like buzz-saw is unrolled whenever needed. For many, they need to keep their tongue rolled up. Our Proverb teaches that a wise man is cautious in what he says; he thinks before he talks and does not gab. This reveals that he is even-tempered (able to keep one's cool). Restraint in talking may even cause a fool or an arrogant fellow to be considered wise. (cf. v.28) Only by practice, prayer, and persistence will one learn how to spare his words and not buzz-saw those around him. The ability to keep a calm spirit during an emotional crisis when words are flying like sawdust will deescalate an explosive circumstance.

So, take a step back, pause, and ask yourself, is this the best time to roll out my tongue? God can help you with this. Try prayer.

⟶ PRAYER ⟵

*"Lord, I'm fast on the trigger when it comes to speaking.
Help me to spare my words. In Jesus' name. Amen."*

PROVERBS 18:21

*"Death and life are in the power of the tongue,
and those who love it will eat its fruit."*

THE POWER OF THE TONGUE

*T*here is a story in the Jewish Talmud about a king who sent two jesters on an errand. In instructing them, he said, "Foolish Simon, go and bring me back the best thing in the world. And you Silly John, go and find for me the worst thing in the world." Both clowns were back in short order, each carrying a package. Simon bowed low and grinned. "Behold, Sire, the best thing in the world." His package contained a tongue. John snickered and quickly unwrapped his bundle. "The worst thing in the world, Sire." Another tongue!

Our Proverbs states the principle illustrated in the story above. The tongue's "fruit" refers to consequences, good or evil, that follow one's words. The point would be that one must bear the consequences of one's words. A witness in a court, for example, can help determine by his words whether a defendant lives or dies. Those who love it (the tongue) refers to people who love to talk. "In the multitude of words sin is not lacking, but he who restrains his lips is wise." (Proverbs 10:19.) It inevitable that we're going to sin if we keep on talking.

So, let's not take lightly the power of our words, for it will be by our words whether our life will be as joyful as a wedding, or as sad as a funeral.

PRAYER

*Lord, help us to always speak words of life in what we say
and shun the heartache of death. In Jesus' name. Amen."*

PROVERBS 19:26

*"He who mistreats his father and chases away his mother
is a son who causes shame and brings reproach."*

A DIM VIEW

The earliest Christmas I remember was the one when I found a pocketknife in my stocking. Excitedly, I opened it, grabbed a piece of wood, and began cutting. About the sixth stroke, I cut my finger. The cut soon healed, but more than seventy years later the scar remains. Nothing was wrong with the knife. It was a gift of love. The trouble was I abused the gift rather than used it.[5]

In love, God has given us the powers of our bodies and minds. Used within His will, they bless us. Outside His will, they harm us.

A grown son who robs (assaults or mistreats) his father (cf. 28:24) and drives . . . his mother off their property, brings shame and disgrace to himself and his society. God takes a dim view on those who abuse their parents physically. "Whoever curses his father or his mother, his lamp will be put out in deep darkness." (Proverbs 20:20) This type of disregard for proper authority and respect upends the whole structure of authority and ultimately disregards God, Himself.

⟶ PRAYER ⟵

*"Lord, may we never abuse our first authorities, our parents,
for this will only lead to God's final disapproval—Hell.
In Jesus' name. Amen."*

5. Hobbs, H. H. (1990). *My Favorite Illustrations* (p. 245). Nashville, TN: Broadman Press.

PROVERBS 20:7

*"The righteous man walks in his integrity;
his children are blessed after him."*

GOOD CONSCIENCE

Character is a victory, not a gift.[1]

General William F. Dean was a prized prisoner of the Communists during the Korean struggle. One day, the General was advised that he had five minutes in which to write a letter to his family. It appeared to be the end. Calmly he accepted the order and proceeded to write. In the body of this now-historic letter appears a single line worthy of remembrance: "Tell Bill the word is integrity."[6]

Integrity is defined as, "being honest and having strong moral principles." Our illustration and Proverb illustrate the virtue and benefits of a man's righteous life. A righteous man has a steady, even hand in governing himself; he keeps good conscience with his morals; and his children will inherit its benefits. If it is your hope to "train up a child in the way he should go . . .," (Proverbs 22:6) then model by example the life you want your children to follow, and they'll love your memory and live your life

PRAYER

*"Lord may my life be my children's example.
In Jesus' name. Amen."*

---

6. Jones, G. C. (1986). *1000 Illustrations for Preaching and Teaching* (p. 195). Nashville, TN: Broadman & Holman Publishers.

May 21

PROVERBS 21:19

*"Better to dwell in the wilderness,
than with a contentious and angry woman."*

CONTENTIOUS FREE LIVING

It happened in the city of Detroit, Michigan. After applying for a marriage license, a man failed to reappear at the country clerk's office until eleven years later to claim the important document. When asked why he and his fiancée had waited so long to get married, he explained, "We had a few disagreements about details."—Paul R. Van Gorder

I would be leery after eleven years! Today's Proverb teaches that a peevish and angry wife can make a man's life miserable! Peace and love generate peace and happiness. There is no real joy in the union of marriage unless there is one spirit. It is better to have no company than the wrong company. Solomon, the author of Proverbs, teaches than a solitary life is better than a contentious wife; better to be exposed to the harsh elements of loneliness than to the constant drumming of an arguing woman. Many women live by the Italian Proverb: "When a wife sins, the husband is never innocent!"

⟡ PRAYER ⟡

*"Lord, spare good, innocent men from bad,
guilty women. In Jesus' name. Amen."*

PROVERBS 22:3

"A prudent man foresees evil and hides himself,
but the simple pass on and are punished."

STORM CLOUDS

A wastrel grandson of Queen Victoria once begged Her Highness by letter an advance on his allowance. The severe Queen answered with a lengthy rebuke of his way of life and a great deal of additional advice, exhorting him to thrift and diligence. Although no money had been sent, the good Queen shortly received a letter of thanks from the young man, explaining that he had followed her precepts literally by selling her letter.[1]

This humorous story highlights good perception, which is the warning given in our Proverb. A prudent man (acting or showing care for the future) will see evil coming and arm himself for the encounter. Noah saw the flood coming and Joseph the seven years of famine. They did not sit on their hands. The simple man, however, tends to listen to words that flatter his ego, but words of warning go unheeded. They think they are the exception.

Is there a person, place, or thing that tempts you to evil? Hide yourself! Do not be naive; don't be simple for if you are, you will "pass on and be punished."

～ PRAYER ～

"Lord, give me 20/20 vision
in seeing the coming evil. In Jesus' name. Amen."

PROVERBS 23:10–11

*"Do not remove the ancient landmark,
nor enter the fields of the fatherless;
for their Redeemer is mighty;
He will plead their case against you."*

THEIR REDEEMER IS STRONG

For the United States, about 120,000 children were orphaned by the death of their fathers in service during World War II.

Hosea 14:3 says ". . . for in You the fatherless finds mercy."

Psalm 68:5 says "A father of the fatherless; a defender of widows, is God in His holy habitation."

God has his eye on the fatherless and determines mercy and justice for them. A redeemer is a close family member. Those hapless souls who abuse the fatherless find themselves in the hands of Almighty God—not an even match. Stealing land from the fatherless by moving the ancient stones that mark out boundaries is especially appalling. The wicked tend to think because they cannot see any defender for the helpless, that there is *no* defender at all. A catastrophic error.

Do not assume because you cannot see anyone as you abuse another that you're not being seen at all!

PRAYER

*"Lord, You are a Father and protector of the fatherless,
the poor, and the weak. Praise Your holy name.
In Jesus' name. Amen."*

PROVERBS 24:24–25

"He who says to the wicked, "You are righteous,"
him the people will curse; . . . but those who rebuke the wicked will
have delight, a good blessing will come upon them."

"You shall not show partiality in judgment;
you shall hear the small as well as the great;
you shall not be afraid in any man's presence,
for the judgment is God's.
The case that is too hard for you,
bring to me, and I will hear it. (v.17)

NO FAVORITES

*J*ustice Gray of the Supreme Court once said to a man who had appeared before him in one of the lower courts and had escaped conviction by some technicality: "I know that you are guilty and you know it, and I wish you to remember that one day you will stand before a better and wiser Judge, and that there you will be dealt with according to Justice and not according to law."—C. E. Macartney

So, there you have it! Do not approved the wicked though he be as close to you as your brother or condemn the righteous though you personally do not like him. Always, always be fair and just in your daily dealings with people. Right is right and wrong is wrong, regardless.

PRAYER

"Lord, may we never distort justice,
regardless of how it may affect us personally.
In Jesus' name. Amen."

PROVERBS 25:28

*"Whoever has no rule over his own spirit
is like a city broken down without walls."*

THE SAFETY OF SELF-CONTROL

*O*ne of the tortures of a member of the Hohenstaufen family was that of a cell, which, when the prisoner first entered was comfortable and easy. After a few days, he observed the dimensions of his chamber beginning to contract. The fact became more appalling every day. Slowly the sides drew closer; and the unhappy victim at last was crushed to death.—Foster

No lack of walls in this story. Our Proverb teaches us about a different kind of wall, a city without them. This city has no protection against attack, no recourse but to be conquered. Likewise, a person who has no control over himself is just as helpless. His or her lack of self-control will end poorly for them, as surely as a city with no protective walls during the time of the ancient middle East. Their goose is cooked!

If you have no rule over your passions and appetites, if you rebel against good reason and conscience, you will be hurting. A good man has good control; control over his thoughts, inclinations, and personal resentments. However, those who have no "rule over their own spirit," are vulnerable. Even the slightest prick of the ego sends them into triad of obscenities, unreason, and even to jail. They are shieldless and unprotected.

⁓ PRAYER ⁓

*"Lord, keep me protected when I'm tempted to be unruly.
In Jesus' name. Amen."*

PROVERBS 26:20

"Where there is no wood, the fire goes out;
and where there is no talebearer, strife ceases."

TIME TO SHUN

They were a happy little family, living in a small town in North Dakota, even though the young mother had not been entirely well since the birth of her second baby.

But each evening the neighbors were aware of a warmth in their hearts when they would see the husband and father being met at the gate by his wife and two small children. There was laughter in the evening too; and when the weather was nice, Father and children would romp together on the back lawn while Mother looked on with happy smiles.

Then one day a village gossip started a story saying that he was being unfaithful to his wife; a story entirely without foundation. But it eventually came to the ears of the young wife, and it was more than she could bear. Reason left its throne, and that night when her husband came home there was no one to meet him at the gate, no laughter in the house, no fragrant aroma coming from the kitchen—only coldness and something that chilled his heart with fear.

And down in the basement he found the three of them hanging from a beam. Sick and in despair, the young mother had first taken the lives of her two children, and then her own.

In the days that followed, the truth of what had happened came out—a gossip's tongue, an untrue story, a tragedy.

Shun such people. "He who goes about as a talebearer reveals secrets; therefore, do not associate with one who flatters with his lips."

⁓ PRAYER ⁓

"Lord, forgive us and help us to never be a revealer of secrets.
In Jesus' name. Amen."

PROVERBS 27:20

"Hell, and Destruction are never full;
so the eyes of man are never satisfied."

GIVE, GIVE

*A*n Edmonton man had been sentenced to serve a term in the penitentiary, not for capital murder, but for manslaughter. Even though he beat his wife until she died, it seemed to have been an understood thing that by mutual consent each would beat up the other once a month "just for satisfaction." But his turn to beat her proved fatal.—*Prairie Overcomer*

I guess he was not satisfied enough!

Our Proverb teaches us two things are never satisfied—death and sin. Some would like to add taxes to the list, but we will stay with how the Proverb is written. It's a curious fate of our human nature, how an individual can really have it all: a good, loving wife, adoring children, money to live comfortably, but will turn the whole apple-cart over for what he perceives to be more satisfying. Sadly, that perception often proves an illusion. Paul teaches, and for good reason, "Now godliness with contentment is great gain." (Timothy 6:6) Paul understood that the nature of life is transitory; it passes rather quickly. The beautiful wife grows old, the excitement of money loses its thrill, and the mundane routine of life has no real meaning apart from God.

The solution *is* God. Know Him and enjoy Him through His Son Jesus Christ. Then, trust God with your possessions, status, and place in life. To be dissatisfied with your circumstances will eat you alive with heartache. Try thanking God for you present circumstance, change what you can, and trust God for the outcome.

❧ PRAYER ☙

"Lord, may I ever be mindful that You
are my greatest satisfaction. In Jesus' name. Amen."

PROVERBS 28:26

"He who trusts in his own heart is a fool,
but whoever walks wisely will be delivered."

A DEAD END

Falling down a flight of stairs caused a middle-aged Kansas City man not only a broken ankle but also an acute case of embarrassment.

As a judge in a Cub Scout safety poster contest, he had just selected the winning entry. It had read: "Always watch your step while walking on stairs."[1]

A fool man is a man who trusts in himself, his own judgment, and his own strength. He doesn't seek counsel, nor does he abide by it. Why should he? He is sufficient. However, the Bible teaches, "The heart is deceitful above all things, and desperately wicked; who can know it?" (Jeremiah 17:9) Our heart can and does deceive us. We all have experienced this. We think *this is what I want, this is the way I'll go*, all the while knowing this was against God and His ways. And how does it end? Just another vain pursuit of heartache. The whole experience leaves us empty. In contrast, the wise man's trust is in God. "Trust in the Lord with all your heart, and lean not on your own understanding; In all your ways acknowledge Him, and He shall direct your paths. (Proverbs 3:5-6)

When your heart rages against God's way, remember, only the fool trusts his heart.

PRAYER

"Lord, 'There is a way that seems right to a man,
but its end is the way of death.' (Proverbs 14:12)
In Jesus' name. Amen."

May 29

PROVERBS 29:25

*"The fear of man brings a snare,
but justice for man comes from the Lord."*

A STRONG TOWER

A woman who had just returned from a trip to Mexico called the Los Angeles police to report that a rattlesnake was loose in her overnight bag. Police went rushing to the scene with sirens screaming. They approached the bag which the woman had heaved out of a window onto the sidewalk. Cautiously, they scattered the contents of the bag only to find that the rattle was caused by an electric toothbrush that was accidentally turned on!—Anthony Paul

Now, that is embarrassing. Fear of man brings uncontrolled imaginations, often unfounded, and usually leaves us looking like the fool. It only hampers our potential, robs us of sleep, and wears us down. There comes a time when our true hope has to be in God. Man can cause us to fear, but at one point do you say, "Look, I'm trusting the Lord on this and moving forward." To continue to imagine what you think will happen will always haunt you. Every rustling leaf will stir you to run. Stop the insanity; justice comes from God. "The name of the Lord is a strong tower; the righteous run to it and are safe." (Proverbs 18:10) This word "safe" means "to be inaccessibly high or to be exalted."

⮞ PRAYER ⮜

*"Lord, may I remember that Your security
removes my insecurity. In Jesus' name. Amen."*

PROVERBS 30:8–9

"Remove falsehood and lies far from me;
give me neither poverty nor riches—
feed me with the food allotted to me;
lest I be full and deny You . . .
or lest I be poor and steal
and profane the name of my God."

THE SNARE OF PROSPERITY
AND THE TEMPTATION OF POVERTY

From the Baker, Oregon, *Democrat-Herald*: "To whoever stole the fire extinguisher out of my 1970 Ford station wagon: *Where you are headed, you'll probably need it.*"

Today's Proverb teaches that we should pray that we not become so rich that we sin by denying God, nor so poor and sin by stealing. Prosperity tends to make people forgetful of God, poverty tempts one to be dishonest. Jesus taught us to pray for "our daily bread," (Matthew 6:11), and to be delivered from temptation. (Matthew 6:13) The solution is God and our prayers to Him. He is the only one that can keep you keen to lies and falsehood and is able to deliver us from the snares of prosperity and the temptation of poverty.

PRAYER

"Lord, deliver me from the downhill slide
of prosperity or poverty. In Jesus' name. Amen."

PROVERBS 31:4–5

*"It is not for kings, O Lemuel,
it is not for kings to drink wine,
nor for princes intoxicating drink;
lest they drink and forget the law,
and pervert the justice of all the afflicted."*

JUSTICE IS FOR ALL

"Not guilty by reason of insanity." This was the unbelievable sentence recited by Judge Barrington Parker following each of the thirteen charges leveled against John Warnock Hinckley, Jr., for the attempted assassination of President Ronald Reagan. The trial is said to have cost $2.5 million. As would be expected, reactions to the verdict varied from clever maneuvering of language to a travesty of justice. Arthur Eads, District Attorney of Bell County, Texas, declared: "Only in the US can a man try to assassinate the leader of the country in front of 125 million people and be found not guilty." Many echoed the sentiment of Eads that the verdict was symptomatic of a runaway leniency in the justice system.

What a miscarriage of justice. This travesty is not the first. Our Proverb teaches that injustice can also carry the day, when one in authority, a king, is intoxicated. Drunkenness blurs the judgment and pervert's justice, Proverbs warns against this. "It is not good to show partiality to the wicked, or to overthrow the righteous in judgment." Likewise, for Christians, it is not wise to drink in excess. They debase themselves and lose any witness for God. People can drink away their sound judgment. "Wine is a mocker, strong drink is a brawler, and whoever is led astray by it is not wise." (Proverbs 20:1)

·~ PRAYER ~·

*"Lord, grant us grace to restrain our passions,
lest we lose our justice. In Jesus' name. Amen."*

PROVERBS 1:7

*"The fear of the Lord is the beginning of knowledge,
but fools despise wisdom and instruction."*

TWO KINDS OF PEOPLE

A hotel manager in Raleigh, NC, reports that a guest woke up everyone in the hotel screaming, "It's in the phone book! It's in the phone book!" The manager got the house detective, and they let themselves into the man's room where they found him in the middle of a nightmare. "I was having a horrible dream," the man explained when awakened. "I dreamed the income-tax people wanted to send me a big refund, but they'd lost my address!"—*Raleigh Times*

He did not want to miss out! None of us do. There is another way to miss out, though easily avoided—ignore God. Our Proverb teaches that the "beginning of knowledge" starts with God. You can have treasures, power, and esteem, but only reverence for God can brings us understanding about life and how to live it with satisfaction.

In bold relief, the "fool" in Proverbs 1:7 is the person who, in their arrogant, coarse way, rejects God and wisdom (cf. v.29). Two kinds of people are contrasted in this verse: those who humbly fear God and thus acquire true knowledge, and the arrogant fools who, by their refusal to fear God, demonstrate that they hold wisdom and discipline in contempt.

PRAYER

*"Lord, help me not to be so proud
as to ignore the wisdom of being humble before You.
In Jesus' name. Amen."*

PROVERBS 2:7

"...He is a shield to those who walk uprightly..."

"But You, O Lord, are a shield for me,
my glory and the One who lifts up my head."
Psalm 3:3

MY SHIELD OF PROTECTION

Francis E. Clarke, founder of *Christian Endeavor*, told of a young man in the Maine woods with his camera on a pleasant outing, who stopped at the entrance of a cavern on a rocky hillside, and impulsively thought: "Let me see what kind of a photograph I can get out of that cave."

Steadying the camera just a little way from the mouth of the cavern, he gave the sensitive plate a long-time exposure into the darkness of the interior. Then he went heedlessly on his way.

When later he developed the plates, a thrill of astonishment passed over him as the exposure of the cave revealed in the center of the opening—but concealed from his eyes by the darkness within—a huge lynx crouched and ready to spring. Danger, disfigurement, perhaps death, had confronted him; yet he had been quite unaware of the peril, in the thoughtless gaiety of holiday freedom.[1]—Christian Victory

God is our shield. (v.7b) He guards our path (v.8a), and he preserves our way. (v.8b) What He asks of us in return is to receive His words and treasure His commands. (v.1) God honors those who honor Him. Treasure God's commands with obedience and enter the joy of having God as your shield in life's many paths, decisions, and snares.

∾ PRAYER ∾

"Lord be my shield as I treasure Your commands.
In Jesus' name. Amen."

June 3

PROVERBS 3:3–4

"Let not mercy and truth forsake you;
bind them around your neck,
write them on the tablet of your heart,
and so find favor and high esteem
in the sight of God and man."

A FAVORABLE FORMULA

Psychologists say that if you refuse to respond to a stimulus, in time the stimulus goes away. The stimulus may return, but it is usually weaker than before. After several occurrences, the stimulus ceases or else the person becomes hardened and unable to feel it. Thus, the person loses the ability to respond positively.[7]

May we never grow so hard as to ignore the promptings of loyalty and love. The Hebrew word *"hesed"* translates as love, kindness, and loyalty to one's covenant or commitment. Those qualities, along with dependability, should grace one's life like a neck chain. A noble goal is to make our words, deeds, and life a reflection of love and faithfulness. The result will be favorable to us.

PRAYER

"Lord, favor me as I strive for loyalty and faithfulness
to my commitments. In Jesus' name. Amen."

7. Hobbs, H. H. (1990). *My Favorite Illustrations* (p. 80). Nashville, TN: Broadman Press.

PROVERBS 4:18–19

"But the path of the just is like the shining sun,
that shines ever brighter unto the perfect day.
The way of the wicked is like darkness;
they do not know what makes them stumble."

TWO PATHS TWO DESTINIES

A distinguished painter was conducting a class for aspiring artists. He was speaking about artistic composition. He emphasized that it was wrong, for example, to portray a woodland, a forest, or a wilderness, without painting into it a path out of the trees. When a true artist draws any kind of picture, say a landscape, he always gives picture an "out." Otherwise the tangle of trees and the trackless spaces depress and dismay the onlooker.

Solomon appeals to his children (v.1) to take the path of wisdom, the only way "out"of the forest; to walk in the way of wisdom (morally upright) and to avoid the path of the wicked. The contrast is between two paths; one is wise, straight, safe, and without unnecessary obstacles. The way of the wicked, however, is tortuous and marked with all manner of hazards. One road is a path of light, growing more obvious, like the dawning of a new day; the other is full of darkness like a setting sun, causing those who walk on it to stumble. The path of the wise is marked by reverence and Godly obedience; the other is characterized by wickedness and ignorance of God and His ways. One lives in the perfect light of God's love; the other in moral darkness, miserable, and wondering why their lives are so empty; like darkness—without God and without hope. Which path are you on?

PRAYER

"Lord, may I not confuse myself on which path to take.
Am I enjoying righteousness, peace, and God's presence,
or are my feet on a path of darkness, misery and heartache?
In Jesus' name. Amen."

PROVERBS 5:1–4

"My son, pay attention to my wisdom;
lend your ear to my understanding . . .
for the lips of an immoral woman drip honey,
and her mouth is smoother than oil;
but in the end she is bitter as wormwood,
sharp as a two-edge sword."

BITTER, BITTER, BITTER

*J*udge Beatrice Mullaney of Fall River, Massachusetts, affirmed that women are almost entirely to blame for lowered moral standards in the United States.

"Women are anxious to exercise freedoms and permissiveness promoted by the women's movement, and the result is dissolution of marriages, homes, and families. In nearly two decades as a judge, I've heard more than 10,000 divorce, separation, and custody cases. And I've seen moral decay, especially in family responsibilities, divorce, permissiveness, and shirking of duties. I blame women almost entirely for lowering the moral standards of this country."[1]

I am sure the above illustration is not going to sit well with many women, but today's Proverb does describe such a woman. Solomon teaches his son to ignore the words (lips) (v.3) of an adulteress. Her deceptive, seductive words are persuasive; sweet like honey, the sweetest substance in ancient Israel, and smoother than olive oil, the smoothest substance in Israel. But what seems attractive at first becomes bitter and sharp later. Involvement in adultery is like tasting gall, the bitterest substance from a plant in ancient Palestine. Those involved in this sin of adultery are to be reminded they are but one step from hell, (v.5) "For her house leads down to death, and her paths to the dead." (Proverbs 2:18)

PRAYER

"Lord, remind me if I want a future of peace,
then I need to be a blameless man now. In Jesus' name. Amen."

PROVERBS 6:6–11

TWINS

*R*arely a week goes by when I do not fly somewhere. Friends kid me about arriving at the airport so early. I have reached the age when I do not hurry, so I start in time to prevent it. I arrive in time to check in, go through security, and drink a cup of coffee while I read the paper. When they call my flight, I am at the gate and ready to go.

But always someone rushes in just before the flight attendant closes the door. I say to myself, "If you had gotten up even fifteen minutes earlier, all that rush would have been unnecessary." Some insist on "a little sleep, a little slumber, a little folding of the hand."(Proverbs 6:9–10)

"No folding of the hands" for the ant. Ants are models of diligence in that they work tirelessly despite having no taskmaster to goad them on, and they prepare for the winter in spite of having no indication that winter is coming. Ants seem to know that the future will provide what they need. They have no commander or overseer, yet they work better than many people under a leader!

This lesson is simple: keep at your responsibilities, be industrious, do not excuse your laziness, or your "poverty will come on you like a prowler, and your need like an armed man." (v.11)

∼ PRAYER ∼

"Lord, remind me that laziness and poverty are twins.
In Jesus' name. Amen."

PROVERBS 7:18–20

"Come, let us take our fill of love until morning;
let us delight ourselves with love.
For my husband is not at home;
he has gone on a long journey . . ."

EXPRESS TRAIN TO HELL

*L*atimer was raised to the bishopric of Worcester in the reign of Henry VIII. It was the custom of those days for each of the bishops to make presents to the King on New Year's Day. Latimer went with the rest of his brethren to make the usual offering; but, instead of a purse of gold, he presented the King with a New Testament, in which was a leaf doubled down to this passage: "Whoremongers and adulterers God will judge."[1]—Walter Baxendale

Beware, this is one bad woman. Watch as she spins her web around her victim. She anticipates his objection of being another man's wife. Never fear," she says, "the good man is not at home."(v.19) What if he should return suddenly? Not a problem. "He has gone a long journey; he has taken a bag of money with him, and will come home on the appointed day (new moon). (vv.19–20) At last the man yields. He is both docile, like the ox going to slaughter; and stupid, like a deer or bird going into a trap. (vv.21–23) He is about to pay the full fee for her services—his life. (v.23)

The science is simple; to be forewarned is to be forearmed.

PRAYER

"Lord, we don't have to wonder about this sin.
Help us not to 'stray into her paths.'
In Jesus' name. Amen."

PROVERBS 8:20–21

*"I traverse the way of righteousness,
in the midst of the paths of justice,
that I may cause those who love me to inherit wealth,
that I may fill their treasuries."*

DRINK FROM THE WELL

Our Proverb today teaches us a simple fact: if you will "traverse" or travel in the way of what is right and justice, God will cause His favor to fall upon you. You'll never lack as long as you stay near the well of what is right and justice.

There is a connection between righteous living and just work ethics that result in prosperity and wealth. The mechanic who is known and trusted can make a very profitable livelihood, because people trust him. He will not insist on a repair that really isn't needed, or do more than what is required, or jack up his price because you're in trouble. But there is another dimension to this Proverb. God's favor in our lives consistently flows from those who love Him.

A simple application: love God, live for what is right and fair, and enjoy God's favor.

✎ PRAYER ✎

*"Lord, keep us in the path of fairness and justice,
and we'll thank You ahead of time for Your favor.
In Jesus' name. Amen."*

PROVERBS 9:9

"Give instruction to a wise man,
and he will be still wiser; teach a just man,
and he will increase in learning."

100 BLOWS

"Rebuke is more effective for a wise man than a hundred blows on a fool." (Proverbs 17:10)

The more a wise man learns, the more he loves wisdom. A wise man wants to know how life and things work; it is to his advantage; whether it be working successfully with people or repairing a car. The more you know, the better the life. The more wisdom a man has, the more desirous he should be to have his weaknesses shown him, because a little folly is a great blemish to the person who is viewed as wise.

It is as great an instance of wisdom to take a reproof well as to give it well. A man has to be humble in order to receive instruction, or a rebuke, or to be taught. The proud (an assumed superiority) do not receive instruction because they view themselves as much too smart to need it. You cannot view yourself as too wise to learn or so good that you could not be better.

PRAYER

"Lord, may we never be so proud as to stop learning.
In Jesus' name. Amen."

PROVERBS 10:19

"In the multitude of words sin is not lacking,
but he who restrains his lips is wise."

A SHORT FUSE AND A LONG TONGUE

After telling his fair patient to put out her tongue, the doctor continued writing out the prescription. When he had finished, he turned to her and said, "There, that will do."

"But, doctor," protested the lady, "you never even looked at my tongue."

And the MD replied, "It wasn't necessary. I just wanted you to keep quiet while I wrote the prescription."

Wisdom is found more in those who are silent than in those who are verbose! The message here is that you should be careful about who you listen to and when a person talks too much, that is a good sign that his words are not worth hearing.

"So then, my beloved brethren, let every man be swift to hear, slow to speak, slow to wrath (v.19); for the wrath of man does not produce the righteousness of God." (v.20) Constant talking will get a person in trouble. Slow down, listen more than you speak, and avoid anger. It will not turn out favorably for you if you have a short fuse and a long tongue.

⌁ PRAYER ⌁

"Lord, I have learned . . . 'it often shows a fine command of language to say nothing.' (The Irish Digest) In Jesus' name, Amen."

PROVERBS 11:2

"When pride comes, then comes shame;
but with the humble is wisdom"

PRIDE ENDS POORLY

In the year 1847, a doctor from Edinburgh, Scotland, Sir James Simpson, discovered that chloroform could be used as an anesthetic to render people insensible to the pain of surgery. From his early experiments, Dr. Simpson made it possible for people to go through the most dangerous operations without fear of pain and suffering. Some people even claim that his was one of the most significant discoveries of modern medicine. Some years later, while lecturing at the University of Edinburgh, Dr. Simpson was asked by one of his students, "What do you consider to be the most valuable discovery of your life?" To the surprise of his students, who had expected him to refer to chloroform, Dr. Simpson replied, "My most valuable discovery was when I discovered myself a sinner and that Jesus Christ was my Savior."

A proud man would not have said that, but a humble man would. The Bible teaches that "God resists the proud, but gives grace to the humble." (James 4:6)

So, if you want the wind of God's favor on you back, you better set aside your "assumed superiority,"or you'll be peddling uphill against the hand of God.

PRAYER

"Lord, there's not a one of us who is free of pride.
Help us to get over ourselves. In Jesus' name. Amen."

PROVERBS 12:4

"An excellent wife is the crown of her husband,
but she who causes shames is like rottenness in his bones."

A CROWN OR A CURSE

An angry woman wrote to a columnist complaining that her husband was living in a tree house. The husband had built the tree house and moved into it to get away from his wife's nagging. The wife complained that the tree house was out front where passers-by could see her husband, and that it had become an embarrassment to her. While she sat behind closed doors, her husband would swing in a hammock on his porch, gaily chatting with curiosity seekers.

The columnist advised the wife to quit nagging or continue to put up with her husband's antics.

A little reverse psychology, but I suspect the wife got the point. If not, it gave the neighbors plenty to gossip about. A wife can make a happy home, a little bit of heaven on earth, even though the husband is less than favorable! She can also make it a preview to hell itself. It is all in the character of the woman.

Wives, make it your determined goal to be the "crown of your husband," otherwise you will end up being his personal curse.

PRAYER

Lord, thank You for the countless women
whose lives exemplify this Proverb;
they deserve more than they often receive.
In Jesus' name. Amen."

PROVERBS 13:16

*"Every prudent man acts with knowledge,
but a fool lays open his folly."*

THE ROOT OF ALL BAD DECISIONS

"*A* cigar store Indian was elected Justice of the Peace in Allentown, New Jersey in 1883. The statue, clothed with the fictitious name of Abner Robbins, was duly placed on the ballot and elected with a majority of seven votes over the incumbent Sam Davis. Judge Davis, who held office many years, resigned in indignation when he learned his successful opponent was a wooden Indian."[1]

These people need to be better informed. In contrast, our Proverb teaches that every prudent man acts with knowledge. A wise man is prudent (one who considers seriously the consequences of his actions), and acts with caution and knowledge. He seeks counsel when he needs to expand his knowledge and will accept guidance in areas where he is uninformed. Any successful endeavor is an informed one. However, there are those who impulsively act first and think afterward; after the consequences settle in. Long term serious consequences, like a prison term! Their folly is displayed before all.

PRAYER

*"Lord, deliver us from ill thought out
and ill-informed decisions. In Jesus' name. Amen."*

PROVERBS 14:29

"He who is slow to wrath has great understanding,
but he who is impulsive exalts folly."

THAT FACE

The camel, although a very useful animal, is one of the ugliest, stubborn, and dangerous of all the so-called tame animals. The camel can kick sideways as well as forward and backward, and it has a very nasty bite. It can stretch its long neck around and bite. It can also turn around and spit in the face of its rider. Sometimes it turns its face around and simply stares at its rider. The camel can drop its head between the two front legs and look backward with an upside-down face; and what a face!

Try to picture being bitten by a camel or having one kick you sideways. That is about as impressive as a guy that flies off the handle at the slightest provocation. He acts impulsively (acting or doing something without forethought), and his folly (lack of good sense) is exalted for all to see! Just what you want your spouse and children to see, right?

So, slow down. When you feel the anger building, try to remember, and this is extremely hard, you are about to be kicked sideways by it. Perhaps picturing a camel looking at you between its legs with an upside-down face will be enough to bring a little humor into the picture.

∼ PRAYER ∼

"Lord, keep me from spitting in my own face
by my quick temper. In Jesus' name. Amen."

PROVERBS 15:4

*"A wholesome tongue is a tree of life,
but perverseness in it breaks the spirit."*

WORDS THAT WORK

*P*lato is credited with this quote: "Wise men talk because they have something to say; fools, because they have to say something."

If you must speak, try words of encouragement. They will bring life to any conversation, and people will hate to see you go. Remember, words can encourage a person or depress them. Words can bring healing and emotional health; that is why they are a "tree of life." But there are others who seem to camp in the negative, the down, the black. Perverse people (a person showing a deliberate desire to behave in an unacceptable or unreasonable way) use words like a machete, chopping, slicing, and hacking. Their words have the effect of a fragmentation grenade! People are glad to see them go and sad to see them coming!

Discouraging words and discouraging people can change, but it will take time. Start with being thankful to God for His goodness in your life. Surely there is something to be thankful for? Even if it's just a loving cat or dog. Thankfulness will lead to encouraging words; the two go hand in hand. Then, take the dare and say something encouraging to another person. Lift them up. Be certain the encouragement is based on reality, not to flatter.

PRAYER

*"Lord, may I always use my tongue to uplift another soul,
not to push them down. In Jesus' name. Amen."*

PROVERBS 16:1

*"The preparations of the heart belong to man,
but the answer of the tongue is from the Lord."*

"GOD CONTROLS EVEN THE TONGUE"

—B. G. Bosh

A person may make plans, like placing soldiers in a battle line, but the Lord determines the outcome. "There are many plans in a man's heart, nevertheless the Lord's counsel—that will stand. God guides what comes out of the heart (the reply of the tongue), one's heart and speech are closely related, but God will ultimately have His will prevail." A man's heart plans his way, but the Lord directs his steps.

Not all that is said is of God, as our above quote illustrates. Hopefully, most of what we do say is that God delights in blessings. However, we are not in as much control of our lives as we may believe. Today's Proverb teaches the humble principle that God ultimately controls outcomes, plans, and even the desires of our heart, as expressed in words that are spoken. Trust God for your life's outcomes, change what you can, control the tongue, and be content with Godliness. (I Timothy 6:6)

PRAYER

*"Lord, You're in control, even if I think I am.
In Jesus' name. Amen."*

PROVERBS 17:3

*"The refining pot is for silver and the furnace for gold,
but the Lord tests the hearts."*

PERFECT AND COMPLETE

In Coventry, England, a man called at the Citizens' Advice Bureau and asked to have his wife traced. It transpired that they had parted three days after their wedding nearly 25 years before and hadn't seen each other since. Asked whether he was thinking of a divorce, the man replied, "Oh, no. I was just thinking it would be nice to get together to celebrate our silver wedding anniversary."—*Weekly News*, London

This of course is no marriage, simply because there is nothing to celebrate. A silver wedding anniversary celebrates the trials and joys of being married for twenty-five years, which is no little task. Our Proverb celebrates the idea that as silver is tried by fire, so God tries the hearts of his children. Silver and gold are purified under intense heat; likewise a believer's heart is purified by the heat of trials which the Lord brings. God in His love tests our devotion and faith. He reveals us to ourselves when we are severely tested. We are often unaware of our own problems. Testing will bring them out! God's will show you whether you are patient, forgiving, complaining, or a wimp. Are you willing to trust God when it does not make sense? Are you willing to forgive others while they continue to sin against you? Are you willing to endure pain while you wait for God?

"My brethren, count it all joy when you fall into various trials, knowing that the testing of your faith produces patience. But let patience have its perfect work, that you may be perfect and complete, lacking nothing."(James 1:2–4)

PRAYER

*"Lord, purify my soul, even if it's painful.
In Jesus' name. Amen."*

PROVERBS 18:21

*"Death and life are in the power of the tongue,
and those who love it will eat its fruit."*

LIFE OVER DEATH

A woman once came to one of the old Puritan divines (a person who adheres to strict moral or religious principles) of London and told him that the bands which he wore with his pulpit gown were altogether too long, and that they annoyed her greatly. She would like his permission to shorten them. Confident of his acquiescence, she had come armed with a pair of scissors. The minister mildly agreed and handed over the offending bands to the woman, who shortened them according to her taste with her scissors and then handed the fragments back to the minister.

When he received them, he thanked her and said: "Now, my good woman, there is something about you that is altogether too long, and which has annoyed me greatly, and since one good turn deserves another, I would like permission to shorten it."

"Certainly," said the woman, "you have permission to do so, and here are the shears."

Whereupon the worthy divine said, "Very well, madam, put out your tongue."—C. E. Macartney

A man may do a great deal of good, or a great deal of harm, both to others and to himself, according to the use he makes of his tongue. There is only one way to use your tongue in a positive and encouraging way, a way that brings life; and that is to yield it to God's control. "So then, my beloved brethren, let every man be swift to hear, slow to speak, slow to wrath, for the wrath of man does not produce the righteousness of God." (James 1:19-20)

∽ PRAYER ∾

*"Lord, help me to choose life and not death.
In Jesus' name. Amen."*

PROVERBS 19:21

*"There are many plans in a man's heart,
nevertheless the Lord's counsel—that will stand."*

RELAX, GOD'S GOT THIS

When Lincoln was on his way to Washington to be inaugurated, he spent some time in New York with Horace Greeley and told him an anecdote which was meant to be an answer to the question which everybody was asking him: Are we really to have Civil War? In his circuit-riding days, Lincoln and his companions, riding to the next session of court, had crossed many swollen rivers. But the Fox River was still ahead of them; and they said one to another, "If these streams give us so much trouble, how shall we get over Fox River?"

When darkness fell, they stopped for the night at a log tavern, where they fell in with the Methodist presiding elder of the district who rode through the country in all kinds of weather and knew all about the Fox River. They gathered about him and asked him about the present state of the river. "I know all about the Fox River. I have crossed it often and understand it well. But I have one fixed rule about Fox River—I never cross it till I reach it."

We all have our Fox Rivers to cross here on earth, and often we worry or fear about what *may have happened*, or anticipate what *may yet happen*. There is a real sense that all has been foreordained, though we ourselves are actively involved in the planning and execution, God still overrides for His own purposes.

"The counsel of the Lord stands forever, the plans of His heart to all generations." (Psalm 33:11)

The Lord of hosts has sworn, saying, "Surely, as I have thought, so it shall come to pass. And as I have purposed, so it shall stand." (Isaiah 14:24) Relax and trust, the outcome is in God's hands. He's got this!

PRAYER

*"Lord, I trust your wise counsel, help me to so live.
In Jesus' name. Amen."*

PROVERBS 20:3

*"It is honorable for a man to stop striving,
since any fool can start a quarrel."*

AROUND AND AROUND

In one of the "Big Three"conferences during World War II, Roosevelt and Churchill were trying to get Stalin to agree with some proposed strategy. When Stalin gave his reason or excuse for not agreeing with them, they said, "That is no reason for your refusal!" Stalin replied with a story of two Arabs.

One Arab asked the other to lend him his rope. The latter replied, "I can't. I need it to tie my camel." The first Arab reminded his companion that he did not own a camel. To which the companion replied, "I know that. But when you do not want to lend your rope, one excuse is as good as any other."

Excuses offered to God are in the same category. They reveal that we simply do not want to do what He tells us to do.

Once you've figured out the argument is going nowhere, no profit, no good reason, it's best to abandon ship. Any fool can argue, and most fools do, continually.

⁓ PRAYER ⁓

*"Lord, help us all to abandon these worthless arguments
before things really get out of hand. In Jesus' name. Amen."*

PROVERBS 21:9

"Better to dwell in a corner of a housetop,
than in a house shared with a contentious woman."

ON OCCASION AND NO OCCASION

*J*ohn Brentz, a friend of Luther, and one of the stalwarts of the Reformation, incurred the hatred of Charles V who made many attempts to kill the minister. Hearing that a troop of Spanish cavalry was on the way to arrest him, he cast himself upon God in prayer. At once the guidance came: "Take a loaf of bread and go into the upper room where you will find a door open, enter and hide yourself under the roof."

He acted accordingly, found the only open door, and hid himself in the loft. For fourteen days he laid there while the search continued. The one loaf of bread would have been insufficient, but day by day, a hen came up to the garret, and laid an egg without cackling. The fifteenth day it did not come, but John Brentz heard the people in the street say, "They are gone at last," and he came out.[1]

Sometimes a man, even in his own house, feels as this reformer did, hiding from his predator. Unfortunately, sometimes the predator is his own wife!

The Bible is shockingly accurate. Out Proverb makes the point that it is better to live in cramped quarters (v.9) or in a desert (v19) with peace and quiet, than in a spacious house with an argumentative and contentious wife. Some wives argue over the little, the insignificant, the minor, all the while feeling justified to do so. May God help the man so married.

"A continual dripping on a very rainy day and a contentious woman are alike. Whoever restrains her restrains the wind, and grasps oil with his right hand." (Proverbs 27:15-16)

⮞ PRAYER ⮜

"Lord, deliver good men from bad women.
In Jesus' name. Amen."

June 22

PROVERBS 22:4

*"By humility and the fear of the Lord
are riches and honor and life."*

SELF-IMPORTANCE

There is a church in Palestine, the doorway of which is so low that one must stoop to enter it. This was to prevent medieval raiders from riding their horses into the church and disrupting the worship. The door is called "Humility Gate."[1]

Humility has been defined as a "modest or low view of one's own importance."

We are not to view ourselves as indispensable. Mistake! Most people can smell this attitude a mile away, plus God "resists the proud but gives grace to the humble." (James 4:6) We must so reverence God's majesty and authority over us as to submit with humility to His commands. Also, a humble man will accept God's divine providence in his life. What God permits and orders, he accepts by faith. What he can and should change he does, but he does not rail against God about those things that cannot be changed, for example, untimely death, end to a marriage, or an unpleasant circumstance.

The riches and honor and life are more spiritual than material, though at times it is material, as God sees fit. It is better to have "peace with God" than a large piece of this world.

PRAYER

*"Lord, help me to suppress my striving self-importance.
In Jesus' name. Amen."*

PROVERBS 23:24–25

"The father of the righteous will greatly rejoice,
and he who begets a wise child will delight in him.
Let you father and your mother be glad
and let her who bore you rejoice."

RIGHTEOUS AND WISE

One of the most heartwarming commercials on television pictured a mother in tears. When asked why, she said to her husband, "Our son called (long distance) today." Her husband asked if anything was wrong. When she replied in the negative, he inquired, "Well, why are you crying? Why did he call?" Smiling through her tears, she answered, "He said, 'I just called to tell you that I love you, Mom.'"

Children will be a joy to their parents if they be righteous and wise. Righteousness is being godly, doing the right thing before God and God's laws, and before man and man's laws. To be wise is to be prudent, "one who considers carefully consequences." A lifestyle of righteousness and wisdom will benefit the individual and delight the parents.

PRAYER

"Lord, may I always be a delight to Mom and Dad.
In Jesus' name. Amen."

PROVERBS 24:27

*"Prepare your outside work,
make it fit for yourself in the field,
and afterward build your house."*

THE RIGHT ORDER AT THE RIGHT TIME

*I*n London, England, there is a strange house. It looks like any other house on the block. But wait! Nobody ever comes out of No. 23 Leinster Gardens. There is neither a doorbell nor a letter box. From the windows, no one at all peers out. And nary a soul ever sits on one of the balconies.

Simply put, No. 23 Leinster Gardens, in the tree-lined Bayswater section of London, is "The House that Never Was."

Yes, No. 23 is a sham. It is a dummy house whose door and windows are merely painted on a cement wall. Behind this dividing oddball facade there is nothing except a network of girders, some train tracks, and the entrance to a tunnel. Every so often a fresh coat of paint is applied to the facing wall to keep it looking exactly like the neighboring buildings.

"The House That Never Was" was put up by London's Metropolitan Railway (the so-called Underground), whose officials decided it would be the best way to hide the entrance to the subway tunnel and fill the gap in the row of houses so as not to spoil the harmonious look of the street.

Israelites, most of whom farmed land, needed to plow and sow seed (to get their fields ready) before they attended to more immediate creature comforts, such as a house. Make sure the income is in-coming before you start building a house. The house may be literal—wood and stones—or figurative—marriage, a wife, and children. Make sure you have the right priorities in the right order, then you will be able to complete what you start.

∽ PRAYER ∼

*"Lord, help me not to put the cart before the horse.
In Jesus' name. Amen."*

PROVERBS 25:21

"If your enemy is hungry, give him bread to eat;
and if he is thirsty, give him water to drink;
for so you will heap coals of fire on his head,
and the Lord will reward you."

COMPASSION OVER REVENGE

Sam Foss was an enthusiastic traveler as well as a writer, and on one of his trips through rustic England, weary and thirsty, he came to a small unpainted house that stood atop a steep hill. Near one side of the road was a crude signpost finger pointing to a well-worn path and a sign that read, "Come in and have a cool drink." Following the path a short distance, he found a spring of ice-cold water above which hung an old-fashioned gourd dipper. On a bench nearby was a basket of summer apples with another sign: "Help Yourself."

His curiosity aroused, Foss sought out the old couple who lived in the little house and questioned them about the signs and the fruit. He learned that they were childless, and that their poor farm yielded them a scant living. But because they had such an abundance of cold spring water and fruit they felt rich and wanted to share it with anyone who might pass that way. "We're too poor to give money to charity," the old gentleman said, "but we thought maybe in this way we could add our mite and do something for folks who pass our way."[1]—*Evangelistic Illustration*

Kindness to one's enemy—giving him food and water—is like heaping burning coals on his head. Sometimes a person's fire went out and he needed to borrow some live coals to restart his fire. Giving a person coals in a pan to carry home "on his head" was a neighborly, kind act; it made friends, not enemies. Compassion over revenge will bring a better world and blessings from God.

PRAYER

"Lord, remind me daily that You prefer compassion from us,
not revenge. In Jesus' name. Amen."

PROVERBS 26:27

*"Whoever digs a pit will fall into it,
and he who rolls a stone will have it roll back on him."*

SCHEMERS

Some years ago, a vase hermetically-sealed, was found in a mummy-pit in Egypt by the English traveler Wilkinson, who sent it to the British Museum. The librarian there, having unfortunately broken it, discovered in it a few grains of wheat and one or two peas—old, wrinkled, and hard as stone.

The peas were planted carefully under glass on the 4th of June 1844, and at the end of thirty days, these old seeds were seen to spring up into new life. They had been buried probably about three thousand years ago, perhaps in the time of Moses, and had slept all that long time, apparently dead, yet still living in the dust of the tomb.—Gaussen

A few grains of wheat and two peas, over 3000 years old, were able to spring to life. This illustrates the concept of you reap what you sow. "Do not be deceived, God is not mocked; for whatever a man sows, that he will also reap." (Galatians 6:7) God often takes the evil designs of men and turns them back on themselves.

So, do not plot evil against another; don't design, coordinate, or participate. God has His ways of turning it all back on the schemers of evil.

⁓ PRAYER ⁓

*"Lord, may we be mindful that You are merciful
and precisely just. In Jesus' name. Amen."*

PROVERBS 27:2

*"Let another man praise you, and not your own mouth;
a stranger, and not your own lips."*

THE PUFFER FISH

There is a legend of a man so much beloved of the angels for his saintliness that they asked God to bestow upon him some new power. They were permitted to ask him to make the choice of a gift. He said he was content and wanted nothing. But on being urged to make some request, he asked for the power to do a great deal of good in the world without knowing it.

And so, ever afterward his shadow, when it fell behind him where he could not see it, had wondrous healing power; but when it was cast before him where he could see it, it had no such power.—J. H. Bomberger

It is deeply ingrained in our nature to want recognition, so when we are feeling inadequate, we tend to brag. The problem with bragging is it is distasteful when you hear it, and it only goes to minimize the one bragging. It does not make him look bigger, only smaller. The puffer fish has the ability to quickly ingest huge amounts of water to turn themselves into a inedible ball several times their normal size. Some species have spines on their skin to make them less palatable.

So, if you are in the habit of "puffing yourself up" by bragging, remember you're less attractive, and people will tend to leave you alone, i.e., not want to be around you.

☙ PRAYER ❧

*"Lord, help me to not 'puff myself up,'
lest you choose to deflate me through humiliation.
In Jesus' name. Amen."*

June 28

"Those who forsake the law praise the wicked,
but such as keep the law contend with them."

THE TOOL OF JUSTICE

In a courtroom drama written by Judge Curtis Bok, the plaintiff, who was a sculptor, at one point asked the judge in frustration, "Isn't this a court of justice?"

"No," replied the judge. "It is a court of law. Justice is an ideal like truth or beauty. As you try to achieve beauty with your mallet and chisel, so law is our tool in the pursuit of justice."[1]

If you want justice for the wicked, be sure you are striving to keep the law yourself. Wicked people will speak well of one another, and so strengthen one another's hands in their wicked ways. But law keepers oppose the injustice of the wicked, for they know that only through obedience to the laws will justice be for all. Such keepers of the law will also incur another benefit—a blessing from God! Which speaks volumes about God.

"But those who rebuke the wicked will have delight, and a good blessing will come upon them." (Proverbs 24:25)

PRAYER

"Lord, remind us that we become the tools of justice
when we keep the laws ourselves. In Jesus' name. Amen."

PROVERBS 29:9

*"If a wise man contends with a foolish man,
whether the fool rages or laughs, there is no peace."*

NO PEACE WITH A FOOL

A citizen of Tel Aviv once went to court against a stone mason who refused to chisel A.D. dates on his father's gravestone. The court referred the case to the Rabbinate (the highest religious body) for an opinion. The Rabbinate rejected the citizen's appeal, saying that the Christian-Gregorian calendar was unacceptable since it was based on the birth of Jesus. The court, however, overturned the Rabbinate's opinion, noting ruefully that the rabbis' statement was dated 1972! The Jewish calendar was 5733 then.

The setting of this verse is in a court. The fool vents his foolishness by raging or laughing, both inappropriate in court. There is no peace with a fool. The best approach is to leave off personal contending and allow the courts to settle the dispute if it is severe enough. With some people, you will never be right or just. Ultimately, your best approach is to leave it with God. God knows how to handle fools.

⟶ PRAYER ⟵

*"Lord, my I not add to the problem
by becoming a fool myself when contending with a fool.
In Jesus' name. Amen."*

PROVERBS 30:5

*"Every word of God is pure;
He is a shield to those who put their trust in Him."*

EVERY WORD IS PURE

*D*r. Robert Dick Wilson, former professor of Semitic philosophy at Princeton Theological Seminary, said, "After forty-five years of scholarly research in biblical textual studies and in language study, I have come now to the conviction that no man knows enough to assail the truthfulness of the Old Testament. Where there is sufficient documentary evidence to make an investigation, the statements of the Bible, in the original text, have stood the test."

And the noted Dr. J. O. Kinnaman said: "Of the hundreds of thousands of artifacts found by the archaeologists, not one has ever been discovered that contradicts or denies one word, phrase, clause, or sentence of the Bible, but always confirms and verifies the facts of the Biblical record."

The Bible is a shield during in a hostile and aggressive world. To trust it is to have a lamp to your feet through life's darkest paths. (Psalm 119:105) To believe it is to bring you to the eternal "streets of gold." (Revelation 21:21) To obey it is to bring the weary soul to "green pastures by still waters. (Psalm 23:2)

Oh, weary sinner, take Christ as Savior, and walk with Him as Lord, and you will have God as your "shield and the horn of your salvation." (Psalm 18:2)

⟶ PRAYER ⟵

*"Lord, I take Christ as my Savior. Save me from my sins
and wayward path. In Jesus' name. Amen."*

PROVERBS 1:32–33

"For the turning away of the simple will slay them,
and the complacency of fools will destroy them;
but whoever listens to me will dwell safely,
and will be secure, without fear of evil."

INDIFFERENCE

*M*any years ago, two Massachusetts state senators wound up in an angry debate, in which one told the other he could "go to ——." The man, thus consigned, protested to Governor Coolidge and asked him to intervene over the outrage. To which Coolidge replied: "I've looked up the law, Senator, and you don't have to go there."

"Turn at my rebuke; Surely I will pour out my spirit on you; I will make my words known to you." (Proverbs 1:23)

To reject "Lady Wisdom" is to hate knowledge (cf. v.22) and to refuse to fear the Lord. (cf. v7) So, fools will suffer the consequences of their actions. (v.31) They reap what they sow. (v. 7) "Do not be deceived, God is not mocked; for whatever a man sows, that he will also reap." (Galatians 6:7) In contrast, to heed the way of wisdom will bring safety and security. (cf. vs 33)

Do not reject the Lord's call through His Son, Jesus Christ. "For whosoever calls on the name of the Lord shall be saved." (Romans 10:13) Whosoever includes whosoever reads those words.

PRAYER

"Lord, remind us that You stretch your hand of forgiveness
toward us all day long. In Jesus' name. Amen."

PROVERBS 2:9

*"Then you will understand righteousness and justice,
and equity and every good path."*

THERE IS NO SECRET

*F*amous men of the past have bequeathed us statements that have become mottoes. History declares that Henry Clay was about to introduce a certain bill in Congress when a friend said, "If you do, Clay, it will kill your chance for the presidency."

"But is the measure, right?" Clay asked, and on being assured it was right said, "I would rather be right than be president."[1]—*The Watchman Examiner*

If you live in an honest and upright fashion, God will be your shield (cf. v.7), he will preserve your life (cf. v.8), and give you understanding on what is the next right decision to make. (cf. v.9)

God's blessing in our lives is directly rated; not to our wealth, not to our education, and not to our background, but to our moral integrity. Doing what is always right before God is what God will bless.

⟶ PRAYER ⟵

*"Lord, may we never forget that pleasing You is no secret,
we simply need to obey. In Jesus' name. Amen."*

PROVERBS 3:5–6

*"Trust in the Lord with all your heart
and lean not on your own understanding;
in all your ways acknowledge Him,
and He shall direct your paths."*

TRUST AND LEAN NOT

A little faith will bring your soul to heaven; a great faith will bring heaven to your soul.[1]—Spurgeon

To trust in the Lord wholeheartedly means one should not rely (lean) on his understanding, for human insights are never enough. God's ways are incomprehensible. "For My thoughts are not your thoughts, nor are your ways My ways," says the Lord. "For as the heavens are higher than the earth, so are My ways higher than your ways, and My thoughts than your thoughts." (Isaiah 55:8,9) Yet in all of this, He is still trustworthy. Cannot figure it out? Makes no sense? Learn to trust God and not your own insight. It may be amusing to watch a cat chase its tail, but in practice, it is no fun. It just leaves you dizzy. Trying to figure out the puzzling pieces of our own life, likewise, leaves us dizzy. Lean on God. He will make your paths smooth. He will remove obstacles; not all of them though. It may not be the easiest road, but those who follow this Proverb will have an easier life.

PRAYER

*"Lord, help us to trust you and not ourselves
when life goes beyond reason.
In Jesus' name. Amen."*

PROVERBS 4:23

"Keep your heart with all diligence,
for out of it spring the issues of life."

THE HEART OF THE PROBLEM

It was necessary for me some years ago to get some passport photographs. Awful agony! When I received the photograph from the photographer, I opened it and, well, I was a little disappointed. So, I wrote to the photographer and he said, "Well, that is only a passport photograph. Would you like some touched-up prints?" That sounded better, so I ordered some. But to my disappointment, the American consulate only wanted the passport photograph. I offered them the other, but no, they wanted the passport photograph that was not touched-up. The two were completely the same person. The touched-up photograph was what I wanted other people to think that I was; but the passport photograph was the ugly reality. And all I could do was to submit to the diagnosis and give the man the thing he wanted.[1]—Alan Redpath

We may want to "touch up" some of our speech and actions by blaming others or circumstances, but the "ugly reality" is that our sins originate in our heart, are formulated in our mind, and then executed through our will. Not always a pretty picture. Jesus put it this way: "A good man out of the good treasure of his heart brings forth good things, and an evil man out of the evil treasure brings forth evil things." (Matthew 12:35-36)

"For out of the heart proceed evil thoughts, murders, adulteries, fornications, thefts, false witness, blasphemies." (Matthew 15:19)

⮞ PRAYER ⮜

"Lord, we accept your assessment of our heart,
therefore, may we seek your remedy through salvation
and Lordship of our thoughts. In Jesus' name. Amen."

July 5

PROVERBS 5:21

*"For the ways of man are before the eyes of the Lord,
and He ponders all his paths."*

GOD'S EYES ARE ON US

In 1623, Baker and Lukas published a Bible in England, since called "The Wicked Bible" because the little word "not"was omitted in the seventh commandment: "Thou shalt not commit adultery." The printers were heavily fined by the High Commission and the whole edition destroyed.

The ways of man, all his characteristics and habits, all his actions, are before the eyes of the Lord, even that which is done ever so secretly and disguised so cleverly. "For God will bring every work into judgment, including every secret thing, whether good or evil. (Ecclesiastes12:14) God takes the time to ponder (to think about carefully before deciding) our behavior). The context is faithfulness to your wife, (v.18) and the perils of adultery. (v.3)

Simple science again: you do not have to be brilliant to please God, but you do have to be obedient.

PRAYER

*"Lord, help us to always be enraptured
with the wife of our youth. In Jesus' name. Amen."*

PROVERBS 6:1–5

"My son, if you become surety for your friend,
if you have shaken hands in pledge for a stranger . . .
Deliver yourself like a gazelle from the hand of the hunter,
and like a bird from the hand of the fowler."

THE FOWLER'S SNARE

*I*n Abyssinia, when a man is convicted of an offense for which he has to pay a fine, he must find a friend who will offer himself as a security that the culprit will not run away until the fine is paid. The prisoner and the man who has the misfortune to be his friend are then chained leg-to-leg and turned loose to roam about, sharing one another's misfortunes, and begging together for the money necessary to pay the fine, until either they are able to regain their liberty or the death of one puts an end to their existence.—E. A. De Cosson

Surety is defined as a person who takes responsibility for another's debt. Surety is not a good idea. It's like being chained to a prisoner who has committed a crime that you have not committed. Miserable! The warning is clear: if you have shaken in agreement on another's debt, make every effort immediately to withdraw your obligation, or you will soon be hating life.

⟨∾ PRAYER ∾⟩

"Lord, help us when our compassion overrides
our good sense. In Jesus' name. Amen."

PROVERBS 7:22–23

*"Immediately he went after her, as an ox goes to the slaughter,
or as a fool to the correction of the stocks . . .
He did not know it would cost his life."*

FOOLS MAKE A MOCK OF SIN

One day a fairy came to a man and told him she would grant him any favor he might wish. The man thought a few minutes, and then said, "My wish is to see a newspaper published one year from today."

Immediately the fairy handed him a newspaper printed one-year in advance. He turned quickly to the financial page, ran his fingers nervously up and down the list of stocks, and leaping from chair shouted, "Hurrah, I'm worth fifteen million dollars." Then carelessly turning over to the obituary page his glance fell on a report that made him gasp. "I died two days ago!"[1]

Solomon devotes three chapters to the topic of adultery or immorality in general. He must be concerned! Considered the wisest man to have lived, he does this for good reason. It's not just the initial encounter that costs him his life; it's the change of heart that results from it. It sets a man upon a course that he favors; one that changes his thought process, one that eventually sets his character so he can never be faithful to just one woman. Mindsets have outcomes, and Solomon warns men that a sexually immoral lifestyle will eventually cost one his life. Maybe not literally; sometimes yes. Many have died at the hand of a jealous husband. But spiritually, one can lose his soul. Paul says, "Do you not know that the unrighteous will not inherit the kingdom of God? Do not be deceived. Neither fornicators, nor idolaters, nor adulterers, nor homosexuals . . . will inherit the kingdom of God." (I Corinthians 6:9-10) That loss of life will be eternal. The "Good News" is God will take away your sin if you believe and repent."

PRAYER

*"Lord, may I never view as casual what You view as critical.
In Jesus' name. Amen."*

PROVERBS 8:11–12

*"For wisdom is better than rubies,
and all the things one may desire
cannot be compared with her.
I, wisdom, dwell with prudence,
and find out knowledge and discretion."*

2,783 DIAMONDS

The crown of Queen Elizabeth II has 2,783 diamonds, 277 pearls, 18 sapphires, 11 emeralds, and 5 rubies—all priceless gems.

Wisdom will give you prudence (care, caution, and good judgment). Discretion is the ability to avoid speaking in a way as to avoid causing offense. Prudence and discretion as well as knowledge (facts, information, and skill) are in high demand today. Too many live their lives in complete absence of them. True wisdom will always start with reverence for God (Proverbs1:7), for to live life in the absence of its creator is truly foolish. Wisdom's value is to live successful before God and man. This virtue far exceeds the value of a crown with 2,783 diamonds, 277 pearls, 18 sapphires, etc. To have material prosperity without wisdom is to eventually be penniless. To have true wisdom with meager means, is the only virtue that will bring you safely into the arms of God.

∽ PRAYER ∼

*"Lord, may I never get so short-sighted
as to trade the temporal for the eternal.
In Jesus' name. Amen."*

PROVERBS 9:10–12

"The fear of the Lord is the beginning of wisdom,
and the knowledge of the Holy One is understanding.
For by me your days will be multiplied,
and years of life will be added to you.
If you are wise, you are wise for yourself,
and if you scoff, you will bear it alone."

PROLONGED LIVING

*B*ats are said to live longer for their size than any other animal. They have a life span of twenty years. It has been suggested that the secret of their longevity is their ability to relax and go quickly into the deep sleep of hibernation. Right after fighting, one of them can almost immediately slow its heartbeat from 180 beats per minute to three, and it can retard its respiration from eight breaths a second to one every eight minutes.

Longevity, at least in bats, rests on their ability to relax and sleep. However, for people, longevity comes as a reward for reverence toward God. "The fear of the Lord prolongs days, but the years of the wicked will be shortened." (Proverbs 10:27)

To understand life, how it works, both with people and God, is directly related to understanding God Himself. Such understanding will leave you with hope and purpose, even in the midst of life's conundrums (a confusing and difficult problem or question). In contrast, men's foolishness and lack of self-control will shorten their lives.

In the end, those that are wise can thank God, but those that are wicked can thank themselves, for God is not the author of their sin.

PRAYER

"Lord, may I always reverence Your name and enjoy my days.
In Jesus' name. Amen."

PROVERBS 10:12

"Hatred stirs up strife, but loves covers all sins."

TO KILL A RAT

*H*ating people is like burning down your own house to get rid of a rat.[1] —Harry Emerson Fosdick

When hate burns beneath the surface, it will erupt in some form of strife (disagreement over fundamental issues). We may think hate is circumstantial, and circumstances certainly play a role, but hate (to feel passionate dislike for someone) usually takes time for the fire to start and then for it to be continually stoked to overflowing.

"He who covers a transgression seeks love, but he who repeats a matter separates friends." (Proverbs 17:9)

So, at some point, if you are in a constant state of hating someone, you must either decide you will forgive (put away) and thus cover the sin, or you choose not to and eventually go your separate ways. It is suggested that honest, fair, and respectful conversations be tried, and accountability for all involved, plus a willingness to repent of sin, reconcile, and go on.

Keep in mind, we're all flawed. We all have personality weaknesses. These should be covered in love because we are human, but likewise, serious sins can be forgiven, if there's true repentance and love.

PRAYER

*"Lord, help us to forgive and to give forgiveness
In Jesus' name. Amen."*

PROVERBS 11:25

*"The generous soul will be made rich,
and he who waters will also be watered himself."*

A SEEMING PARADOX

Mrs. Sam Saddoris moved her car to get a penny that rolled beneath it. The car lurched, hit a parking meter, broke a window as it bounced against a building, rolled half a block down the sidewalk, and stopped.

Damaged to the car was $102. Damage to the window and parking meter was not estimated. Police said they were not even sure whether Mrs. Saddoris found the penny.[1]

Some cling to money much too tightly. In the economy of God, the greedy ultimately lose even the material things they try so hard to keep, while the generous only prosper more and more. Paul the Apostle put it this way: "This I say: He who sows sparingly will also reap sparingly, and he who sows bountifully will also reap bountifully." (II Corinthians 9:6)

So, take any opportunity to give to others in genuine need; do not hold back. If you have it, give it, whether money, material goods, or service, and you'll find a strange thing happening to you. God will see fit to return to you many of the same favors you give to others. Most importantly, you'll have God's favor on your soul, and that favor is always through His Son, Jesus Christ. (cf. John 14:6)

PRAYER

*"Lord, help me to open my hands, not to close them.
In Jesus' name. Amen."*

PROVERBS 12:26

*"The righteous should choose his friends carefully,
for the way of the wicked leads them astray."*

CHOOSE CAREFULLY

When in Rhodesia, now Zimbabwe, I asked a friend why Cecil Rhodes did not participate in the gold rush days to augment his fortune in diamonds. "The story goes," he said, "that during the early leasing of the better gold fields, a friend of Rhodes lay desperately ill. The popular and immensely wealthy Rhodes denied himself the privilege of participating in the bidding to sit by his friend's bed, day and night, until he died."[8]

A righteous person does not take on just anybody as a friend; he chooses his friends carefully.

The friends you choose will reflect your own character. Usually, what your friends do and like is what you do and like as well, thus friendship. "Birds of a feather flock together" for good reason. Ducks do not hang with woodpeckers, and geese don't fly with eagles. So, carefully evaluate what your friends like and do, for if you hang with them for long, you'll be doing the same. Do they value church? The Bible? Service? If so, you are on the right path. Do they do drugs? Unemployed? And in general, get in trouble? Beware. It will not be long before you're doing the same. ". . . do you not know that a little leaven, leavens the whole lump?" (I Corinthians 5:6)

⸻ PRAYER ⸻

*"Lord, help me to think about what friends I choose,
because before long, I'll be thinking like them.
In Jesus' name. Amen."*

8. Jones, G. C. (1986). *1000 Illustrations for Preaching and Teaching* (p. 48). Nashville, TN: Broadman & Holman Publishers.

PROVERBS 13:3

"He who guards his mouth preserves his life,
but he who opens wide his lips shall have destruction."

DON'T BE A QUICK DRAW

In France, there once lived a poor, blind girl who obtained the Gospel of Mark in raised letters and learned to read it by the tips of her fingers. By constant reading, these became callous, and her sense of touch diminished until she could not distinguish the characters. One day, she cut the skin from the ends of her fingers to increase their sensitivity, only to destroy it.

She felt that she must now give up her beloved Book, weeping, pressed it to her lips, saying, "Farewell, farewell, sweet word of my Heavenly Father!" To her surprise, her lips, more delicate than her fingers, discerned the form of the letters. All night she perused with her lips the Word of God and overflowed with joy at this new acquisition.—Selected

I'll have to say unusual, but a better use of our lips than what our Proverb warns against. Being careful about what you say will keep you out of a lot of trouble. Thoughtless words often reveal private information, offend unnecessarily, and make promises hard to keep. So, the best policy is to remain silent, speak with grace, and then not so often. It is better to remain silent and thought to be a fool than to speak and remove all doubt!

"Whoever guards his mouth and tongue keeps his soul from troubles." (Proverbs 21:23)

PRAYER

"Lord, help me to put a lock on my lips,
and open them only so slowly. In Jesus' name. Amen."

PROVERBS 14:12

"There is a way that seems right to a man,
but its end is the way of death."

I WASN'T EXPECTING THIS!

Where is happiness found? John D. Rockefeller, a Christian millionaire, said, "I have made many millions, but they have brought me no happiness. I would barter them all for the days I sat on an office stool in Cleveland and counted myself rich on three dollars a week." Broken in health, he employed an armed guard.[1]

W. H. Vanderbilt said, "The care of 200 million dollars is too great a load for any brain or back to bear. It is enough to kill anyone. There is no pleasure in it." John Jacob Astor left five million but had been martyr to dyspepsia and melancholy. He said, "I am the most miserable man on earth." Henry Ford, the automobile king, said, "Work is the only pleasure. It is only work that keeps me alive and makes life worth living. I was happier when doing a mechanic's job." Andrew Carnegie, the multi-millionaire, said, "Millionaires seldom smile."[1]

The above illustration shows that outside the conscripts of God's laws, life is not nearly as pleasurable as some might think. Those who pursue life without regard for God and His Word, often find themselves in the most desperate straits. It has been said that "you don't really break God's law; you just break yourselves on them." Excellent!

So, if there is a course you consider wise, but is clearly contrary to the Bible, reconsider. It most likely will end up poorly.

∽ PRAYER ∼

"Lord, how often we imagine what is our greatest good,
all the while not realizing that the whole endeavor
will end in disaster. In Jesus' name. Amen."

PROVERBS 15:11

"Hell, and Destruction are before the Lord;
so how much more the hearts of the sons of men."

DO NOT BE LED ASTRAY

On an American troopship, the soldiers crowded around their chaplain asking, "Do you believe in hell?" "I do not." "Well, then, will you please resign, for if there is no hell, we do not need you, and if there is a hell, we do not wish to be led astray."[1]—Christian Beacon

This is a "how much more" Proverb; if Hell is clearly seen by God, how much more the hearts of men. Hell has always been a curiosity for people. There are those who do not believe in Hell, such as our chaplain above and others who make fun of the idea, such as this one: "And, O my brethren," quavered the preacher at the end of his sermon on Hell, "for the wicked there will be wailing in the next world, weeping and wailing and gnashing of teeth."[1] "But, Reverend," said a member of the congregation, "how about those who have no teeth?" "Brother," said the preacher sternly, "teeth will be provided." People continue to mock in disbelief, but Christ Himself preached more on Hell than heaven. "It is better for you to enter into life with one eye, rather than having two eyes, to be cast into hell." (Matthew 18:9)

This is a rather stern warning. Be careful what you set your mind on, for God does see it. If it be righteousness, kindness, and purity, God be pleased, but if it is lust, hate, revenge, and the pursuit of riches, be careful, for God sees that, too. Do not add your soul to the vast hordes of unbelievers who now desperately wish they were not in Hell.

PRAYER

"Lord, may I remember that you never doubted
the existence of Hell. In Jesus' name. Amen."

PROVERBS 16:33

"The lot is cast into the lap,
but its every decision is from the Lord."

THE OUTCOME IS DETERMINED

*A*t a meeting in London, Winston Churchill gave the story of his escape from a South African military prison in Pretoria. Churchill told how, after wandering in the region round Pretoria for two or three days, and feeling at the end of his tether, he made up his mind to present himself at the door of one of the houses whose lights were twinkling in the valley below.

Although a price had been set upon his head, he thought there was a chance of some friendly soul in the heart of that enemy country, and he prayed earnestly that he might be guided to the right house. Then he went up to the door of one of the houses and knocked. A man opened the door and asked him what he wanted. "I am Winston Churchill," he replied. "Come in," said the friendly voice. "This is the only house for miles in which you would be safe."[1]—Bernard M. Allen

"A man's heart plans his way, but the Lord directs his steps." (v.9) We're not quite in control of things as we may think. God has a plan, prepared beforehand, and it is His purpose that we follow it. We can rebel, but that only makes it harder on us. We can complain, but that also makes it harder on us. We can compromise with it, but we can never escape it. The better part of wisdom is to submit to it in faith. We trust the character of God to do right, for it is impossible for Him to do wrong. We can doubt this, but it will only make the ride that much more uncomfortable, or we can relax, live in faith and obedience and thankfulness, and He will, in turn, surround us with favor. (Psalm 5:12)

⁖ PRAYER ⁖

"Lord, You do not condone our sin,
but You do determine our course. In Jesus' name. Amen."

PROVERBS 17:22

*"A merry heart does good, like medicine,
but a broken spirit dries the bones."*

BODY AND SOUL

In a letter to a friend, Robert Louis Stevenson wrote, "For fourteen years I have not had a day of real health. I have wakened sick and gone to bed weary. I have done my work unflinchingly. I have written in bed and out of bed, when torn by coughing and when my head swam for weariness. The battle goes on. Ill or well is a trifle, so long as it goes on. I was made for conflict. The powers that be have willed that my battlefield shall be this dingy, inglorious one of the bed and the medicine bottle."

Here is an example of the broken spirit, but Stevenson continued to write. Two books of his were *Treasure Island* and *The Strange Case of Dr. Jekyll and Mr. Hyde.* Wonderful!

The best medicine for a healthy life is to be cheerful. This cheerful attitude to life comes from being thankful. Paul exhorts us to "Rejoice always, pray without ceasing, in everything give thanks; for this is the will of God in Christ Jesus for you." (I Thessalonians 5:16-17)

The formula is simple: pray and thank God constantly for His riches. This brings a cheerful heart, which brings health to the body. The alternative is brokenness. The sorrows of the mind will produce psychological sickness and physical devastation.

PRAYER

*"Lord, thank You for Your Word,
which brings health to body and soul.
In Jesus' name. Amen."*

July 18

PROVERBS 18:12

"Before destruction, the heart of man is haughty,
and before honor is humility."

SOW HUMILITY, REAP HONOR

The attitude of humanism relegates God to a place of unimportance in our lives. Its philosophy is, "I have done great things today. I will do greater things tomorrow."[9]

Proverbs paints this picture of reality: "The fear of the Lord is the instruction of wisdom, and before honor is humility." (Proverbs 15:33) To honor God as Creator and Sustainer requires humility (a modest or low view of one's importance). To parade around as though one has created his own success is short-sighted. What role did such people have when they were in their mother's womb, growing day by day? Did they shape their own hands, design their own feet, fashion their own eyes? They had zero to do with that, yet they take those very hands, feet, and eyes and sometimes achieve great success; all the while denying God his rightful honor! That's how pride (having an excessively high opinion of one's importance) expresses itself. Ruin will be the end of such people. God will see to it. Having a low opinion of one's own importance is a favorable position before God Almighty. Such a person God will honor.

⟨ ⤝ PRAYER ⤞ ⟩

"Lord, help us to remember how important You are,
and how honored we are to serve You.
In Jesus' name. Amen."

---

9. Hobbs, H. H. (1990). *My favorite Illustrations* (p. 213). Nashville, TN: Broadman Press.

PROVERBS 19:14

*"Houses and riches are an inheritance from fathers,
but a prudent wife is from the Lord."*

THE CHOICE IS YOURS

*A*t her Golden Wedding celebration, my grandmother told guests the secret of her happy marriage: "On my wedding day, I decided to make a list of ten of my husband's faults which, for the sake of our marriage, I would overlook."

As the guests were leaving, a young matron whose marriage had recently been in difficult times, asked her grandmother what some of the faults were that she had seen fit to overlook. Grandmother said, "To tell you the truth, my dear, I never did get around to listing them. But whenever my husband did something that made me hoping mad, I would say to myself, "Lucky for him that's one of the ten!"—Selected

Blessed be the man who has such a wife! This Proverb highlights the thought that there are gifts that men give to men (houses and riches), but those from the Lord far out step these. A "prudent"(-God-fearing) woman is from the Lord. "Who can find a virtuous wife? For her worth is far above rubies." (Proverbs 31:10)

Finding the right spouse is a blessing from God. If you do not, you will suffer the women of verse 13 ". . . and the contentions of a wife are a continual dripping." This is misery on the installment plan.

So, be very cautious who you choose for a wife. The best way to do that is to leave the choice to God. For this to happen, you will need to value God and God's Word. If not, do not be surprised if you end with a contention's woman. (cf. v.13)

PRAYER

*"Lord, may we believe that leaving critical choices
to You is worth the wait. In Jesus' name. Amen."*

PROVERBS 20:10

*"Diverse weights and diverse measures, they are both alike,
an abomination to the Lord."*

SHADY TRADE PRACTICES

Passing a cemetery one day, the Irishman paused at a startling inscription on a tombstone. He read the words: "I still live." After scratching his head in puzzlement for a moment, the Irishman ejaculated: "Be jabbers, if I was dead, I'd be honest enough to own up to it!"[1]

This is cute and entertaining, but the point is well made; honesty is paramount. Our Proverb for today highlights the importance of honesty before God, for He is honest. Abomination means "something that causes disgust or hatred." If you are out to disgust God, dishonesty will do it. Our Proverb warns that anyone who uses weights that are lighter or heavier than their stated amounts is the type of person God has his eyes on. "For the eyes of the Lord run to and from throughout the whole earth, to show Himself strong on behalf of those whose heart is loyal to Him." (2 Chronicles 16:9)

So, simply put, may God's eyes be viewing you favorably. You always want to stay on the "sunny side" of God's love, or one day you may face its absolute justice.

⤙ PRAYER ⤚

*"Lord, remind me of the simple adage,
'honesty is the best policy.' In Jesus' name. Amen."*

July 21

PROVERBS 21:21

"He who follows righteousness and mercy finds life,
righteousness, and honor."

UNCOMPLICATING THE COMPLICATED

*J*eremy Taylor once said, "Mercy is like the rainbow which God hath set in the clouds: it never shines after it is night. If we refuse mercy here, we shall have justice in eternity."

This Proverb states as a general principle that there are exceptions,:three blessings—life, righteousness, and honor.

Life: the idea is abundant life; life in the spirit that issues into eternal life at death. It's not wealth alone. "For what will it profit a man if he gains the whole world, and loses his own soul?" (Mark 8:36)

Righteousness: defined as the "quality of being morally right." Do life God's way, and the quality of your life will be marked with kindness, goodness, and joy shown to you. For as you give, you receive: ". . . for whatsoever a man sows, that will be also reap." (Galatians 6:7)

Honor: defined as "high respect; great esteem. When you follow honor as a pattern of life, righteousness and mercy, defined as "forgiveness shown toward someone whom it is within one's power to punish or harm," you'll be held in high esteem in the eyes of God and man. "Let not mercy and truth forsake you; bind them around your neck, write them on the tablet of your heart, and so find favor and high esteem in the sight of God and man." (Proverbs 3:3-4)

Really, life does not have to be that complicated. Practice these virtues and you'll find true life.

PRAYER

"Lord, we ask for help, so our lives are marked
by righteousness and forgiveness. In Jesus' name. Amen."

Pastor Dan Butcher | 203

PROVERBS 22:8

*"He who sows iniquity will reap sorrow,
and the rod of his anger will fail."*

THE FUTURE IS OURS

"*I* am not so much of a farmer as some people claim," said Honorable W. J. Bryan in his lecture on 'The Price of Peace.' "But I have observed the watermelon seed. It has the power of drawing from the ground and through itself 200,000 times its weight, and when you can tell me how it takes this material and out of it colors an outside surface beyond the imitation of art, and then forms inside of it a white rind and within again a red heart, thickly inlaid with black seeds, each one of which, in turn, is capable of drawing through itself 200,000 times its weight—when you can explain to me the mystery of a watermelon, you can ask me to explain the mystery of God."[1]

We may not understand the process of how a small watermelon seed can produce fruit 200,000 times its own weight, but there are realities we can clearly understand, one of which is warned against in today's Proverb. Trouble is the end of wickedness. If you sin, and you know it is sin, then you are storing up for yourself trouble. Sin is pleasurable for a season. (Hebrews 11:25) However, it has a short shelf life, and then it turns rancid. Something that may cool your jets if you are pursuing a lifestyle contrary to the Bible is that you're saving up for a future of heartache. The Good News is this: God has mercy for all who turn in faith and repent. "As a father pities his children, so the Lord pities those who fear Him." (Psalm 103:13) God has no pleasure in the death of the wicked, but that the wicked turn from his way and live. (Ezekiel 33:11)

✎ PRAYER ✎

*"Lord, may we anticipate a future of joy and peace,
not sorrow and dread. In Jesus' name. Amen."*

PROVERBS 23:6–8

*"Do not eat the bread of a miser, nor desire his delicacies;
for as he thinks in his heat, so is he. "Eat and Drink!" he says to you,
but his heart is not with you, the morsel you have eaten,
you will vomit up, and waste your pleasant words."*

BEWARE THE MISER

The French millionaire miser, M. Foscue, to hide his treasure securely, dug a cave in his wine cellar so large and deep that he could go down only with a ladder. At the entrance was a door with a spring lock, which would automatically shut itself. After some time, he disappeared. A search was made for him but to no avail. At last, his house was sold.

The purchaser of the house began to rebuild it and discovered a door in this cellar, and, descending, found him lying dead on the floor with a candlestick nearby. His vast wealth amassed and hidden was with him. He had apparently gone into the cave, and the door accidentally closed, shutting him in. He died for lack of food. He had eaten the candle and gnawed the flesh off both his arms. Thus, died this avaricious wretch amongst the treasure which he had accumulated. Unbelievable! How can some people be so miserly while enjoying God's riches here on earth?

Cultivating the rich is a waste of time, according to this Proverb, and rightly so. Christ warns his disciples to avoid corrupt lifestyles, based on corrupt philosophies. "But if your eye is bad, your whole body will be full of darkness. If therefore the light that is in you is darkness, how great is that darkness!" (Matthew 6:23) Misers (people who hoard wealth and spend as little money as possible) believe they are the smart ones! They hoard their riches with little to no desire to help the genuinely poor or needy; all the while patting themselves on the back for being so smart! These misers know what to say to sound generous. "Eat and drink!" But their hearts are not with you; they begrudge your feasting, especially since it is at their expense.

PRAYER

*"Lord, your hand is always open to us. May ours be as well.
In Jesus' name. Amen."*

PROVERBS 24:10

"If you faint in the day of adversity, your strength is small."

THE UNVEILING DAY

Meyer Berman was one stockbroker who was happy when the stock market fell. In 1969, while most people got ulcers over the market's Niagara-like descent, Mr. Berman made money. A confirmed skeptic, he did not believe what he heard about a stock's rosy prospects unless he investigated. When he did, he often found reason to believe it would go down instead of up, and he was right often enough to have a fourteen-room house with a four-car garage.[1]

Difficult times for Mr. Berman made him rich! Difficult times for some people break them. Their strength is small. It is good to be tested, to experience trials and encounter adversity. It will do the following: 1. The day of adversity can also reveal yourself to yourself. Many people sit in luxury, wealth, and favorable positions, all the while dolling out free advice as to what they would do if they were in that position. However, when the other shoe falls on them, they fall to pieces! These types have never been tested, never been in the crisis, never on the front line. They just give orders from a safe distance. 2. The day of adversity can also show your strength. You may be surprised at how well you responded. These types of people are often quiet and unassuming but have tremendous strength of character.

◦— PRAYER —◦

*"Lord, without Your strength, I have no true strength.
In Jesus' name. Amen."*

PROVERBS 25:28

*"Whoever has no rule over his own spirit
is like a city broken down, without walls."*

SELF-CONTROL OR NO CONTROL

The great Maestro, Toscanini, was as well-known for his ferocious temper as for his outstanding musicianship. When members of his orchestra played badly, he would pick up anything in sight and hurl it to the floor.

During one rehearsal, a flat note caused the genius to grab his valuable watch and smash it beyond repair. Shortly afterward, he received from his devoted musicians a luxurious velvet-lined box containing two watches, one a beautiful gold timepiece; the other a cheap one on which was inscribed, "For rehearsals only."[1]—Selected

This story illustrates well the high cost of losing your temper. If you want to embarrass yourself and those you love, a lack of self-control is made to order. You will not go far if you cannot control yourself. Anger will waste you. You will never get promoted, never really achieve, and never be happily married. The wise man rules his own thoughts, his own desires, and his own inclinations. All good leaves, and all evil breaks in on a man when he loses control of himself. "He who is slow to anger is better than the mighty, and he who rules his spirit than he who takes a city." (Proverbs 16:32)

PRAYER

*"Lord, remind me that to be slow to anger is to be like You.
In Jesus' name. Amen."*

PROVERBS 26:17

"He who passes by and meddles in a quarrel not his own,
is like one who takes a dog by the ears."

HOW TO BE BITTEN
NINE TIMES OUT OF TEN

*R*otterdam, New York (UPI)—A young bride who got into an argument with her husband of a few hours ran him down with a car and killed him on the way home from the wedding reception, authorities said.

The County District Attorney said 21-year-old Joan Kenison drove over her 23-year-old husband, Lewis, after the couple argued on their way from the cocktail lounge where the reception was held.

Today's story illustrates well the wisdom of staying out of trouble that is not yours. It could be deadly!

If you tend to be a busybody, and interject yourself into others business, watch out, you'll likely to be bitten like a dog would if picked up by his ears. Let them end it the way it began, between themselves!

⤞ PRAYER ⤝

"Lord, keep me from meddling in other people's troubles.
I have enough troubles of my own. In Jesus' name. Amen."

PROVERBS 27:22

"Though you grind a fool in a mortar with a pestle along with crushed grain, yet his foolishness will not depart from him."

FOOLS AND THEIR FOLLY

There was a certain nobleman who kept a fool, to whom he one day gave a staff, with a charge to keep it till he should meet with one who was a greater fool than himself. Not many years after, the nobleman was sick, unto death. The fool came to see him.

His sick lord said to him. "I must shortly leave you."

"And whither are you going," said the fool.

"Into another world," replied his lordship.

"And when will you return? Within a month?"

"No."

"Within a year?"

"No."

"When, then?"

"Never!"

"Never?" said the fool. "And what provision hast thou made for thy entertainment there, whither thou goest?"

"None at all."

"No?" said the fool. "None at all? Here, then take my staff; for, with all my folly, I am not guilty of any folly such as this."—Bishop Hall

Force must be used with those who will not be ruled by reason, and love, and their own interest. This story illustrates the Proverb that some fools will not depart from their folly (lack of good sense), even if this lack of good sense causes them harm. Force must be used when reason, love and self-interest does not win the day. Some continue to drink in such excess that they lose it all—job, family, and home. They end up at the Rescue Mission, penniless, dirty,, and in bondage. Thankfully, even when they are at their lowest, Christ can free them and any who come to Him in humble faith. ". . . whoever commits sin is a slave to sin. And a slave does not abide in the house (heaven) forever, but a son abides forever. Therefore, if the Son makes you free, you shall be free indeed." (John 8:34–36) The Good News still stands: find your freedom in Christ, and stop the foolishness, finally.

⟨ PRAYER ⟩

"Lord, may no one ever believe that bondage is forever.
In Jesus' name. Amen."

PROVERBS 28:6

*"Better is the poor who walks in his integrity,
than one perverse in his ways, though he be rich."*

BETTER THAN

Famous men of the past have bequeathed us statements that have become mottoes. History declares that Henry Clay was about to introduce a certain bill in Congress when a friend said, "If you do, Clay, it will kill your chance for the presidency."

"But is the measure, right?" Clay asked, and on being assured it was right said, "I would rather be right than be president."[1]—*The Watchman Examiner*

We need more of this type in Congress today! In society, we need more men and women who stand up moral uprightness (integrity), than the profit that so often awaits them if they are dishonest. The Bible deals in opposites. In this Proverb, many would argue that riches would be a better choice, even if it meant an occasional dishonest act, than poverty. They see no value in integrity, i.e. honesty, if it means forfeiting riches, unless of course, they are the ones being lied to or stolen from, then the virtue is paramount!

God sees things almost opposite of what we see. Better to be poor and honest than rich and perverse. Yes, indeed, God deals in opposites.

☙ PRAYER ☙

*"Lord, we tend to strain at a gnat (honesty)
and swallow a camel (dishonesty).
Lord, help us with our own opposites.
In Jesus' name. Amen."*

July 29

PROVERBS 29:26

*"Many seek the ruler's favor,
but justice for man comes from the Lord."*

HEAVEN'S APPELLATE COURT

Some years ago, Richard Speck allegedly murdered eight student nurses in Chicago in cold-blooded deliberateness. He was tried and sentenced to death. Acknowledging his guilt, the Supreme Court of the United States later ruled that the death sentence was illegally passed upon him because there was no one on the jury opposed to a death penalty! Therefore, the imposition of the death penalty was illegal.[1]

This man escaped the justice of man, but not God's. Payday some day!

Our Proverb instructs us that ultimate justice comes from God. We tend to the hands of our superiors far more than God Himself! We are willing to offend the Almighty by seeking justice from relatives, friends, or neighbors, while ignoring the ultimate Justice of all.

Isaiah put it this way: "For the Lord is a God of justice; blessed are all those who wait for Him." (Proverbs 30:18) So, have you been wronged? Cheated? Abused? Wait for God. His eyes are upon you, and His ears are open to your cry. (cf. Psalm 34:15) Seek justice through the courts, but eventually justice will come from God.

PRAYER

*"Lord, may we first call upon Heaven's court for justice
before we trust men. In Jesus' name. Amen."*

PROVERBS 30:20

*"This is the way of an adulterous woman:
she eats and wipes her mouth,
and says, "I have done no wickedness."*

JUST ANOTHER MEAL

The sphinx in ancient mythology was supposed to have propounded a riddle: "What animal goes on four legs in the morning, on two at noonday, and on three in the evening?" The riddle remained unsolved till Oedipus appeared and gave the right answer—"Man." In infancy the human babe goes on all fours; during life's course, he walks upright on two legs; and in the eventide of life he leans on a staff.[1]

Even more of a riddle is how some people can do wrong and have no conscience about it. Like our Proverb above, sexual liaisons for these type of women are taken rather lightly, like eating a noon day meal. After they're finished, they are on their way, with no thought of conscience; soon to be forgotten like most meals are.

However, God's perspective is rather clear. "Marriage is among all, and the bed undefiled; but fornicators and adulterers God will judge." (Hebrews 13:4) God will judge you if you continue, but the Good News is this: "The Lord is merciful and gracious, slow to anger, and abounding in mercy . . . as a father pities his children, so the Lord pities those who fear Him." (Psalm 103:8,13) Do you want God's mercy, grace, and pity? Then stop all illicit sexual encounters and honor God and His ways, for God prefers mercy of judgment. (cf. James 2:13) He has no pleasure in the death of the wicked. "I have no pleasure in the death of the wicked, but that the wicked turn from his way and live . . ." (cf. Ezekiel 33:11)

⟶ PRAYER ⟵

*"Lord, may I not lightly esteem what You highly esteem.
In Jesus' name. Amen."*

PROVERBS 31:30

"Charm is deceitful, and beauty is passing,
but a woman who fears the Lord, she shall be praised."

INADEQUATE

*T*here are eight reasons why a woman buys something: because her husband says she can't have it; it will make her look thin: it comes from Paris; the neighbors can't afford it; nobody has one; everybody has one; it's different; because.[1]—*True Story Magazine*

There are some women who buy, buy, and buy, and the husband pays, pays, and pays. In the end, such women bring heartache. However, Chapter 31 of Proverbs concludes the entire book by saying, "but a woman who fears the Lord, she shall be praised." (Proverbs 31:30) The book ends as it started, with reverence for God. (cf. 1:7)

Solomon states, "Charm (the power of giving delight) is deceitful (misleading) and beauty is passing. (cf. v. 30) Charm and beauty are not enough to marry a woman. They are inadequate! What you want is a woman who has reverence for God and God's ways, that will not fade. It is the long view you want to have in mind. How will a beautiful and charming woman be in twenty years? If she's Godly, she will grow in Christ-like characteristics (kindness, gentleness, patience, forgiveness, etc.), if not, you never really know how it will end. For some of my readers, a Godly woman is the last thought that comes across the radar. So, beware, God has a better plan. Do not find out the hard way.

PRAYER

"Lord, I have learned, 'Do not let your adornment be merely out-
ward—arranging the hair, wearing gold, or putting on fine apparel—
rather let it be the hidden person of the heart, with the incorruptible
beauty of a gentle and quiet spirit, which is very precious in the sight
of God.' (I Peter 3:3–4) In Jesus' name. Amen."

PROVERBS 1:7

*"The fear of the Lord is the beginning of knowledge,
but fools despise wisdom and instruction."*

WISDOM'S WAY

*A*n old funeral custom that prevailed in Scotland until recent times was to carry out the casket of the deceased, not through the front door, but through an opening made in the side of the house which was walled-up immediately after serving its purpose. Thus, the ghost was prevented from re-entering the house because the only door that it knew was gone.—Selected

Foolish for certain! But even more foolish is to neglect God, ignore reverence, and pursue life as if God were only there for your personal enjoyment. "The fool has said in his heart, 'There is no God.'" (Psalm 14:1) Fools (lacking good sense) do not fear God. Yet Solomon, considered the wisest man to have lived, begins his whole discourse on wisdom with the affirmation that true wisdom and knowledge of life begins with God. As you pursue wisdom in the shadow of the Almighty, there will be many who will be going in the opposite direction. (cf. vv.10–19) If you follow suit, you will never be satisfied with your life, no matter how successful you are. One must understand, if you start at the wrong place, your destiny will be wrong as well. Start with God first, do not be a fool and reject wisdom and instruction.

⟶ PRAYER ⟵

*"Lord, we have so many roads to travel.
Don't let us miss the one marked wisdom.
In Jesus' name. Amen."*

August 2

PROVERBS 2:7–9

"He stores up sound wisdom for the upright . . .
Then you will understand righteousness and justice,
equity and every good path."

A CONUNDRUM

On March 2, 1977, the House of Representative approved by a 402–22 vote a Code of Ethics for its members. It contained a strong financial accounting (gifts totaling $100 in one year from a single source) and set a limit on outside earnings (15 percent of a member's current salary or $8,625).

No doubt these figures are outdated, but the idea of accountability and honesty is so ingrained in our culture that a law was passed to keep members of Congress accountable. If you have a difficult problem, then follow this prescription: Be morally upright yourself. (v.7.) Do what is just and holy. (v.8) Jesus put it this way: "You will know them by their fruits. Do men gather grapes from thorn bushes or figs from thistles? (Matthew 7:16) Wisdom will not come to the wicked, nor will the unrighteous understand justice. Why? Because they are wired wrong. If you're yearning to know "every good path," (v.9) then seek God's way first, so when circumstances present themselves that pose a genuine conundrum (a confusing or difficult problem), God will show you "every good path." (v.9)

PRAYER

"Lord, may I live a righteousness life first
before I seek a righteousness decision. In Jesus' name. Amen."

PROVERBS 3:11

"My son, do not despise the chastening of the Lord,
nor detest His correction;
for whom the Lord loves He corrects,
just as a father the son in whom he delights."

DESPISING DISCIPLINE?

Thomas Edison invented the phonograph at age 30, and he was almost totally deaf from childhood. He could hear only the loudest noises and shouts. This kind of delighted him, for he said, "A man who has to shout can never tell a lie!"[1]

This is a good example of useful pain. Edison's pain (deafness) kept him honest. Likewise, when God disciplines us, and who is without discipline, the end is our good. We come to learn over time, that God is incapable of doing wrong and too good to hurt. You may have a hard time believing this, but enduring discipline from God due to known sin, will ultimately lead to life. ". . . but He (God) disciplines us for our profit, that we may be partakers of His holiness." (Hebrews 12:10) Holiness is the end, why, because holiness brings life, fulfilling life. Sin, on the other hand, brings sorrow and death. "What fruit did you have then in the things of which your are now ashamed? For the end of those things is death. But now having been set free from sin, and having become slaves of God, you have your fruit to holiness, and the end, everlasting life." (Romans 6:21, 22)

PRAYER

"Lord, help me not to despise Your hand of discipline,
but rather trust You for the life-giving outcome.
In Jesus' name. Amen."

PROVERBS 4:7

"Wisdom is the principal thing; therefore, get wisdom."

THE "PRINCIPAL" THING

*I*n January 1970, Max Born died. A close friend of Albert Einstein and a colleague of Max Planck and Otto Hahn, the nuclear physicists, he was one of the great minds of the twentieth century. In an interview on German television before his death, Born commented: "I'd be happier if we had scientists with less brains and more wisdom."[1]

In our day, a premium is put on brains, but brains without wisdom (moral integrity) can destroy the earth, as was the concern of nuclear physicist Max Born. Proverbs teaches the principal goal of life is to "get wisdom," but how does one do this? It all begins with the beginning. The beginning of wisdom is reverence for God. (cf. 1:7) Any daily wisdom based on another foundation is to miss life's true mission, such is the exhortation of Solomon. Why was the nuclear physicist Max Born so concerned about scientists who had less brains and more wisdom? Because he knew if you did not use nuclear power wisely, it could literally destroy mankind, all with all her brainy scientists! Wisdom, according to the Bible, is moral uprightness. Without sound morals, mankind can be likened to an ape in a room full of dynamite playing with matches! If you think I exaggerate, just watch the evening news.

Make moral uprightness your primary working principal (adjective use: first in order of importance). If you do, she will promote you and honor you. (cf. v. 8)

PRAYER

"Lord, help us in our daily struggle to do what is morally right, the outworking of wisdom. In Jesus' name. Amen."

PROVERBS 5:18

*"Let your fountain be blessed
and rejoice with the wife of your youth."*

DEVOTED FOR LIFE

Michael Faraday, who died in 1867, was one of the most brilliant scientists of modern times. He was a pioneer in electrical discoveries.

Faraday received practically no education, but in the bookbindery where he found work, he also found a few volumes of science. He read and studied these, and then embarked on the experiments that were to become his religious convictions, so that we are not surprised at these words he uttered with his dying breath: "I bow before Him who is the Lord of all."[1]

Faraday was devoted to discoveries in the electrical field. As a result, he was considered a brilliant scientist, though he had little formal education. Devotion (loyalty to a person or cause) is our Proverb for today. Solomon exhorts us to be devoted to the wife of our youth. Stay with that one person all the days of your life, and you will be blessed (happy). It seems in life that you only get one chance to make certain critical decisions. Who you marry is one of them. If you marry well, especially if you have children, you and your family will be far ahead in the game of life. This especially true if you remain with the wife of your youth. You are able to build a foundation of shared memories and devotion over the years, while your children avoid the heartache and devastation of divorce, divided allegiance between parents, and the general mistrust of life itself.

So, be wise, be devoted to your wife, the wife of your youth. Don't multiply wives through divorce; you'll only be multiplying trouble.

∾ PRAYER ∾

*"Lord, help us to be wise with the wife of our youth,
and remain devoted to her for life. In Jesus' name. Amen."*

PROVERBS 6:9–11

"How long will you slumber, O sluggard?
When will you rise from your sleep?
A little sleep, a little slumber, a little folding of the hands to sleep—
so shall your poverty come on you like a prowler,
and your need like an armed man."

THE LOVE OF EASE

A loud-voiced, drunken man, followed by his wife and small son, swaggered aboard a railroad train that was soon steaming across the lowlands of Scotland. Across the aisle sat a Christian temperance worker who felt led to sing an old hymn with the hope that the drunkard would be quieted and perhaps go to sleep. Soon he was snoring vociferously. After a nap of some hours, he awakened somewhat sobered. As the temperance lecturer left the train, the fellow held out his hand, bade him good-bye, and thanked him for his singing.

Fifteen years passed and the temperance worker was again touring Scotland. After a particularly successful meeting, a well-dressed man and wife came forward and inquired of the speaker if he remembered them. He shook his head. "Why, I'm the man who was drunk that day on the train," confessed the stranger, "and you sang me to sleep. But I never could get away from those hymns, and it was not long before I was led to Christ. Our son Joseph, who was also with us that day, is now in school preparing for the ministry."[1]

This Joseph was, in years to come, to be the great Dr. Joseph Parker, who was for a long-time pastor in one of London's largest churches. This ends well, God be praised. But our Proverbs illustrates the dangers of missed opportunities due to laziness and excessive rest. In contrast to this, verses 6–8 of this same Chapter highlight the diligence of the ants, who with no administrator or leader, prepare for the future as they diligently work, day to day. The sluggard (vv. 9–11), however, would rather sleep in, call in sick to work, or in general avoid work's demands. Poverty will claim him as its victim.

PRAYER

"Lord, we pray for favor to go about our daily labor, and to resist the self-destructive ways of laziness. In Jesus' name. Amen."

PROVERBS 7:25–27

*"Do not let your heart turn aside to her ways,
do not stray into her paths; . . . her house is the way to hell,
descending to the chambers of death."*

THE MONSTER BENEATH THE BEAUTY

A Gallup Poll showed most Europeans believe in heaven but not in hell. In Sweden, the least orthodox nation, only 60 percent believed in God.[1]

Europeans may not believe in hell, but Solomon warns that a prostitute or wayward wife will convince a man that "hell" does exist, at least here on earth! ". . . her house is the way to hell." (v.27) This handmade "hell" exists in ruined families, destruction of self-control, loss of self-respect, and the attendant disrespect among upright friends. But it does not stop there. These tragic figures are usually of a corrupt nature whose choices reflect an alienated life from God Himself. Such people will eventually end up in "eternal hell" and that is no joke. Why is it no joke? Because we never find Jesus joking! Interestingly, never once did Jesus joke about life, God, or eternity. Instead he was dead serious. He was especially serious about hell. "And do not fear those who kill the body but cannot kill the soul. But rather fear Him who can destroy both soul and body in hell." (Matthew 10:28) "If your hand causes you to sin (meaning a close sin), cut it off. It is better for you to enter into life maimed, rather than having two hands, to go to hell, into the fire that shall never be quenched." (Mark 10:43)

Solomon warns against making our own hell here on earth, the corruption that results from a life of prostitutes, adultery, and fornication. But the tragedy doesn't end there. This lifestyle will eventually lead to judgment,; "but fornicators and adulterers God will judge." (Hebrews 13:4)

∾ PRAYER ∾

"Lord, we thank You that You do not punish us according to our sins, because of salvation in Christ. In Jesus' name. Amen."

August 8

PROVERBS 8:34–36

*"Blessed is the man who listens to me . . .
for whoever finds me finds life,
all those who hate me love death."*

HOW TO CHOOSE LIFE AND FAVOR

*T*here is a form of deafness known to physicians in which the person affected can hear everything except words. In such a case, the ear, as an apparatus for mere hearing, may be so perfect that the tick of a watch or the song of a bird is really appreciated. But owing to a local injury deeper than the ear, for it is in the brain itself, all spoken words of his mother tongue are as unintelligible to the sufferer as those of a foreign language.

Give him a book and he may read as understandingly as ever, but every word addressed to him through his ear reaches his consciousness only as a sound, not as a word.[1]—W. H. Thompson

Amazing! Some people can hear a bird chirping in the yard, but not a greeting from a loved one.

There is a similarity between this story and our Proverb. The man who listens to wisdom—a reverence for God and God's ways—finds life and obtains God's favor (cf. vs.35); but those tone deaf to God's commands, those who willfully sin against God, wrong their own soul. (cf. v.36)

Solomon, the author of Proverbs, constantly contrasts the ways of wisdom with the ways of death (cf. Chapter 7) and their respective ends. In today's Proverb, it's life and favor, or injury to the soul and the love of death. Choose wisely!

PRAYER

*"Lord, tune our ears to the songs of heaven,
that we may find life and favor. In Jesus' name. Amen."*

August 9

PROVERBS 9: 5–6

"Come, eat of my bread and drink of the wine I have mixed.
Forsake foolishness and live and go in the way of understanding."

THE TRUE PLEASURES OF LIFE

*E*very person confronts three great questions: Where am I from?
Whither am I going? And what must I do on the way?—John
Ruskin.[1]

Today's Proverb invites us to the feast that wisdom offers. We are
encouraged to shun foolishness (lack of good sense or judgment);
in this case, a life lived in the absence of God. It also teaches us "to
go in the way of understanding," that is, to know what pleases the
Creator and understand what gains His favor. If we are to confront
the "big" questions of life, then "what must I do on the way," is
to live as a wise man. A wise man is morally upright, he fears his
Creator, and obeys His commands. He forsakes the self-destructive
life (a life lived primarily in absence of God's concerns) and strives
to please the first priority—God. Consequently, he enjoys life and
the life-giver.

Forsake the self-destructive ways of disobedience to God and
live in the way of understanding.

PRAYER

"Lord helps us to love wisdom
and delight in the way of understanding.
Help us to forsake our foolish disobedience.
In Jesus' name. Amen."

August 10

PROVERBS 10:17

*"He who keeps instruction is in the way of life,
but he who refuses correction goes astray."*

WHAT OF PRIDE?

*P*ride, usually considered a virtue, is, in some circumstances, a basic form of sin. Dr. Karl Menninger in *Whatever Became of Sin?* reminded us that vanity, egocentricity, arrogance, self-adoration, selfishness, and self-love are really synonyms for pride. Theologically, pride asserts itself into pride of power, knowledge, and virtue.

In *Writing in Power, A New Social Analysis,* Bertrand Russell noted, "Every man would like to be God if it were possible; some few find it difficult to admit the impossibility."[10]

A simple manifestation of pride (preferring self-will) is to approach life with little regard for correction (a change that rectifies an error). A wise person receives instruction because he senses his need for guidance. A proud man does not view himself as being wrong. To be corrected for speeding through a school zone will be received by a wise man; a fool, however, is never wrong. There must be some mistake, and it is not me!

Be wise! Receive instruction, and enjoy life, otherwise, you will find your cruising going astray.

∼ PRAYER ∼

*"Lord, help us to be wise enough to receive instruction
lest we miss the way. In Jesus' name. Amen."*

---

10. Jones, G. C. (1986). *1000 Illustrations for Preaching and Teaching* (p. 317). Nashville, TN: Broadman & Holman Publishers.

PROVERBS 11:30

*"The fruit of the righteous is a tree of life,
and he who wins souls is wise."*

A TREE OF LIFE

*O*f all the trees on all continents, the palm tree is most useful. The encyclopedia tells us that there are eight hundred different uses for the palm tree.[1]

As a result of righteous living (fruit) a person becomes a tree of life, a source of a meaningful life for others. This contrasts with a fool who troubles his family. (v.29) As the palm tree is a tree with eight hundred different uses, a righteous life (morally upright) will produce fruit all its life. This fruit will benefit the immediate family. (cf. Proverbs 20:7) "The righteous man walks in his integrity; his children are blessed after him."

So, the exhortation is simple and clear,: live a morally upright life in the sight of God and man, and you'll be a blessing long after you are gone.

She (wisdom) is a tree of life to those who take hold of her, and happy are all who retain her." (Proverbs 3:18)

☙ PRAYER ☙

*"Lord, help us to eat freely from the fruit of life,
that we may be a lasting influence for God on others.
In Jesus' name. Amen."*

PROVERBS 12:2

"A good man obtains favor from the Lord,
but a man of wicked intentions He will condemn."

THE GOOD, THE BAD AND THE WICKED

*M*ark Hopkins, educator, ordained minister in the Congrega-
tional Church, and president of Williams College from 1836
to 1872, is quoted as having said to a graduating class:

"If the only option available to Williams were to graduate men
with the highest learning but without any interest in the welfare of
mankind, or to graduate men with less mental capacity but possess-
ing an aspiration to do good, I would choose the latter for Williams
because it would render a more essential service.[11]

It is better to be good (approved) than to be intelligent! So says
the advice of Mark Hopkins, President of Williams College. Things
have changed! Today, a premium is put on intelligence, personal
abilities, and prosperity. For many to aspire to be good is not even
on the radar! Yet God's favor remains with the good man, whether
he be rich or poor, smart or simple, influential or not. However,
God will condemn the wicked man and his bad plans.

If you're seeking God's acceptance and approval, be good. A
good man receives Christ as Savior, (cf. (Romans 10:9, 13) and
obeys Him as Lord (boss). (cf. Hebrews 5:9)

PRAYER

"Lord, may we always be in your favor as good people.
In Jesus' name. Amen."

11. Jones, G. C. (1986). *1000 Illustrations for Preaching and Teaching* (p.112).
Nashville, TN: Broadman & Holman Publishers.

PROVERBS 13:5

"A righteous man hates lying,
but a wicked man is loathsome and comes to shame."

LIAR, LIAR, PANTS ON FIRE!

A "Truth in Government Act" proposed by Representative Donald M. Fraser (D-Minn.) would make it illegal for federal officials to lie to private citizens. Right now, Fraser says, honesty is a one-way street. "Under current law, it is a crime for a private citizen to lie to a government official, but not for a government official to lie to the people." Perhaps officials should take an oath of honesty when they are sworn in.[1]

People do not like to be lied to. I do not; you do not. Why? Because people who speak the truth hate it when others do not. It is repulsive. Plus, liars often get their way and sometimes our money. When one lives day to day in the practice of being honest and without lies, then lying is naturally foreign and despised. "The fear of the Lord is to hate evil; pride and arrogance and the evil way and the perverse mouth I hate." (Proverbs 8:13)

Do not lie, or you will end up on God's list of those with behaviors He hates. Plus, there is the added heartache of bringing shame on yourself. A liar is a "double loser."

∽ PRAYER ∽

"Lord, keep us honest, always speaking the truth in love.
In Jesus' name. Amen."

PROVERBS 14:8

*"The wisdom of the prudent is to understand his way,
but the folly of fools is deceit."*

FOLLY'S FRUIT

The United Press International reported on an angry Israeli judge who refused to allow a lady to be her own age. The 1975 story said:

"In 1955, Miss Melania Neubart decided she wanted to be ten years younger in hopes of paving an easier road toward marriage. Claiming there was an error in the official records, Miss Neubart obtained a court declaration stating she was born in 1923 instead of 1913 (she would have been age 62 in 1975).

"Several months ago, she went to the magistrate's court to change her year of birth back to 1913 and admitted she had lied the first time because she wanted to find a husband. Still single, she realized she was officially too young to qualify for a national insurance pension.

"The judge refused the applicant's behavior as 'bold impertinence,' saying she made the court 'an unwitting accomplice in the perpetration of a lie.'"[1]

She got what she wanted, but I do not think she liked what she ended up with. Our Proverb for today is clear: those who deceive often are deceived themselves. Fools are deceived into thinking their folly (acts that lack good sense) have no consequences! She deceived the court regarding her age, received her request for an age change (folly), then realized years later she could not qualify for a retirement (deceived). The way of sin is hard.

❦ PRAYER ❦

*"Lord, help us to think about our behavior,
lest we receive what we don't want. In Jesus' name. Amen."*

PROVERBS 15:1

"A soft answer turns away wrath, but a harsh word stirs up anger."

KEEP COOL AND KEEP FACE

*I*n the 1890s, a book appeared entitled *Beside the Bonnie Briar Bush*. It was authored by John Watson, who wrote under the pen name of Ian Maclaren. In the volume is the story of a lad who decided to enter the ministry. Before finishing school, however, his saintly mother died, and he went to live with an aunt. By and by, the young man completed seminary and was ready to take his first church; indeed, to preach his first sermon as pastor. The bright boy labored long on his sermon, then proudly read it to his aunt. When he asked for criticism, his aunt expressed appreciation for its beauty but reminded him that many of his parishioners had had little schooling. It was then she shared his mother's words of admonition just before her death: "When you stand up to preach, always say a good word for Jesus Christ."[12]

A soft answer in the middle of a verbal firestorm is extremely difficult, but it can be done.

On the occasions that I've been able to do this, the result is almost like magic. Silence. The recipient is almost dumbfounded and a more equitable end can be reached. A soft answer requires forethought, patience, self-control, and kindness—virtues worth having and highly prized in the book of Proverbs.

But, if you prefer "verbal combat," a harsh word will do it. It's like tripping a land mine; sudden and disastrous results will follow.

◦◦ PRAYER ◦◦

*"Lord, help me with my soft answers.
I'm through with harsh words. In Jesus' name. Amen."*

---

12. Jones, G. C. (1986). *1000 Illustrations for Preaching and Teaching* (p. 196). Nashville, TN: Broadman & Holman Publishers.

PROVERBS 16:2

"All the ways of a man are pure in his own eyes,
but the Lord weighs the spirits."

LOVE IS THE BEST MOTIVE

A major television network carried a news story showing a convoy of trucks entering a Thai village. The trucks were loaded with food sent to that village by people from the state of Michigan. The state governor had visited the village and observed the hunger of the people. He returned to Michigan and attempted to do something about it. The people of that little Thai village probably knew little of this place in the United States. Nevertheless, they did know that somewhere there were some people who cared enough to help. Love is reason enough.[13]

If you are trying to evaluate your motives, be certain they are based on your love for God. "The refining pot is for silver and the furnace for gold, but the Lord tests the hearts." (Proverbs 17:3) A person may think nothing is wrong with what he does; outwardly it may seem innocent. But God knows his heart and whether the motives behind his actions are pure or not.

So, check your motives. We check the oil in our cars to see if it is dirty; likewise we need to check our own motives to see if they are pure before God or just plain dirty. How can you tell? Check your motives against God's Word, the Bible. You cannot be running contrary to what God has said. If you're still not sure, seek a mature Christian friend for counsel. They can be an unmeasured help in times of need. Consider circumstances, but do not make circumstance the sole guide. And last, but certainly not least, pray, pray, and pray.

⸺ PRAYER ⸺

"Lord, help us not to be deceived by our improper motives.
Deliver us from Satan's crafty deceptions. In Jesus' name. Amen."

13. Hobbs, H. H. (1990). *My Favorite Illustrations* (p. 171). Nashville, TN: Broadman Press.

PROVERBS 17:9

*"He who covers a transgression seeks love,
but he who repeats a matter separates friends."*

OVERLOOK THE OVERSIGHTS

If you really want to know who your friends are, just make a mistake.—*The Bible Friend*

A true friend will forgive a mistake; others will keep reminding you of it. If you are in the habit of bringing up past mistakes or sins, lose that fault immediately, or you will end up friendless. Nobody wants to be reminded of their failures. Instead, seek to cover an offense and leave it buried with a "Do Not Disturb" sign on the site. Your life will be much simpler and happier. The person who is forgiving and compassionate will enjoy life and will be enjoyed by others.

"A perverse man sows' strife, and a whisperer separates the best of friends." (Proverbs 16:28)

Be a peacemaker, not a talebearer.

PRAYER

*"Lord, help us not to recite or recall the sins of others.
In Jesus' name. Amen."*

PROVERBS 18:13

*"He who answers a matter before he hears it,
it is folly and shame to him."*

HOW TO SHAME YOURSELF
IN ONE EASY STEP

A legend says that the Devil once came to a sinner during confession, saying that he came to make restitution. On being asked what he would restore, he said, "Shame. For it is shame that I have stolen from this sinner, making him shameless in sinning; and now I have come to restore it to him, to make him ashamed to confess his sins."—Foster[1]

Shame is defined as a feeling caused by consciousness of wrong or foolish behavior. Giving an answer before you hear the whole matter will do it! Speaking before you hear all the facts is difficult to control. It usually stems from impatience, the inability to rule your spirit. If you take pride in a quick response, you will soon learn the hard way that your first thoughts are usually not the best. If you speak rashly, shame will wrap its arms around you like a wet blanket. So, stop the craziness of sudden responses; put your impatience on hold and listen. You'll feel better about life.

PRAYER

*"Lord, help us not to be wise in our own eyes,
help us instead to put the brakes on a quick reply.
In Jesus' name. Amen."*

PROVERBS 19:3

*"The foolishness of a man twists his way,
and his heart frets against the Lord."*

THE BLAME GAME

In 1967, Japan's largest Protestant denomination, the United Church of Christ (Kyodan), adopted a statement publicly condemning the Church's guilt and complicity in World War II. The declaration acknowledged that the Japanese church actively cooperated in the war, failing thereby to uphold the purity of the faith.[1]

It is unusual for people to own their mistakes, but in the illustration above, this church accepted their culpability in the second World War. However, a foolish person subverts his own life, then he turns and blames God! Characteristically, this type of person has the inability of owning up to their decisions, so once the consequences settle in, they blame others, and ultimately God Himself.

There is a solution to this: accept your sin, confess your wrong to God (cf. I John 1:9), and make the necessary changes that come with repentance. Such a flaw will not die easily, but with humility and hard work, the battle can be won. James tells us, ". . . let every man be swift to hear, slow to speak, slow to wrath, for the wrath of man does not produce the righteousness of God." (James 1:19)

PRAYER

*Lord, help us not to blame You for our foolishness.
In Jesus' name. Amen."*

PROVERBS 20:30

"Blows that hurt cleanse away evil,
as do stripes the inner depths of the heart."

THE BLOWS THAT HEAL

*T*here are not any hard-and-fast rules for getting ahead in the world—just hard ones. As if life's lessons are not hard enough, we still experience pain.

Today's Proverb illustrates that cleansing of the soul is often done by pain. We may receive this pain directly from God, who disciplines us for our good, as Hebrews 12:11 teaches: "Now no chastening seems to be joyful for the present, but painful; nevertheless, afterward it yields the peaceable fruit of righteousness to those who have been trained by it." Or the pain may come from a supervisor who disciplines you for being late. Whatever source the pain, it is well for us to take a closer look at ourselves to see what the issue is. Nobody enjoys pain, but pain is how God gets our attention. It is like He's using a megaphone to call our name.

So, the simple solution is to listen, examine, and compare our behavior to the Bible. If you're clearly in the wrong, allow the pain to teach you about God's love, for He only allows pain in our lives for the good of His children; even though that may be hard to believe.

PRAYER

"Lord, may we listen to our pain
and allow it to cleanse our hidden faults.
In Jesus' name. Amen."

PROVERBS 21:23

"Whoever guards his mouth and tongue keeps his soul from troubles."

TAKE GUARD!

The heathen philosopher Xanthus, expecting some friends to dine with him, ordered his servant Aesop to provide the best things the market could supply. Tongues only were provided; and these the cook was ordered to serve up with different sauces. Course after course was supplied, each consisting of tongue.

"Did I not order you," said Xanthus in a violent passion, "to buy the best victuals the market afforded?"

"And have I not obeyed your orders?" said Aesop. "Is there anything better than a tongue? Is not the tongue the bond of civil society, the organ of truth and reason, and the instrument of our praise and adoration of the gods?"

Xanthus ordered him to go again to the market on the morrow and buy the worst things he could find. Aesop went, and again he purchased tongues, which the cook was ordered to serve as before. "What! Tongues again?" exclaimed Xanthus.

"Most certainly," rejoined Aesop. "The tongue is surely the worst thing in the world. It is the instrument of all strife and contention, the inventor of lawsuits, and the source of division and wars: it is the organ of error, of lies, calumny, and blasphemies."[1]

If you have mastered your tongue, as best as possible being mortal, then your life is full of God's blessing and man's favor. However, if not, you will continue to struggle. James illustrates the struggle in controlling the tongue. "With it we bless our God and Father, and with it we curse men, who have been made in the likeness of God. Out of the same mouth proceed blessing and cursing. My brethren, these things ought not to be so." (James 3:9,10)

Make guarding the tongue one of your daily goals. With God's help, things will get better.

~ PRAYER ~

"Lord, put a guard on my lips,
lest I trouble my own soul. In Jesus' name. Amen."

PROVERBS 22:1

*"A good name is to be chosen rather than great riches,
loving favor rather than silver and gold."*

TOO HIGH A PRICE

A young man employed by a Sunday school board told the following searching story. He was invited at the last minute to preach at a church in Nashville. On impulse, he used as his text, "Thou shalt not steal." The next morning, he stepped on the bus and handed the driver a dollar bill. The driver handed him back his change. He stood in the rear of the bus and counted the change. There was a dime too much. His first thought was, "The bus company will never miss this dime."

Then quickly came the realization that he could not keep money that did not belong to him. He made his way to the front and said to the driver, "You gave me too much change." Imagine his surprise when the driver replied, "Yes, a dime too much. I gave it to you purposely. You see, I heard your sermon yesterday, and I watched in my mirror as you counted your change. Had you kept the dime, I would never again have had any confidence in preaching."

If a person obtains riches and wealth at the expense of a respected character, he has paid too high a price. The greatest life to have ever lived, Jesus of Nazareth, had neither riches nor gold, but it was said of Him that "He grew in the favor of God and man." (cf. Luke 2:52)

Riches are of no value if in gaining them you destroy your self-respect and character. "So are the ways of everyone who is greedy for gain; It takes away the life of its owners." (Proverbs 1:19)

⋙ PRAYER ⋘

*"Lord, help us value the immaterial riches of a good character
over the material riches of this world. In Jesus' name. Amen."*

PROVERBS 23:17–18

*"Do not let your heart envy sinners
but be zealous for the fear of the Lord all day;
for surely there is a hereafter, and your hope will not be cut off."*

PRESENT SUCCESS IS NOT THE FINAL OUTCOME.

*E*nvy shoots at others and wounds herself.[1] It is tempting to envy (feelings of discontentment aroused by someone else's possessions, luck, or success) those who have what you do not. But our Proverb teaches that the present success of someone does not mean it will be the outcome. There is a future state in which the righteous will be rewarded and the wicked judged. Jesus put it this way: "Do not marvel at this; for the hour is coming in which all who are in the graves will hear His voice and come forth—those who have done good, to the resurrection of life, and those who have done evil, to the resurrection of condemnation." (John 5:28,29)

So, keep doing the next right thing before God. God sees and God hears "and your hope will not be cut off." (v.18)

⟿ PRAYER ⟿

*"Lord, may we not lose heart in doing good,
however unrecognized it may be. In Jesus' name. Amen."*

PROVERBS 24:11

*"Deliver those who are drawn toward death
and hold back those stumbling to the slaughter."*

DELIVERANCE

Someone has said that if you could convince a man there was no hope, he would curse the day he was born. Hope is an indispensable quality of life.

Years ago, the S-4 submarine was rammed by another ship and quickly sank. The entire crew was trapped in its prison house of death. Ships rushed to the scene of disaster off the coast of Massachusetts. We do not know what took place down in the sunken submarine, but we can be sure that the men clung bravely to life as the oxygen slowly gave out.

A diver placed his helmeted ear to the side of the vessel and listened. He heard a tapping noise. Someone, he learned, was tapping out a question in the dots and dashes of the Morse Code. The question came slowly: "Is . . . there . . . any . . . hope?" This seems to be the cry of humanity: "Is there any hope?" Hope, indeed, is the basis of all human existence in Christ![1]

Currently, our nation is suffering from the Coronavirus, the lock down of our economy, and protests and rioting where cities are burning and people are dying. During these difficult times, the question is asked, is there hope for peace? Peace of mind? Peace in our society? Today's Proverbs teaches that the godly are to deliver those "drawn toward death and hold back those stumbling to slaughter." The only true rescue of those "stumbling to death" is found in Christ. Jesus said it well: "Peace I leave with you, My peace I give to you, not as the world gives do I give to you. Let not your heart be troubled, neither let it be afraid." (John 14:27)

Have you found your peace in Christ?

PRAYER

*"Lord, I believe in Jesus Christ as my Deliverer and my Peace.
In Jesus' name. Amen."*

PROVERBS 25:27

*"It is not good to eat much honey;
so, to seek one's own glory is not glory."*

COURTING APPLAUSE

John Wanamaker told of meeting a boyhood friend who had experienced nothing but hard luck in his career. He had been locked out of his meager hotel room, and he was half starved. Deeply moved, Mr. Wanamaker fed him in his own restaurant and urged him to order every delicacy on the menu. Then he handed him enough to pay his hotel bill and ordered him to report to him for a good job the next morning.

The man never came. The hotel clerk, to whom the jubilant fellow had related the whole incident, called Mr. Wanamaker about noon. The man had died during the night—of acute indigestion.

Excess, in almost anything, can kill you. Our Proverb warns us about the dangers of seeking recognition, praise, or glory. It's as bad as eating too much honey. Recognition is pleasant, but to actively to pursue it will leave you and others nauseated.

The solution is found in Proverbs 27:2. "Let another man praise you, and not your own mouth; a stranger, and not your own lips." True praise, that which is spontaneous and appropriate, comes from other mouths, not our own.

∽ PRAYER ∽

*"Lord, may we be so busy praising You
that we'll have no time to praise ourselves.
In Jesus' name. Amen."*

PROVERBS 26:10

*"The great God who formed everything
gives the fool his hire and the transgressor his wages."*

GOD IS GOOD EVEN TO THE FOOL

*T*his story was told of General Robert E. Lee. Hearing General Lee speak in the highest terms to President Davis about a certain officer, another officer, greatly astonished, said to him, "General, do you know that the man of whom you speak so highly to the President is one of your bitterest enemies and misses no opportunity to malign you?"

"Yes," replied General Lee, "but the President asked my opinion of him; he did not ask for his opinion of me."[1]—*Sunshine Magazine*

It would be extremely difficult to speak well of another who's past comments have been so vitriolic. Yet, today's Proverb describes how God Almighty is good even to the fool. Jesus expressed it this way: ". . . for He (God) makes His sun rise on the evil and on the good, and sends rain on the just and on the unjust." (Matthew 5:45) God's character is such that His goodness falls on those who don't deserve it or appreciate it. Amazing!

Such love should constrain every disobedient son and daughter to surrender their will to God. God is good even to the ungrateful and unbelieving. How much more so to those who love God?

PRAYER

*"Lord, may Your goodness always keep us close to Your side.
In Jesus' name. Amen."*

PROVERBS 27:12

*"A prudent man foresees evil and hides himself;
the simple pass on and are punished."*

FOR TIME AND ETERNITY

When Clarence Darrow was a young lawyer, he was presenting a suit for damages in a civil court in a small town. The jury that was selected appeared to be even lower than average in intelligence. However, one man seemed much superior to the rest and would probably be elected foreman by the jury—according to the local legal customs. Throughout the case, therefore, Darrow concentrated on this man, and addressed all his oratory to him. The case finally went to the jury.

"Gentleman," said the judge, "have you reached a decision?"

"No, Your Honor," answered the foreman "We've come back to ask for some information. There are two words which have been used throughout this trial which we don't know the meaning of."

"What are they?" asked the judge.

"One word is 'plaintiff' and the other is 'defendant.'"[1]

This story humorously illustrates the danger of ignorance. Today's Proverb warns us of another type of ignorance: a willful disregard for future evil. A prudent man can see the evil coming. He considers what the outcome will be and then decides what his best course of action should be in the present. In contrast, a simple man does not do this. He will deal with it when it arrives. Like the man who does not save for retirement, or secure medical insurance. Such lack of forethought can be devastating. Likewise, those who don't make future plans for meeting a holy and just God will suffer eternal devastation. This can all be avoided by prudently placing your hope in Christ. As Paul the Apostle said, "For He (God) made Him (Christ) who knew no sin to be sin for us, that we might become the righteousness for God in Him." (2 Corinthians 5:21)

◦── PRAYER ──◦

*"Lord, help us to be prudent for time and eternity.
In Jesus' name. Amen."*

PROVERBS 28:14

*"Happy is the man who is always reverent,
but he who hardens his heart will fall into calamity."*

HAPPY IS THE MAN

Not in Unbelief—Voltaire was an infidel of the most pronounced type. He wrote, "I wish I had never been born."

Not in Pleasure—Lord Byron lived a life of pleasure if anyone did. He wrote, "The worm, the canker, and grief are mine alone."

Not in Money—Jay Gould, the American millionaire, had plenty of that. When dying, he said, "I suppose I am the most miserable man on earth."

Not in Position and Fame—Lord Beaconsfield enjoyed more than his share of both. He wrote, "Youth is a mistake; manhood a struggle; old age a regret."

Not in Military Glory—Alexander the Great conquered the known world in his day. Having done so, he wept in his tent, because he said, "There are no more worlds to conquer."[1]

Where then is happiness found? The answer is simple—in Christ alone. In today's world, happiness is defined as favor, luck, or fortune, but the Bible presents a completely different picture. To be happy is to be reverent, to honor God. This honor demonstrates itself in faith in Christ as our Savior and obedience to His commands. (cf. John 14:15) "If you love Me, keep My commandments." If people would pursue God on a daily basis, reading the Bible and praying, God will bless his way. "And in His law, he mediates day and night. He shall be like a tree planted by the rivers of water, that brings forth its fruit in its season, whose leaf also shall not wither; and whatever he does shall prosper." (Psalm 1:2-3)

So, don't grow bitter at God or God's ways. He has a plan for your life. Trust Him for it and live in the "shadow of the Almighty," and He will be your "refuge and fortress." (Psalm 91:1-2)

PRAYER

*"Lord, keep our heart soft towards You.
Keep us from the hardness of bitterness. In Jesus' name. Amen."*

PROVERBS 29:20

*"Do you see a man hasty in his words?
There is more hope for a fool than for him."*

A QUICK DRAW

Calvin Coolidge wisely expressed it: "One of the first lessons a president has to learn is that every word he says weighs a ton."[14]

A fool tends to blurt out foolish and ill-reasoned thoughts and often the first thought that comes to mind. He lacks self-control, which is the hallmark of any successful living. The wise man has learned to control himself, especially in what he says. "The tongue of the wise uses knowledge rightly, but the mouth of fools pours forth foolishness." (Proverbs 15:2)

The fool's fool answers before he finishes hearing, believing he knows the facts beforehand. "He who answers a matter before he hears it, it is folly and shame to him. (Proverbs 18:13)

Speaking in haste and being conceited (excessively proud of oneself) are two things for which there is less hope than for being a fool. (cf. 26:12) "Do you see a man wise in his own eyes? There is more hope for a fool than for him." A fool speaks first and thinks later, after the consequences settle in, like the blast from a stick of dynamite.

Strive earnestly to control what you say, or eventually your words will control you, for good or for ill.

⟶ PRAYER ⟵

*"Lord, help us to keep a close watch on our speech,
lest we play the role of one lower than a fool.
In Jesus' name. Amen."*

---

14. Jones, G. C. (1986). *1000 Illustrations for Preaching and Teaching* (p.305). Nashville, TN: Broadman & Holman Publishers.

PROVERBS 30:11–12

*"There is a generation that curses its father,
and does not bless its mother; there is a generation
that is pure in its own eyes yet is not washed from its filthiness."*

A NOON DAY FEEDING
FOR A GREAT WHITE

Disrespect for parents is nothing new. The New Testament predicts it! II Timothy 3:1-2 says it this way: "But know this, that in the last days perilous times will come: for men will be lovers of themselves, lovers of money, boasters, proud, blasphemers, disobedient to parents . . ."

Disrespect for parents extends itself to disrespect for authority in general. If children don't learn the value of respecting their first authorities, their parents, it extends into adulthood. They will struggle!

I recently was watching a series on shark attacks off the coast of Australia. They had on video a surfer who was frantically fighting off an attack of a great white. Fortunately, he survived. Immediately the police put up signs warning surfers of possible shark attacks. About an hour later, another surfer showed up, completely aware that a shark had attacked a surfer earlier that day. He figured enough time had passed for the shark to be out of the area, plus the waves were perfect. So off he goes. Well, as expected, he was attacked, too! Again, the surfer survived, but not without bite marks on his leg.

There is a whole generation who think this way. If they can get away with something, it's okay. But to disregard authority is to disregard God. "For there is no authority except from God, and the authorities that exist are appointed by God." (Romans 13:1)

This present lawless generation, (the current rioting in Minneapolis, New York, Portland) illustrates well Paul's description in 2 Timothy 3:1–5. A whole generation who believe they are justified in their acts of anarchy "yet is not washed from its filthiness."

⟶ PRAYER ⟵

*"Lord, keep us from believing we are justified
in breaking Your laws by breaking man's. In Jesus' name. Amen."*

PROVERBS 31:10

"Who can find a virtuous wife? For her worth is far above rubies."

A RUBY IN THE ROUGH

A remarkable story is told about an exceedingly costly jewel that for many years was considered of no more value than a mere pebble.

Gustaf Gillman, a Chicago lapidary, was at work in his shop, according to the narrative, when John Mihok, of Omaha, entered. Mihok, who was a laborer, drew out of his pocket a rough, red stone and handed it to Gillman. "I want you to cut and polish this," said Mihok. "Where did you get it?" gasped Gillman, as his eyes almost popped out of his head. "My father picked it up in Hungary fifty years ago," was the reply of Mihok. "He thought it was a pretty pebble. When I landed in this country, I found it in my valise. It has been lying around the house ever since. The children played with it. My last baby cut his teeth on it. One night I dreamed it was a diamond worth a lot of money, but it's not a diamond. It's red." "No, it's a pigeon-blood ruby," said Gillman. "What might it be worth?" was the question of Mihok. "I'd say anywhere from one-hundred-thousand to two-hundred-fifty-thousand dollars," answered Gillman; and Mihok leaned against the door. The big, rough stone, we are told, cut to a flawless ruby of 23.9 carats. It is believed to be the largest ruby in this country and possibly the largest in the world.[1]

Only God could bring such a woman into a man's life. Solomon concludes his book the same way he started with the "fear of the Lord." (cf. 1:7 with 31:30) A woman who reverences and respects God with heartfelt love is of surpassing value. Such women are rare.

⟿ PRAYER ⟿

"Lord, we may be rubies in the rough,
but help us to strive toward the example.
In Jesus' name. Amen."

PROVERBS 1:28–29.

*"Then they will call on me, but I will not answer,
they will seek me diligently; but they will not find me,
because they hated knowledge and did not choose the fear of the Lord."*

GOD IS NO FOOL

*T*here was a certain nobleman who kept a fool, to whom he one day gave a staff, with a charge to keep it till he should meet with one who was a greater fool than himself. Not many years after, the nobleman was sick, unto death. The fool came to see him.

His sick lord said to him. "I must shortly leave you."

"And whither are you going," said the fool.

"Into another world," replied his lordship.

"And when will you return? Within a month?"

"No."

"Within a year?"

"No."

"When, then?"

"Never!"

"Never?" said the fool. "And what provision hast thou made for thy entertainment there, whither thou goest?"

"None at all."

"No?" said the fool. "None at all? Here, then take my staff; for, with all my folly, I am not guilty of any folly such as this."—Bishop Hall

Some have the misconception of living a godless life and then repenting at the end. Today's Proverb puts an end to that thinking. God sees, God hears, and God judges. True wisdom is to reverently follow God by trusting His Son for salvation and reverently obeying Him through faith.

Don't deceive yourself into thinking you can out-think God. God is merciful but He's no fool.

⟶ PRAYER ⟵

*"Lord, may we live our days in humility and reverence,
for You will honor those who honor You.
In Jesus' name. Amen."*

September 2

PROVERBS 2:21–22

*"For the upright will dwell in the land,
and the blameless will remain in it;
but the wicked will be cut off from the earth,
and the unfaithful will be uprooted from it.*

DELAYED AGAIN

*A*n unfaithful husband reportedly has been cured of his infidelity by electric shock treatments. The treatment was administered by two psychiatrists in a London hospital who reported the experience in an issue of *Pulse*, an English medical journal.

The psychiatrists showed the guilty man (Mr. X) colored pictures of his wife and mistress alternately on a screen in a darkened room for thirty minutes each day for six days. When his mistress' picture was flashed on the screen, the unfaithful husband received a 70-volt electric shock on the wrist. When his wife's pictures appeared, a tape recording told him of the harm he was doing to her and to their marriage by the affair he was having with his neighbor's wife. The unfaithful husband had been married for ten years and his adulterous relationship had gone on for two years before he sought help.[1]

There are plenty of women who would like to try this one. Though unorthodox, it illustrates the idea of reward for good behavior and punishment for ill. Today's Proverb is a summary statement for the whole Chapter. The basic concept is a "payday someday." God will see to it that the righteous are rewarded and the guilty punished. It's a simple concept but often challenging to practice due to the reward or punishment not being immediate. Evil people are not always punished instantly by God; if it were so, they would stop. Rewards do not come soon enough, so we may leave off on our good behavior. God delay's punishment or reward due to the idea that a life lived before God is to be from the heart, even though reward or punishment is delayed.

❧ PRAYER ❧

*Lord, help me to be patient with delays, knowing that
the ultimate reward will be Your presence in Your kingdom,
while the wicked are banished from both. In Jesus' name. Amen."*

PROVERBS 3:7–8

"Do not be wise in your own eyes;
fear the Lord and depart from evil.
It will be health to your flesh, and strength to your bones."

LESS BRAINS AND MORE WISDOM

*I*n January 1970, Max Born died. A close friend of Albert Einstein and a colleague of Max Planck and Otto Hahn, the nuclear physicists, he was one of the great minds of the twentieth century. In an interview on German television before his death, Born commented: "I'd be happier if we had scientists with less brains and more wisdom."[1]

"Less brains and more wisdom." Well said. That is the essence of today's Proverb. Some have been blessed with a keen intellect, understanding of facts and concepts come easily, and they seem to remember them for years. But knowledge is not everything! A proper use of knowledge (wisdom) is the difference between using atomic power as a blessing or as a bomb; as a servant or as a tyrant; to sustain life or to end it.

Sadly, because of our achievements, many believe reverence for God is old-fashioned, outdated, and primitive. Meanwhile, back in reality, we all live under the MADD policy: "Mutually Assured Destruction." We will not attack you with our nuclear warheads because our own destruction is assured when you retaliate. If we are so "wise," why do we live in a world that now has the capacity to destroy all living creatures? In contrast, our Proverb exhorts us to reverence God in all our ways, warning against being "wise in our own eyes," as to rule out God and His laws.

PRAYER

"Lord, we live in a world of such technical advancement,
we have come to believe we do not need You!
Deliver us Lord from ourselves. In Jesus' name. Amen."

PROVERBS 4:5–6

"Get wisdom! Get understanding!
Do not forget, nor turn away from the words of my mouth.
Do not forsake her, and she will preserve you;
love her and she will keep you."

TWO PATHS, TWO DESTINIES

*A*ltamont the infidel, cried out his last words: "My principles have poisoned my friend; my extravagance has beggared my boy; my unkindness has murdered my wife. And is there another hell? Oh, thou blasphemed, yet most indulgent Lord God! Hell is a refuge if it hides me from thy frown."[1]

Wisdom has been defined as the successful use of knowledge. Our Proverb exhorts us to get wisdom and understanding. "The fear of the Lord is the beginning of wisdom." (Proverbs 9:10) Infidels and atheists do not die well, as the above story illustrates. They have pursued life in the absence of God's wisdom (reverence for God), and their understanding has only hardened their hearts. This all is a choice, you know. We either pursue God or the absence of God. Each path is considered wise. One will preserve and keep you as the Proverb says, the other will poison you.

PRAYER

"Lord, help us to be wise in Your eyes,
not wise in our own eyes. In Jesus' name. Amen."

PROVERBS 5:18

*"Let your fountain be blessed
and rejoice with the wife of your youth."*

FAITHFULNESS AS A FOUNTAIN

Someone has said that in war Providence is on the side of the strongest regiments. And I have noted that Providence is on the side of clear heads and honest hearts; and whenever a man walks faithfully in the ways that God has marked out for him, Providence, as the Christian says—luck, as the heathen says—will be on that man's side. In the long run, you will find that God's Providence is in favor of those who keep His laws, and against those that break them.—Henry Ward Beecher[1]

God favors the faithful. Our Proverb today teaches the joy of marital faithfulness. "Drink water from your own cistern . . . and rejoice with the wife of our youth." (vv.15,18) For our Proverb to refer to a wife as a "well" was a high compliment. In an arid country like Israel, a well was a prized possession. So is a wife. Marriage is a struggle at times, but two faithful people before God can work out any "dry spots." Let you and your family be blessed before God by rejoicing with the wife of your youth, otherwise, you may find out that the other "well" was only an illusion.

PRAYER

*"Lord, grant us Your grace to rejoice with the wife of our youth,
otherwise, we may find in our old age we are dry and parched.
In Jesus' name. Amen."*

PROVERBS 6: 27–29

"Can a man take fire to his bosom, and his clothes not be burned?
Can one walk on hot coals, and his feet not be seared?
So, is he who goes into his neighbor's wife ..."

A BURNING EXPERIENCE

Two farmers had adjoining farms. One man was a Christian, the other an unbeliever. The Christian farmer faithfully observed the Lord's Day. He and his family always worshiped in the Lord's house. The unbelieving farmer ignored God and tilled his farm seven days a week. At harvest time, his farm showed a larger yield than that of his Christian neighbor. When he taunted his neighbor about this, the latter replied, "God does not settle his accounts in October."

But eventually God does settle them.

Our Proverb today gives a stern warning about the consequences of marital unfaithfulness by asking a simple question: "Can a man take fire to his bosom, and his clothes not be burned?" No! There are those who beg to differ, but God does not settle his accounts in October as the story illustrates.

Because God may delay regarding the devastating consequences of adultery, that delay is not denial. He will judge the unfaithful, often in broken homes, broken hearts, and broken lives. Not to mention the financial ruin that often follows this sin. God pleads with you eloquently by saying, "Can one walk on hot coals, and his feet not be seared? (v.28) No, he can't.

Stay clear of the coals!

⟶ PRAYER ⟵

"Lord, help us not to burn our own clothes
or sear our own feet with another man's wife.
In Jesus' name. Amen."

PROVERBS 7:25–26

*"Do not let your heart turn aside to her ways,
do not stray into her paths, for she has cast down many wounded,
and all who were slain by her were strong men."*

GUARD YOUR HEART

In 1974, the research firm of Daniel Yankelovich, Inc. surveyed thirty-five-hundred young people, ages sixteen to twenty-five. The interviews sought to learn what these selected individuals felt about "every important value" in today's world.

The study indicated that only 31 percent considered premarital sexual relations as morally wrong compared with 52 percent in a 1969 survey. Opposition to abortion dropped from 58 percent to 45 percent in the same period. The proportion who considered "living a clean moral life a very important value" fell from 71 percent to 52 percent. Standards are shifting into the patterns that existed in the days of Noah.

The above survey illustrates well what our Proverb is teaching: "Do not let your heart turn aside to her ways." What you think matters. What you set your mind on matters. Proverbs 4:23 says "Keep your heart with all diligence, for out of it spring the issues of life." If you set your mind on illicit sex, then you'll eventually find yourself in an illicit relationship.

Our Proverb reminds us well that the heart of the matter is the heart.

PRAYER

*Lord, help us to guard our heart, what we think;
for some thoughts are not noble ones.
In Jesus' name. Amen."*

PROVERBS 8:13

*"The fear of the Lord is to hate evil; pride and arrogance
and the evil way and the perverse mouth I hate."*

A FEW THINGS GOD HATES

Okay. Hurray for what God loves; look out for what God hates. Two brothers grew up together on the family farm; the younger stayed home and worked the farm while the other older made his way to the city to make a name for himself. The older brother went to college, became an attorney, and was hired by a well-known law firm. The other brother continued on the farm. One day, the attorney came to visit his younger brother and remarked, "Why don't you leave this farm and make a success for yourself, hold your head up high like me?" The younger thought about it for a while and then pointed his finger to a field of wheat. "Look closely. You'll notice that the empty heads stand up, those that are filled always bow low."

Pride has been defined as "an assumed superiority." Let's talk about skin color for a moment. I've met people who believe that just because of the color of their skin that somehow (this is the "assumes" portion of the above definition) they have a status above others with a different color. Go figure? I do not get it, and neither does God. As facts stand, that type of attitude puts them on the A team for what God hates. God hates to see anyone treat others as though they were beneath them. A man or woman may have great talent and conclude they are better than others, but one simple question reveals the fallacy of this type of thinking. What do they have that was not given them? Where were they when God in His majesty was knitting together their feet, their eyes, and their mind in their mother's womb? What part did they have in this process? Zero! I understand that and get it about the self-discipline and sacrifice great athletes, composers, and scientists make to achieve. But do not forget, we would never be able to achieve anything had not God at the beginning put His hand in.

☙ PRAYER ☙

*"O, Lord, keep us from inflating ourselves so large that we believe
that we have an inherit superiority over others.
In Jesus' name. Amen."*

September 9

PROVERBS 9:17

PROVERBS 9:17

"Stolen water is sweet, and bread eaten in secret is pleasant."

AMBUSHED BY CONSEQUENCES

*H*arry Olson of Chicago had his automobile stolen and turned hitchhiker to get a ride home. He was picked up by his own car, in which was the man who had stolen it.

This humorous but sad story illustrates well our Proverb. With every temptation to steal, there is the sweet enjoyment of gaining something that is not yours. The context of our Proverb is a prostitute who is tempting her clients with the thought that illicit sex is the best "bread eaten in secret . . .." To one extent, I suppose this is true. That's why such sin is so tempting. But the Proverb doesn't end with the sweetness of stolen goods or behavior. Verse 18 warns us: ". . . but he does not know that the dead are there, that her guests are in the depths of hell."

Such temptations never advertise the consequences (loss of self-esteem, broken homes, financial ruin), only the immediate gratification. The hook must be covered by the bait or you will catch no fish.

PRAYER

*"Lord, keep us from thinking that heaven
is in what God calls hell. In Jesus' name. Amen."*

PROVERBS 10:4

"He who has a slack hand becomes poor,
but the hand of the diligent makes rich."

INEXCUSABLY LAZY

While other men paint, or water or weed,
I'm curled up in a chair, with a good book to read.
While other men shop, or shovel, or mow,
I'm having a drink while watching some show.
I offer to help, but my wife says,
"Forget it, if you lend a hand, I know I'll regret it."
And therein's my secret,
I'm very adept at only one thing, and that's being inept."[15]

It seems that some have made avoiding work a new art form. Our Proverb for today warns of the danger of a "slack hand." Poverty! Some people have little to nothing because they do little to nothing to earn it. Paul gives a stern warning to those who refuse to work due to laziness. He says, "But if anyone does not provide for his own, and especially for those of his household, he has denied the faith and is worse than an unbeliever." (I Timothy 5:8) Laziness is serious business in the eyes of the Lord!

Hard work rewards! "The diligent hand makes rich." Some jobs are not conquered unless you are tenacious as a bulldog, but the rewarding satisfaction and provisions are worth it in the end. Somewhat surprising is you tend to forget just how hard that job was, but you're still smelling the fragrance long after it's done.

⟶ PRAYER ⟵

"Lord, I'd rather be lazy, but I'd much rather be pleasing.
In Jesus' name. Amen."

---

15. *Illustrations for Biblical Preaching.* Edited by Michael P. Green, pg. 213, 214, #749, Baker Book House, Grand Rapids, Michigan.

PROVERBS 11:5

*"The righteousness of the blameless will direct his way aright,
but the wicked will fall by his own wickedness."*

UNQUESTIONABLY THE RIGHT CHOICE

*B*efore the days of modern navigational aids, a traveler made the Atlantic crossing in a boat equipped with two compasses. One was fixed to the deck where the man at the wheel could see it. The other compass was fastened up on one of the masts, and often a sailor would be seen climbing up to inspect it.

One day, a passenger asked the captain, "Why do you have two compasses?"

"This is an iron vessel," replied the captain, "and the compass on the deck is often affected by its surroundings. Such is not the case with the compass at the masthead; that one is above the influence. We steer by the compass above."—*Prairie Overcomer*

Are you steering your life by the compass above? The Bible is your true compass. Follow it and you'll walk in righteousness, and it will keep you from falling for the tempting but evil influences around you. Life is full of decisions. Just one bad choice can change the course of your life. Righteousness, however, will always guide you to a safe harbor.

PRAYER

*"Lord, I have so many decisions to make
and sometimes it's confusing,;
remind me that a righteous choice
is always the right choice. In Jesus' name. Amen."*

PROVERBS 12:22

*"Lying lips are an abomination to the Lord,
but those who deal truthfully are His delight."*

WANTON LIES

A "Truth in Government Act" proposed by Representative Donald M. Fraser (D-Minn.) would make it illegal for federal officials to lie to private citizens. Right now, Fraser says, honesty is a one-way street. "Under current law, it is a crime for a private citizen to lie to a government official, but not for a government official to lie to the people." Perhaps officials should take an oath of honesty when they are sworn in.[1]

The temptation to lie is inherent in the human heart. The fact is, you do not need to teach a child to lie; it comes naturally.

"Did you hit your brother?" No!

"Did you hide your sister's shoes?" No!

I did, however, hear one boy's complete candor when asked, "Why did you hit you brother?"

"Because I wanted to!"

Yes, we want to lie if it benefits us. It can keep us from being spanked by our parents or even from being fired at work. The beauty of the Bible is if man wanted to write the Bible, they wouldn't! Why? Because it so often chides us for wrong that we want to do, such as lie.

Lying causes the Lord to be disgusted. That is the definition of "abomination." God does hate somethings; one of those "somethings" is lying.

⟜ PRAYER ⟞

*Lord, remove far from me lying lips,
lest you remove Yourself far from me.
In Jesus' name. Amen."*

PROVERBS 13:1

"A wise son heeds his father's instruction,
but a scoffer does not listen to rebuke."

MY HANDSOME SON

Someone said there is a point in the Rocky Mountains where raindrops fall ever so close together. However, those falling on one side of the ridge flow westward toward the Pacific Ocean; those falling on the other side of the ridge flow southeastward toward the Gulf of Mexico. The raindrops fall so near each other but wind up so far apart.

This is an apt illustration of people making decisions for Christ. Persons may be in the same family or social group, yet their decisions for or against Christ determine whether their eternal destiny is heaven or hell. Now the difference may seem so slight. But destinies are bound up in the decisions they make. Persons are to ponder long in deciding about so vital a matter.

Heed your father's instruction, trust Christ, and obey Him. Amazing the nature of decisions! How one decision can cast the future of your life and eternity for good or for ill. Our Proverb today encourages a son to heed his father's instruction. This can be as simple as to how to fix a flat tire or as complicated as interpersonal relationships. A wise father will guide his son not only in this life, but the one to come.

Don't mock a father's counsel about this life, and more critically, about the life to come. To do so is to close off your earthly father and your Heavenly Father as well.

❧ PRAYER ❧

"Lord, there's a babel of advice these days,;
tune my ears to my father's wise counsel.
In Jesus' name. Amen."

PROVERBS 14:13

*"Even in laughter the heart may sorrow,
and the end of mirth may be grief."*

*"Laughter can conceal a heavy heart,
but when the laughter ends, the grief remains."
(New Living Translation)*

THE BIBLE IN ONE HAND AND THE NEWSPAPER IN THE OTHER

*M*y college Bible professor, Dr. Edward Simpson, use to say, "Read the Bible with one hand and the newspaper with the other." So, here is what the *Salt Lake Tribune* headlined September 14, 2019. "Mental Health Survey Paints a Bleak Picture." The article goes on to say that 40 percent of Utah's college students reported feeling so depressed that it was difficult to function. I thought college was a time of excitement! Football, new friends, freedom, adventure, etc., but it's depression; depression so severe that a startling percent had intentionally harmed themselves! This is bad news, but there is good news. The same Bible that describes with astounding accuracy our college students also say this: "I am the light of the world. He who follows Me shall not walk in darkness but will have the light of life." (John 8:12) Many college students set upon campus free from parental control, and little control in their campus life. They are taught that truth is "relevant." Truth not absolute, but *relevant*; applied differently in different circumstances and cultures. The questions is: Is that an absolute truth or just a relevant one? Does that "truth" apply to everyone, or just on campus? You and I live in an absolute world which is ordered by absolute truth. Gravity is the same in the good old USA as it is in India. One plus one equals two, not three. When people live believing there are no absolute "moral truths," they suffer horribly. Is it any wonder they feel depressed, guilty, and full of shame? Christ is the only true fulfillment. "I have come that they may have life, and that they may have it more abundantly." (John 10:10b)

PRAYER

*"Lord, may I find in Christ true meaning in this life.
In Jesus' name. Amen."*

PROVERBS 15:1

"A soft answer turns away wrath, but a harsh word stirs up anger."

TWENTY-SIX SOLDIERS

Karl Marx supposedly said, "Give me twenty-six lead soldiers, and I will conquer the world." He meant the twenty-six letters of the alphabet on a printing press.[1]

We have all experienced the power of words spoken in praise, how encouraging and motivating they are, and we've all experienced its corresponding devastation when a word is spoken in an unguarded moment. Oh, how we all wish we could go back in time and remove those ill-spoken words. It seems the last demon brought under the Holy Spirit's control is that of the tongue. We soon learn that the more obvious sins of the mouth need immediate attention; swearing for instance. But to bring the entire tongue under control is a lifelong task. Our Proverb today highlights a soft word when hard words are flying. One has to admit that saying something that is well deserved but inappropriate feels good, but rarely brings what you wish; in contrast, it stirs up a storm that lasts for hours, days, and in some sad cases, years.

I remember a time in my own experience waiting in line to have the oil in my truck changed. I was in a hurry. The employee was matter of fact about the time frame I was looking at, and my response was less than soft! He immediately got defensive, so I decided to leave, about the only thing I did right at that point. I pulled my truck out of line and then sat on the side of the parking lot stewing. After a few minutes of sanity, I decided to go back and admit my mistake and apologize. I commented that he deserved more help. At that comment, I saw a transformation before my very eyes. To acknowledge his undeserved plight was the soft tongue that I should have started with. He said he had one man on lunch and another did not show up for work. He gave me my customer slip and said he would get to it ASAP. I still had to wait, but it sure made the waiting easier. I also believe it made for a better day for him.

⟩ PRAYER ⟨

"Oh, Lord, help me to wise up to the wisdom of a soft tongue in the midst of hard times. In Jesus' name. Amen."

PROVERBS 16:32

*"He who is slow to anger is better than the mighty,
and he who rules his spirit than he who takes a city."*

STRIPPING THE GEARS

No one treated Abraham Lincoln with more contempt than did Edwin Stanton. Stanton called Lincoln a "low cunning clown." Stanton also nicknamed Lincoln the "original gorilla"and chided explorer Paul Du Chaillu for wandering in Africa attempting to capture a gorilla when one could be easily found in Springfield, Illinois. Lincoln said nothing! Amazingly, Lincoln made Stanton his minister of war! Why, because Stanton was the best man for the job. Years later, when Lincoln lay dying, struck down by an assassin's bullet, Stanton looked down on his so called "original gorilla" and with tears said, "There lays the greatest ruler of men the world has even seen." The patience of love had won in the end.

The Bible teaches, "Love is patient . . .." (I Corinthians 13:4) Hearts have been won and irritable circumstances conquered by men and women who control their temper. To be "slow to anger" is greater than the conquest of a city by the skill of a warrior. So, it is better to let you engine "idle" than stripping the gears through anger. Stripping the gears with harsh words, over-reaction, and poor decisions . . . I've been there.

⟶ PRAYER ⟵

*"Lord, this concept is so simple, but the practice so hard.
Help me to face my circumstances, my day, my life
with the wisdom of knowing that patience wins in the end.
In Jesus' name. Amen."*

September 17

PROVERBS 17:6

"The glory of children is their fathers,"

WHEN I GET TO HEAVEN

A little boy was asked in Sunday school who he wanted to see first when he got to heaven. I'm not going there!" Shocked, the Sunday school teacher asked why? "Because I want to be with my Dad. Mama and sister are going there, but Dad isn't. So, I want to be with Dad." A short time later, the Sunday school teacher met the boy's father, who also was their family physician. He repeated the Sunday school incident and then pointedly asked, "And now, Doctor, just where are you going?" The physician was a confirmed unbeliever, but the incident and question rocked him. He soon started to pace the floor and with tears in his eyes he sighed painfully. "It's just like him to say that. I'll have to change my ways. I have noticed that he always wants to be with me and be like me!"

God has put it in a child's heart to be like their parents! That is why they mimic them. That is why they thrill at making their parents laugh. That is why boys brag that "my dad can beat up your dad." This goes even further; children's self-esteem, confidence, and overall sense of well-being is tied up with the example and life of their parents. When parents succeed, generally the children do as well. Dad is my inspiration; we have heard it before. Even as an adult, I like to brag about my father, a true hero in the war, he fought with the famed 101st Airborne. Why is that? Because that makes *me* feel good about myself. It makes *me* feel that I too can accomplish, succeed, and overcome.

So, here it is. Mom, Dad, you are your children's heroes. Chapter 20:7 puts it another way: "It is a wonderful heritage to have an honest father." (*The Living Bible*) Children will soon forgive a parent who will humble themselves, acknowledge their wrong, and genuinely start behaving the way heroes behave.

PRAYER

"Lord, Please help me to live as I should before You,
that my children would see me as their hero, warts and all.
In Jesus' name. Amen."

PROVERBS 18:6

*"A fool's lips enter into contention,
and his mouth calls for blows."*

BABBLING LIPS

A trick played by magnetic storms can cause a conversation on a telephone line to jump to a radio line nearby and be broadcast without the knowledge of the two persons talking. This occurred in New York a short time ago when such a connection caused an intimate phone call to be heard on a coast-to-coast program.

Would you be embarrassed if what you're saying was broadcast over the telephone's lines? Especially if it was damaging to another? Some words are so inflammable, they've caused lifelong friends to come to blows. Our Proverb tells us that a fool has not quite figured this out. He speaks without reflection. There is no halt to his lips once the mind presents its thoughts; no restraint, no contemplation of consequences. His lips fill his life with contention, all the while not realizing why his life is one verbal blow after another. He may be found amusing, even funny, but eventually he will be found with a fat lip! To control the lips is to control contention.

⸱⸙⸱ PRAYER ⸱⸙⸱

*"Lord, help me to speak with constraint,
lest I live in contention. In Jesus' name. Amen."*

PROVERBS 19:21

*"There are many plans in a man's heart,
nevertheless, the Lord's counsel—that will stand."*

"Man proposes, but God disposes." (The Living Bible)

DISAPPOINTED WITH LIFE?

Napoleon was asked if God was on the side of France. He responded rather sarcastically, "God is on the side that has the heaviest artillery." Then came the Battle of Waterloo where Napoleon lost the battle and his kingdom. He was exiled to the island of St. Helena. Old and humbled, Napoleon quoted the words of Thomas a Kempis: "Man proposes; God disposes." Life and history teach us that God can work his sovereign will-despite man's best efforts otherwise.[1]

Has life not worked out for you? Have your cherished dreams and ideal circumstances been dashed? Do you see life as a disappointment, or at least on some big issues? The Proverb above is just for you. If you're like me, I had my whole future planned out at the ripe old age of eighteen! God's will, however, took a strange and perplexing turn, many turns, and I struggled; but it still has purpose and even joy. If you take a microscope and look at a piece of cloth under it, the outside edges are blurred, but the center is clear, crystal clear. If, as a believer, you can trust God for the blurred edges, those painful circumstances in your life that only bring you down, and instead look at the center of the cloth where the cross of Christ is, where a loving and just God looked on while sinful man crucified His Son. From the cross came the resurrection, and with it salvation, then you can cope with your own tragedies and loss—those blurred edges. God has had his purpose fulfilled in our lives through the disappointments. Those disappointments bring character, a godly character, that can help fellow pilgrims with their disappointments.

━ PRAYER ━

*"Lord, I've been disappointed for sure, but help me to trust that You
have a grander far nobler purpose for my life than
what I originally had in mind. In Jesus' name. Amen."*

PROVERBS 20:22

"Do not say, "I'll pay you back for this wrong!"
Wait for the Lord, and he will deliver you."
—New International Version

THE BITE OF REVENGE

*H*ave you heard about the man who was told by his doctor that he had rabies? Instantly, the patient started to write in a notebook. The doctor, suspecting he was writing out his will, said, "Wait a minute. You're not going to die. There's a cure for rabies." "I already know that," the patient uttered "I'm just writing down a list of people I'm going to bite." —Charles R. Swindoll, *Hope Again*

Friedrich Nietzsche said, "Revenge is the greatest instinct in the human race." Oh, how true that is. However, we violate God's clear teaching when we use revenge. God knows. God knows you were wronged, and He knows the offender's address. Our problem is we are way too impatient. Our thinking is we want God to strike him dead within the next thirty minutes, or at least by the time the commercials are over! If the individual does not repent, God will have his day with them— if not in this life, most certainly in the next. Second, whatever God does, He does it perfectly. He will not violate his mercy or suspend his justice. "For the Lord is a God of justice, blessed are all those who wait for Him." (Isaiah 30:18) There are some things we should never touch; revenge is one of them.

The antidote to revenge is prayer! Sometimes, it demands a lot of prayer. Prayer for grace on your part. And this is the hard part: prayer for the offender's repentance. Revenge is like cancer. If you don't take care of it, it will take care of you. So, remove it with the surgery of forgiveness. Let God be God. He sees, and He knows, and he will act.

⟶ PRAYER ⟵

"Lord, this is, far, far beyond our capacity to do.
If it is going to be done, You will need to walk us through this.
Help me to forgive and not seek to even the score."
In Jesus' name. Amen."

PROVERBS 21:3

*"To do righteousness and justice
is more acceptable to the Lord than sacrifice."*

FRACTIONAL OBEDIENCE

*R*ighteous living and a life of justice is more important than religious rituals with neither. The Old Testament prophet Samuel reproves king Saul by saying, "Has the Lord as great delight in
burnt offerings and sacrifices as in obeying the voice of the Lord?
Behold, to obey is better than sacrifice, and to heed than the fat of
rams." (I Samuel 15:22)

How tempting it is for some to throw money at the Lord, and
then to continue to live in disobedience to God's commands.

How tempting it is to volunteer at the Homeless Shelter at
Christmas and then to continue in a life of stubborn rebellion
against God's laws.

How tempting it is to attend an Easter Service and then call it
good while returning to a life of dissipation.

A grandfather was visiting his six-year-old grandson when his
mother called, "Tommy, it's time for your shower!" Grandfather
asked, "Do you use the shower downstairs or the one upstairs?"
Tommy replied, "Momma says that I can't take a shower upstairs,
and when Momma says no, we'd better do no!"[16]

It's best to do "no" when God says no. Do not be fooled into
thinking that occasional obedience and justice in some form will erase
a life of stubborn disobedience. That is not the "Way of Wisdom."

PRAYER

*"Lord, how tempting it is to throw you some sacrifice hither
and yarn, when humble righteousness is the order of all our days. In
Jesus' name. Amen."*

16. Jones, G. C. (1986). *1000 Illustrations for Preaching and Teaching* (p.
137). Nashville, TN: Broadman & Holman Publishers.

PROVERBS 22:4

"Humility and the fear of the Lord bring wealth and honor and life."

HUMILITY

"*A* woodpecker was pecking on a tree in the middle of an intense thunderstorm when suddenly the tree was struck by lightning. The woodpecker was thrown to the ground, dazed and confused. Upon regaining his senses, he shouted, "What a peck!" This is *not* what Solomon had in mind with this Proverb.

Humility means "ranking low in a hierarchy or scale: insignificant."—*Webster Ninth Collegiate Dictionary*. It's being a Private as opposed to a four-star General. The individual who does not go around asserting his importance is usually a person others are attracted to. To be humble is not to deny gifts or abilities; it just means that you are modest about the display of them. The truly humble person realizes that all gifts are given to us by our Creator, so why should we brag about something God has given? This Proverbs goes further. A person who links a humble attitude with true reverence for God and God's ways, is promised riches and honor and life. Proverbs, by nature, are general principles. There are exceptions. These are not guaranteeing, but in the general world of everyday living, they are true. A humble person, as opposed to someone who believes they have an assumed superiority (proud), does far better at work. Employers prefer them, especially if they have God-given abilities, rather than the gifted person who is difficult to get along with because he views himself so highly. I had an employer tell me that he had to let go an excellent mechanic because he just could not get along with people. Everyone loves the person who has outstanding ability but does not act like it. He behaves like an ordinary person even though he has extraordinary ability.

⟿ PRAYER ⟿

"Lord, help me to keep my attitude in check while I walk in Your light, and may You see fit to honor me with the true riches of life. In Jesus' name. Amen."

PROVERBS 23:29–30, 32

*"Who has woe? Who has sorrow? Who has contentions?
Who has complaints? Who has wounds without cause?
Who has redness of eyes?
Those who linger long at the wine, those who go in search of mixed wine."*

"At the last it bites like a serpent, and stings like a viper."

THE DRINK THAT ENSLAVES

I sat across the table from a young man in his twenties. His looks were Irish, and his quiet demeanor was appealing. We opened the Bible together and read of God's will for his life. The place was a homeless shelter (Rescue Mission of Salt Lake). He told me how his drinking drove him to be homeless, sleeping in a tent along a riverbank. He talked about how in that environment you had to fight for survival, necessities such as food and dry clothes, and the ever-present danger of being attacked for what little you had. In the thirty years I have been volunteering at the Rescue Mission, I've seen fights break out on the very platform I was preaching on, front row attendees vomiting on themselves, and endured the suffocating smell of men who have not showered in months.

Our Proverb today is not over exaggerating the effects of drinking. "Who has woe? Who has sorrow? Who has contentions?" I have seen men give up everything for their drinking. A man who was formerly a physician in California came through the Mission because of his addiction. Drinking and drugs have no class restriction, no educational boundaries, and no race laws.

I recently attended a man's celebration of twelve years of sobriety. He received his twelve-year coin. His message was to walk with Christ and do not give up. He ought to know; he was right off the streets and homeless when he entered the Mission. Now he serves as the CEO of another Rescue Mission. Jesus said in John 8:12, "Therefore, if the Son makes you free, you shall be free indeed."

PRAYER

*"Lord, free me from the tyranny of drink before I become its
complete slave, a slave to utter self-centeredness, unconcerned about
anything other than feeding my master.
In Jesus' name. Amen."*

PROVERBS 24:29

*"Do not say, 'I will do to him just as he has done to me;
I will render to the man according to his work.'"*

ITCHING FOR REVENGE

I like what the old country preacher said about revenge: "I'm not going to get even. I'm going to tell God on you." Sound advice. Then, of course. there is this approach. I was working at a Fred Meyer store years ago while going through Seminary. I recall one of the sales associates telling me she didn't get mad, she just got even. Most people choose to get even! They lay in wait, consuming their mental and physical health while they plot out their revenge. But it is a heavy toll. Revenge usually is not as sweet as they'd hoped for and generally shows itself in poor health years down the road.

God says He'll take care of business. "Vengeance is mine, and recompense; their foot shall slip in due time; for the day of their calamity is at hand, and the things to come hasten upon them." (Deuteronomy 32:35) The problem we have with this verse are the three little words "in due time." If truth be known, most revenge taken by man is immediate, impulsive, and disastrous. We just do not want to wait on anybody, not even God! But waiting on God is always best. We learn this as adults, whether it be airline tickets, food made from scratch, or a duly earned raise. However, it does not satisfy our anger to wait when comes to justice; but a wise man soon learns that waiting on God always brings the best. We know this when it comes to the circumstances of life. It is time we learn it with God: ". . . for the day of their calamity is at hand . . ."

So, don't grab the wheel out of God's hands. He has it under control.

⟨ ⟩ PRAYER ⟨ ⟩

*"Lord, help me to wait on You for any retribution.
Don't let me ruin the ingredients by stirring too quickly.
In Jesus' name. Amen."*

September 25

PROVERBS 25:4–5

"Take away the dross from silver and it will go to the silversmith for jewelry. Take away the wicked from before the king, and his throne will be established in righteousness."

SOME SLICING AND DICING

"*A* famous preacher of many years ago had a clock in his church that was well known for its inability to keep time accurately. It was sometimes too fast, sometimes too slow. Finally, after its fame became widespread, the preacher put a sign over the clock, reading, "Don't blame the hands—the trouble lies deeper.[17]

Many of our troubles are our own doing! We wonder why life has become "one weary round of drudgery after another." Do not blame the hands on the clock, the real issue is within. We all struggle with the dross within, those evil tendencies that we feed and enjoy. Consequently, God seems distant and far away. One of the main objectives the Holy Spirit has in mind is too purify from us the dross. This may involve giving up friends and acquaintances that are harmful, to say the least. We hang with these individuals and after a while we look like them in our attitude, speech, and lifestyle. There is a saying among the homeless: "Same places, same friends, same habits." No wonder. Geese fly with other geese; they do not fly with ducks or eagles. It is a natural order God has established, and it speaks volumes. We cannot expect our "silver" to be pure if we are constantly associating with the evil. For example, we see on TV a constant litany of death, violence, and sex; these have a corrosive effect on our soul. So, do not be surprised if you have no appetite for prayer or God's Word after a couple of hours of this "dross." Jesus wants to emphasize the importance of this, so He advises removing every temptation (dross) of evil, no matter what the cost. (cf. Matthew 5:30)

⊱ PRAYER ⊱

"Lord, You know my dross, and You also know that I like it. Help me to identify anything that alienates You from me and remove it. In Jesus' name. Amen."

17. *Illustrations for Biblical Preaching.* Edited by Michael P. Green, pg. 337. Baker Book House, Grand Rapids, Michigan.

PROVERBS 26:11

"As a dog returns to his own vomit, so a fool repeats his folly."

DOGS AND DRIVING
UNDER THE INFLUENCE

*I*n Charles Colson's book *Born Again*, he details his experiences with President Nixon and Watergate. Colson shares one of President Nixon's problems—he could never admit he was wrong in anything. Even when he had a cold—face red, nose running, sneezing—he would never admit it.[18]

A sure-fire way to repeat your mistake is not to admit it. People of this stripe won't listen to good counsel. Why? Because to admit to their error is for them a complete renouncing of who they are. The problem with this attitude is it places you on the road to destruction. "There is a way that seems right to a man, but its end is the way of death." (Proverbs 14:12)

Many of us repeat small but persistent mistakes that mar our day. Perhaps a closer look at our habits will reveal that we too are repeat offenders. Gross! The image of a dog returning to its own vomit should be enough to keep us from doing the same. Our day will much more effective and enjoyable, and when you do it the Lord's way, the menu cannot be beat.

⟨⟩ PRAYER ⟨⟩

"Lord, you know how often we have repeated the same mistakes repeatedly, and in our insanity expected the outcome to be different. We plead with You for the grace to keep our noses out of where they should not be, and for Your favor to change these blighting habits that keep us from feasting on Your 'abundant life.' (John 10:10) In Jesus' name. Amen."

---

18. *Illustrations for Biblical Preaching.* Edited by Michael P. Green, pg. 290. Baker Book House, Grand Rapids, Michigan.

PROVERBS 27:2

*"Let another man praise you, and not your own mouth,
a stranger, and not your own lips.*

THE LITTLE FISH
WITH A BIG IMPRESSION

"General Earle G. Wheeler, Army Chief of Staff, was observing the induction of a recruit on an inspection trip he was conducting. The young man was asked by the sergeant, "Did you go to grammar school?" "Yes, sir," was the response. "I also went through high school, graduated from Knox College, and took graduate study at Michigan and Harvard, where I got my PhD." The sergeant reached for a rubber stamp and stamped the questionnaire with one word: "Literate."[1]

I would say literate, but not wise. Nobody, and I mean nobody, likes to hear someone brag about themselves. It makes you feel uneasy and leaves you wondering what need the bragger must have to so inflate himself. Inferiority? There is a fish called the "puffer fish" that can puff himself up two to three times bigger than his original size when threatened. I believe that people do this all the time. It is called bragging. This individual will take a tale and exaggerate it to three times what the original was, with him being the hero. *We* all have an inherent need to be valued, to feel important, to feel that we contribute to the overall good in life. When we feel insignificant, there is the temptation to brag. There is an antidote to this. Let someone else do it. That is the heart of today's Proverb. Work hard and be modest. Eventually you will be recognized. Most of your friends and relatives know what you have accomplished; they are just not sure how to say it. One other thing. God sees! (Psalm 33:13) "The Lord looks from heaven; He sees all the sons of men . . . He considers all their works." (Mark 8:36) Jesus said your value as a person exceeds the wealth of the entire planet. Think about that for a moment.

PRAYER

*"Lord, help us when we feel little, of no value. Keep us from bragging.
May we truly believe that your image,
stamped on our heart, is far more valuable. In Jesus' name. Amen."*

PROVERBS 28:13

*"He who covers his sins will not prosper,
but whoever confesses and forsakes them will have mercy."*

A DIFFICULT CONFESSION

"A college freshman went to the dorm laundry room with his dirty clothes bundled into an old sweatshirt. But he was so embarrassed by how dirty his clothes were that he never opened the bundle. He merely pushed it into a washing machine and when the machine stopped, he gathered the bundle up and pushed it into the dryer. Back at his room he discovered that his clothes had gotten wet and then dry, but not washed."[1]

The soul's tendency to hide our sins can be traced back to Adam who tried to palm off his transgression on wife Eve. (cf. Genesis 3:12) He even reminded God that He was the one who brought Eve to him in the first place. Poor fellow, just minding his own business until God gave him Eve.

People nowadays laugh at the Genesis account of Adam and Eve, but to this day will still act like them. We hide our sins, deny our accountability, and fight tooth and claw that we *did not* do it. I've read the paper for years, and rarely do I ever read of a man who is accused of a serious crime plead guilty. You get the impression from these criminals that they are just innocent victims, even when the face on the video is their's. "Is that you sir?" "No, it is someone who looks like me."

I am familiar with a story at work of a man who was caught sleeping on the job. He was asked if he was sleeping on the job and to his supervisor's surprise, he said yes! He had been working two jobs, seven days a week for years and had been overcome by sleep. He confessed upright and said it would never happen again. He lost his raise that year but managed to keep his job.

PRAYER

"Lord, keep us humble and honest. In Jesus' name. Amen."

September 29

PROVERBS 29:11

"A fool vents all his feelings, but a wise man holds them back."

ANGER

"*A*lexander the Great was one of the few men in history who deserved his descriptive title. He was intelligent, energetic, and versatile, but several times in his life, he was defeated by anger. The story is told of one occasion, when a dear friend of Alexander, a general, was drunk and began to ridicule the emperor in front of his men. Alexander was enraged with anger and snatched a nearby spear and killed his childhood friend. Later, overcome with grief, Alexander tried to kill himself with the same spear, but was stopped by his men. For days he lay sick, calling for his friend and chiding himself as a murderer."[19]

Alexander indeed was great, conqueror of countries and major cities, but he lay lame at the feet of his own anger. St. John Climacus is credited with these words: "As long as anger lives, she continues to be the fruitful mother of many unhappy children." (*Climax*) I read an article about hospital Emergency Room where I came across a fascinating statement made by one of the ER physicians. He said that ninety-five percent of the patients in the emergency room were not in life-threatening circumstances. That really surprised me. Wasn't this for emergencies only? Not all perceptions are emergencies. I believe this relates to anger, as well. We perceive the issue we're upset about deserves the righteous venting of our anger, but seldom does. Okay, you were slighted, I get it, but venting all your feelings at that moment will *not* get you what you want. It will get you in trouble, perhaps even thrown into the back seat of a police car. There is a better way—prayer! Sounds foolish to some, but prayer will direct your feelings to the only one that will really give you help—God. The Bible teaches that God will deal with the unjust. "Vengeance is Mine." (Deuteronomy 35:32)God will take of it.

PRAYER

"Lord, 'But I am poor and needy; Make haste to me, O God!
You are my help and my deliverer; O Lord, do not delay.' (Psalm 70:5)
In Jesus' name. Amen."

19. *Illustrations for Biblical Preaching*. Edited by Michael P. Green, pg. 21,#21. Baker Book House, Grand Rapids, Michigan.

PROVERBS 30:5–6

"Every word of God is pure;
He is a shield to those who put their trust in Him.
Do not add to His words, lest He rebuke you,
and you be found a liar."

SHIELDED

And so, I thought, the anvil of God's Word
For ages, the skeptics' blows have beat upon,
But though the noise of falling blows was heard
The anvil is unchanged; the hammers gone.
—John Clifford

In the real world of experience, people have found the Bible to stand. It stands in birth; it stands in life; and it stands in the end. There is no corruption, no mixture of error and truth, no speculation, no imagined encounters, no contemporary philosophy—it is just pure (not mixed with any other material). "The words of the Lord are pure words, like silver tried in a furnace of earth, purified seven times." (Psalm 12:6) "Your word is very pure; therefore, Your servant loves it." (Psalm 119:40) Thus, God becomes your shield when you place yourself under the protection of His Word.

Therefore, do not add to it. It is perfect; it needs no additions. "Whatever I command you, be careful to observe it; you shall not add to it nor take away from it." (Deuteronomy 12:32)

The mind of God is gained by careful reading, trusting what you have read, and then experiencing God as He keeps His word to you.

∾ PRAYER ∾

"Lord, Your Word is my shield.
May I never be so wise as to add to it
and be found out to be a liar. In Jesus' name. Amen."

PROVERB 1:7

*"The fear of the Lord is the beginning of knowledge,
but fools despise wisdom and instruction."*

SKILL IN LIVING

*P*roverbs teaches that to live skillfully in this life, one must have a reverence for God. The above Proverb uses the word fear; actually, it is reverence shown by submission to God's will. The one who consistently submits to God's will has true wisdom. Wisdom has been defined as the successful application of knowledge. True wisdom, according to Proverbs, is to reverence God by obeying Him. Case in point: A young man is making his way down a long stretch of railroad tracks. In the distance, he hears the roar of an oncoming train. Knowledge tells him it is a train, wisdom tells him to get off the tracks!

To reject God's wisdom and instruction in this life by not submitting to His will is like insisting you stay on the tracks while a train is rushing headlong toward you! It can end up in disaster, but people do it all the time. Take for instance the true story of two women talking at a fashionable London restaurant about their husbands. They showed each other photographs and realized they were married to the same man! Consequently, this man spent five years in prison. Bigamy is against God's law and man's. (cf. Deuteronomy 17:17) Lack of reverence for God in this case created untold heartache for this man and those who came to love him. A wise man submits to God's will, but a fool despises such practice.

So, where do you stand, Christian? Are you on the tracks of self- will, rejecting God's will in some form while moral disaster rushes toward you? Or are you submitting daily to God's will in the wisdom of reverence?

PRAYER

*"Lord, may we believe that true wisdom in this life
is found in You. In Jesus' name. Amen."*

PROVERBS 2:7

"He is a shield to those who walk uprightly."

THE GUARDRAILS OF LIFE

People who do what is morally right generally suffer less in this life. There are exceptions, but as a rule this Proverb is true. For example, the story is told of a believer, Frederick Nolan, who was fleeing from his enemies during a time of persecution in North Africa. Pursued by them over hill and valley, he fell exhausted into a wayside cave. Awaiting his death, he watched a spider as it was weaving a web. Within minutes, the little bug had woven a web across the mouth of the cave. When his pursuers arrived, they wondered if Nolan was hiding there, but after looking at the unbroken web, they thought it impossible for him to have entered the cave without destroying the web, so they went on. God saw fit in this case to shield this servant that he might continue his upright life.

The converse is also sadly true. The story is told of an electrician who would clock in at 7 a.m. for his day's shift. He was seen several times that morning, and then he routinely disappeared around noon, not to be seen again until 2 p.m. in the afternoon. Management was growing suspicious, so they paged him to a phone with caller ID; he returned the call from his own residence! This man would typically go home for lunch since he lived nearby and not return to work until around 2 p.m. in the afternoon. He was fired that very day. Life has ample examples of the truth of this Proverb. The promise is that if we will do the right thing, at the right time, God will shield us. This is not a guaranteed, for God does allow us to suffer, even his upright saints, but as a general rule this Proverbs applies. Are you facing a difficult problem or decision? Wondering what to do next? Do the next right thing as God sees it, and then you'll have God as your shield.

⁓ PRAYER ⁓

"Lord, at times I'm tempted to take the shortcut, the easy way, even the dishonest path. Remind me that You always shield, preserve and guard the upright, In Jesus' name. Amen."

October 3

PROVERBS 3:1

"My son, do not forget my law, but let your heart keep my commands;
for length of days and long life and peace they will add to you."

LENGTH OF DAYS

I t has been said that wisdom is the successful application of knowledge. One of the clear voices heard from the book of Proverbs is that wisdom is seen in obeying God and man. To heed a warning is wise, especially if it involves danger. Not everyone is so wise. The October 2, 2003 edition of the *Salt Lake Tribune* ran a front page article entitled, "A Fatal Adventure." The article described how two brothers scuba-diving in an underground siphon were drowned. Ignoring a warning from their father that such a dive could be dangerous, the men set off for what would be their last adventure. The siphon was an irrigation tunnel that channeled water across a ravine. A concrete tube, 9 feet in diameter, ran down the sides of the ravine at various angles to a depth of 96-feet across the ravine floor. By 1 a.m. the following day, search and rescue teams had arrived at the north end of the siphon. None of the rescue divers, some with more than 20 years experience, were willing to enter the siphon until it was drained. After taking more than eight hours to drain the siphon, search crews found the bodies around 10 a.m. Despite clearly marked warnings of the danger and posted "No Trespassing" signs, the divers *still* entered the siphon. The age of the men—23 and 21!

The above Proverb teaches that the man who keeps God's commandments will prolong his days. God clearly teaches that a man's responsibility is to obey the governing authorities that God has in place. "Let every person be in subjection to the governing authorities." (cf. Romans 13:1) Simply put, this means obeying "No Trespassing" signs.

PRAYER

"Lord, help me to heed warnings, especially those that cut into my fun
and time. Remind me these warnings are there for good reason,
and God's voice is often heard in them. In Jesus' name. Amen."

October 4

PROVERBS 4:23

"Keep your heart with all diligence,
For out of it spring the issues of life."

"I think, therefore I am." (René Descartes)

YOU ARE WHAT YOU THINK

They say you are what you eat. Proverbs, the Bible's book on wisdom, asserts you are what you think. The above Proverb teaches us that we must keep a close watch on our private thoughts, for they dynamically impact the life we live. None other than Jesus Himself said in Matthew 15:19-20, "For out of the heart proceed evil thoughts, murders, adulteries, fornications, thefts, false witness, and blasphemies. These are the things which defile a man . . .." A cursory reading of your daily newspaper will argue for the truthfulness of this. A leading Republican candidate for California's governorship publicly apologized for groping and sexually harassing women in years gone by. Sexual abuse is an issue of the heart. This type of behavior does not happen in a vacuum; it originates in the heart, in our thought processes. What you are thinking will influence your emotions, which can influence the words you speak and the action you take.

The good news is the opposite is true as well. As we dwell on what is good, our emotions, attitudes, and actions are impacted positively. Paul the Apostle put it this way: "Finally, brethren, whatever things are true, whatever things are noble, whatever things are just, whatever things are pure, whatever things are lovely, whatever things are of good report, if there is any virtue and if there is anything praiseworthy, mediate on these things." (Philippians 4:8) It is impossible to live in this world without being aware of the sad, the negative, the destructive, but we do not have to dwell on them.

PRAYER

Lord, the toughest daily battle we have with the evil one
is our thought life. Help me to keep this area of my soul especially
lovely. I do have a choice. With Your help, I'll keep my soul's mind
in a good report. In Jesus' name. Amen."

PROVERBS 5:3–4

"For the lips of an adulteress drip honey . . . but in the end she is bitter as gall, sharp as a doubled-edged sword."

IF YOU PLAY YOU WILL PAY

The picture here is a warning against adultery, the seventh commandment. Adultery is still one of the primary reasons why many marriages end in divorce.

Take, for example, the wealthy couple who decided to hire a chauffeur. The wife advertised, the applicants were screened, and four candidates were brought before her for the final interview. She called the four applicants to her balcony and pointed out a brick wall and asked them, "How close do you think you can come to that wall without scratching my car?" The first man estimated he could drive within a foot without damaging her car. The second said he could come within six inches without hitting it. The third candidate not wanting to be outdone said he could come within inches of the wall. The fourth candidate, however, said, "I don't really know how close I could come to the wall without damaging your car. Rather, I would try to stay as far away from it as possible." This candidate had a different mindset. True skill was not based on how close he could get the car to the wall, but in keeping a wide margin of safety.

There are aspects in human nature that are best kept at a distance. Sexual temptation is one of them. A wide margin of safety is the best way to deal with it. Today's Proverb warns us that the steps of the adulteress lead straight to the grave. (v.5) Many a soul will testify of the truthfulness of that. Are you flirting with disaster? Or, as our Proverb puts it, are you being seduced by the looks or words or acts of another that is not your spouse? Perhaps this will help. Picture yourself slowly descending the steps to hell itself, because that is how the experience will end up.

⁖ PRAYER ⁖

"Lord, keep us mindful of consequences, especially those that can alter our entire life. In Jesus' name. Amen."

PROVERBS 6:32

*"The man who commits adultery lacks judgment;
whoever does so destroys himself."*

SEVEN-FOLD HEARTACHE

There are acts in life, which once committed, will alter your future. They will never stop nipping at your feet, regardless of where they may take you. Murder, for instance, is a sad reality, but once committed has devastating consequences; high dollar theft is another one that can get you ten to fifteen years in the state penitentiary; and of course, adultery, our topic for today.

Our Proverb teaches that the man who commits adultery lacks judgment, but what judgment is he lacking? I hold it is the subtle attitude that adultery can be committed without any real consequences.

An excellent example of this oft-repeated danger with no seeming consequence is seen in the Australia outback where an alligator performer would place his head in the jaws of a deadly alligator. His daily performances had earned him quite a reputation as well as the assurance the alligator would behave himself. On one eventful day, he placed his bald head inside the alligator's jaws only to have it clamp down and throw him around like a rag doll. In horror, the viewing audience watched as the zookeepers scrambled to pry open the alligator's tooth-studded jaws. The next day he reappeared on TV conspicuously wearing a hat and assuring his viewers that he had survived his ordeal intact. Rest assured, *you* will not go unpunished if you commit adultery, and verse 29 guarantees that.

There is hope. Jesus forgives, and His forgiveness enables us to forgive others and ourselves (cf. Matthew 6:12)

∼ PRAYER ∼

*"Lord, may we always walk in the shadow of Your presence,
far from this sin. In Jesus' name. Amen."*

PROVERBS 7:1–5

*"My son, keep my words and store up my commands
within you . . . and you will live."*

WRITE THEM ON THE
TABLET OF YOUR HEART

Skillful living before God and man involves memory. Today's Proverb teaches us to bury God's word in our heart.

An excellent true to life example of the power of memorized scripture is seen in the story of Jacob de Shazer. Shazer was sent as one of Jimmy Doolittle's raiders on Japan on April 18, 1942. He was an atheist. During the attack he was shot down by enemy fire and captured. Imprisoned, he watched two of his companions shot by a firing squad and saw another one die of slow starvation. He hated the Japanese, and they hated him. Slowly he began to recall some of the things he had heard about Christianity. Finally, he asked the jailers if they could get him a Bible. At first, they thought it was a joke. As Shazer persisted, they warned him to stop making a nuisance of himself. After a year-and-a half of asking, a guard flung a Bible into his cell and said, "Three weeks you have. Three weeks, and then I take away." Good to his word, the Bible was taken back after just three weeks. However, in those three weeks, he studied and memorized the Bible and contemplated the meaning of life. Released in 1944, Jacob de Shazer returned home. In 1948, de Shazer, his wife, and infant son returned to Japan as missionaries! The profound impact of reading and memorizing the Bible's contents for those three short weeks changed his life.

Are you a believer whose Christian life lacks power and genuine reality? Do you secretly wish things were different between you and our Heavenly Father? Is your Christian experience boring? Try memorizing scripture; you'll be amazed at the vitality and joy that will return to your Christian walk.

PRAYER

*"Lord help us to memorize Your Word,
that we may be favored by You. In Jesus' name. Amen."*

October 8

PROVERB 8:8

*"All the words of my mouth are just;
none of them is crooked or perverse."*

WEIGHING THE WORD

*T*his Proverb makes the boast that all her words are just, and none are wrong or twisted. Proverbs, as well as the Bible itself, claims that the very words are accurate and reliable. Can we trust a book that has been translated hundreds of times as it is passed from one generation to the next?

The words of the Bible can be tested. One such test is the numerous prophecies surrounding the birth, life, and death of Christ. There are over 300 of them, written well before His birth, predicting His birth in Bethlehem, His betrayal by Judas, and His crucifixion on the cross. If you were to take just eight of these prophecies and apply the science of probability to them, the possibility that any one man might fulfill them by chance would be one in ten followed by sixteen zeros. To better understand how large a number this is, it would be the same as if you were to cover the entire state of Texas with silver dollars two feet deep! Then, if one of these coins had a special mark on it, what would be the probability of a blind man finding that coin? It would be the same probability as a man fulfilling just eight of the prophecies surrounding Christ's life by chance. How were the biblical writers able to predict the future? The Holy Spirit supernaturally guarded its contents so only what God wanted written was recorded. (cf. II Timothy 2:15).

We have an inerrant guide for life—the Bible. We have an unfaltering source for wisdom—the Proverbs. Read them, believe them, and trust them. They are just and there is no crooked way in them.

ᴏ— PRAYER —ᴏ

*Lord, thank You for an unerring guide in the Bible,
that gives us a sure guide for life.
In Jesus' name. Amen."*

October 9

PROVERBS 9:7

*"Whoever corrects a mocker invites insults;
whoever rebukes a wicked man incurs abuse."*

INVITATION TO ABUSE

What characterizes an evil person? According to this Proverb, it is the individual who, when corrected for doing wrong, will verbally or even physically abuse you. For example: The assistant administrator of a large cafeteria fired one of her employees for stealing. Two days later, the administrator found her car window smashed and the sides of her car keyed. The concept taught by this Proverb is simple—those who correct a wicked person may end up paying for it.

In another example of the reaction that follows, a legitimate correction is seen in the Annual Convention of the Diocese of Michigan. Two Gay Liberation members spit out Communion wine near the altar and disrupted the convention. Others hugged and kissed in the pews and aisles of St. Paul's Cathedral. Finally, about twenty Gay Libbers marched to the podium carrying signs and shouting slogans. The convention was then adjourned. This disruption took place when a Gay Lib leader was not allowed to speak in favor of a resolution encouraging Episcopal churches to lend their facilities to homosexuals.

The application of this Proverb is obvious. When you are corrected for a legitimate wrong, do not abuse. Likewise, do not be surprised if when you correct an offense you may be verbally or even physically abused yourself!

PRAYER

*"Lord, help us to receive a correction with humility and grace.
In Jesus' name. Amen."*

PROVERBS 10:1

*"A wise son brings joy to his father,
but a foolish son grief to his mother."*

A FATHER'S DELIGHT
OR A MOTHER'S GRIEF

*I*t is natural and right to be proud of a son or daughter. They are your children, and any honor brought their way is honor to you. We like to think they have done so well because of how we raised them. This is what honor will do for you when your children choose wisely. For example, John D. Rockefeller, Sr. said he had to begin work as a small child to help support his mother. His first week's wage amounted to $1.50, He said, "I took the $1.50 home to my mother, and she held the money in her lap and explained to me that she would be happy if I would give a tenth of it to the Lord. I did and from that week until this day, I have tithed every dollar God has entrusted to me. I want to say, if I had not tithed the first dollar I made, I would not have tithed the first million dollars I made." God honored this man, and this honor no doubt brought great joy to his mother's heart, for it was from her lap he learned this lesson.

Conversely, it's a great disgrace to parents to have one of their own children humiliate themselves and thus shame his parents in the process. An edition of the *Salt Lake Tribune* detailed the story of a star professional basketball player from California who was charged with rape. Judging from the testimony of the article, it will not go well with him. Plus, it's sure to disgrace his parents.

When your parents think of you, what comes to mind? Does the memory of you bring joy or grief? It can be joy. It is not too late. That is the good news. The theme of Proverbs is found in Chapter 1:7. "The fear (reverence) of the Lord is the beginning of knowledge . . .." A wise son or daughter respects God's wishes by obeying His Word.

⟶ PRAYER ⟵

*"Lord may our parents be proud when we come to mind.
In Jesus' name. Amen."*

October 11

PROVERBS 11:1

"Dishonest scales are an abomination to the Lord,
but a just weight is His delight.

TRY HONESTY

"The story is told of a driver who slammed into a parked car. He got out of his car and started to write a note to put under the windshield wiper. It read: "I have just smashed into your car. The people who saw the accident are watching me. They think I am writing down my name and address. I am not. Sorry."

Funny, yes, unless of course it is your car. If you really want God's attention, be dishonest. If you want God's delight, be honest. God takes such a dim view of dishonesty He calls it an "abomination." The word abomination is defined as "a thing that causes disgust or hatred." If you want to disgust God, dishonesty will do. Those with a seared conscience have no trouble being dishonest. That is their creed. When in a tight squeeze, go to dishonesty; it will save you, at least for a while, until all the wheels on the wagon come off.

True wisdom is seen in the old adage, "Honesty is the best policy." It may hurt, it may be uncomfortable, it may be embarrassing, but it will not be *near* the heartbreak dishonest lips will bring. There is a better way. Be a delight to God.

PRAYER

"Lord, the temptation to be dishonest, in all its expressions,
is as persistent as a bad cold. Help us all to be honest;
help us to loath what disgusts You. Help us to be a perpetual delight
in Your sight. In Jesus' name. Amen."

October 12

PROVERBS 12:15

*"The way of a fool is right in his own eyes,
but he who heeds counsel is wise."*

THE FOOL'S WAY OR THE WISE MAN'S WAY—WHICH WAY IS YOURS?

Cany Postlethwaite has never been in the military, but a misdirected check from the Veterans Administration made its way to her doorstep for a seventh time, and she couldn't seem to get rid of it.

She received a VA check in the mail made out to one Ronald Lee Vest. She put it back outside for the postman to pick up on his next round. "I got it back about four or five days later in a different envelope," she said. So, she telephoned the VA office and was directed to send the stray check there. "So, I did—and I received it back again, in the same envelope." Next she mailed it to the Treasury Department office in Kansas City where the check was issued, along with a certified letter advising that "I did not know this person and this person did not live here." The check was returned once more, in a different envelope.

"Then I took it down to the White Rock (postal) station and gave it to the postmaster," she recounted." And I got it back again. Then I took it down personally to the Veterans Administration, again—and I got it back, again." They told me to mail it to the State VA headquarters in Waco. And this morning I received it back again."

After the seventh delivery, Mrs. Postlethwaite phoned the Dallas VA people once more. "They just said, "Well, I don't know what else we can do." At one point she called the Secret Service and told one of its agents she intended to destroy the check. The agent told her: "You can't destroy it. That's government property." All right, she would keep it, she told the man. And he replied, "You can't keep it. It's not yours."

⟶ PRAYER ⟵

*"Lord, keep me from thinking like a fool,
one who shuns good advice. In Jesus' name. Amen."*

October 14

PROVERBS 14:12

*"There is a way that seems right to a man,
but in the end, it leads to death."*

A LAMPLESS WAY

*P*erhaps you have experienced it, a short cut that ends up being a dead end! You thought at the beginning it would save you time, but it ends up taking longer.

An old but very rich man with a rather cantankerous disposition visited a rabbi seeking to know why he was so unhappy. The rabbi took the old man to a window and asked him what he saw. Looking into the street he saw people everywhere—women, children, and men. A second time the rabbi took the old man to a mirror and asked him what he saw then. "Why, I see myself." Then the rabbi said, "In the window there is glass, and in the mirror there is glass, but the glass of the mirror is covered with a little silver, and once the silver is added, you cease to see others and can see only yourself."

Money as the cure all for all unhappiness is certainly one way that many pursue, only to find too late that it leads to emotional death.

Christ Himself warned about the perils of the money-loving way. A rich young ruler approached Christ with a question about eternal life. Jesus told him to sell all his possessions and give the money to the poor and come follow Him. The young ruler walked away, and then Christ penetratingly stated, "I tell you the truth, it is hard for a rich man to enter the kingdom of heaven . . . it is easier for a camel to go through the eye of a needle than for a rich man to enter the kingdom of God."

The pursuit of money at the expense of ignoring God and denying people is a way that seems right to many people but will only end up in the ways of death.

⁓ PRAYER ⁓

*"Lord, keep me from being 'wise in my own eyes.'
In Jesus' name. Amen."*

PROVERBS 15:1

*"A gentle answer turns away wrath,
but a harsh word stirs up anger."*

GET ONE'S DANDER UP

A man purchased a paper at a newspaper stand. He greeted the newsman courteously but received a gruff and discourteous reply. He accepted the paper, which was rudely shoved in his face, but the customer politely smiled and wished the newsman a good day.

A friend had observed the entire exchange and asked, "Does he always treat you that way?"

"Yes, he does."

"And are you always so polite and friendly in return?"

"Yes, I am."

"Why are you so nice when he continues to be so rude?"

"Because I don't want him to decide how I 'm going to act."

The next time you find yourself in a similar unpleasant experience, rein in your temper and pray as you speak in gentle words. You'll be amazed how much better it will go for you. I was!

⟶ PRAYER ⟵

*"Lord, help us to speak gentle words, not the word that gouges.
In Jesus' name. Amen."*

PROVERBS 16:32

*"Better a patient man than a warrior,
a man who controls his temper than one who takes a city."*

PRECIOUS PATIENCE

We are a people of action, perpetual motion, and activity. We live it, praise it and watch it. Today's Proverb showcases the wisdom of patience. To live skillfully in life, we are to be patient. So highly esteemed is this virtue that Solomon, the wisest man to have lived, argues that patience is better than being a warrior! Better, better, better is the man who can control his temper than the man who can take a city! This is a hard sell in America. We exalt the virtue of speed, power, and conquest. But patience is better.

A first-grade teacher had just finished putting the last pair of galoshes on her thirty-two students. The last little girl said, "You know what, teacher? These aren't my galoshes." The teacher patiently removed them from the girl's feet. Then the little girl continued, "They are my sister's, and she let me use them today." The teacher quietly put them back on. Patience made this exchange a pleasant and humorous one, rather than a traumatic event.

What a different world we would live in if control such as this were prized as highly as a man who can wield the force that takes a city. Proverb's wisdom teaches us that we are to honor the control of our spirit over the capture of a city. And the reason is simple, there is far less destruction in life if we perfect patience and temper our tempers.

PRAYER

*"Lord, help us control ourselves, the one persistent battle of life.
In Jesus' name. Amen."*

PROVERB 17:9

"He who covers over an offense promotes love,
but whoever repeats the matter separates close friends."

PROTECTIVE COVERING

*L*ove in its truest form is a love that forgives. When an offense is directed personally against you, to forgive goes against the grain of our human nature. Our natural impulse is to payback, bruise for bruise, stripe for stripe, eye for eye. (cf. Lev. 24:20) So crucial is this concept of forgiving those who harm us that in the Lord's Prayer (Matthew 6:12) Christ emphasizes that our own sins will not be forgiven if we refuse to forgive those who have trespassed against us. And then he repeats it in verses 14–15. How much better it is to forgive than to "repeat" an offense. However, there are those who are otherwise persuaded! To continually remind a friend or loved one of a former offense is to punish them on the installment plan. It's like cutting a dog's tail off an inch at a time.

A man was sharing with a friend what happens when he and his wife get into an argument. "I hate it every time we have an argument; she gets historical." You mean hysterical, don't you?" "No," I mean historical. Every time we argue, she drags up everything from the past and holds it against me!" The problem with this approach is it can end up in divorce. Nobody likes to be reminded of their past missteps.

The founder of the American Red Cross, Clara Barton, was once reminded of an especially cruel act committed against her. But Miss Barton seemed not to remember. "Don't you remember it?" her friend asked. "No," came her reply "I distinctly remember forgetting it." It is not possible to be happy if you're collecting and nurturing old grudges.

⟶ PRAYER ⟵

"Lord, this sin is not a misdemeanor, it is a felony.
Keep us far from it. In Jesus' name. Amen."

October 18

PROVERBS 18:22

*"He who finds a wife finds what is good
and receives favor from the Lord."*

CELESTIAL GOOD

If the truth were known, most singles would rather be married! There are exceptions to this, but most would agree that a loving, faithful, and compatible companion is hands down better than facing life alone. The Bible says, the Lord God said, "It is not good for the man to be alone. I will make a helper suitable for him." (cf. Genesis 2:18) Here we have what is not good and then what is good—a wife! A good wife is of such value that Proverbs teaches that a man obtains favor from God when he finds one. But there are struggles. It has been said that marriage is like two porcupines that lived in Alaska. When the snow flew and the temperatures dropped, they drew close to one another for warmth. But, when they were close, they stuck each other with their quills, so apart they went. But after a while, the cold drove them back together again. If they were going to keep warm, they had to learn to adjust to one another. I believe much of the marital combat that occurs today would end if men viewed themselves as favored by God for having a wife. When we were trying to win their favor, they felt favored. Once we won their favor, we became the favored one as our Proverb teaches. And we will continue in their favor if we behave like we have been favored.

PRAYER

*"Lord, grant us men Your favor to favor our wives.
In Jesus' name. Amen."*

PROVERBS 19:2

*"Also, it is not good for a soul to be without knowledge,
and he sins who hastens with his feet."*

A LEAP AND A LOOK

Slow is real! It is also safer. The adage, "Act in hast and repent in leisure" is a true axiom because someone penned their experience to words. Whenever there is an urgency to speak or act and it can wait, you will be glad you did.

In the 1929 Rose Bowl, California was leading Georgia Tech 7–6 when Roy Riegels (playing for the University of California) took the ball. He became confused when his teammates began blocking Tech men behind him. He turned and ran in that direction.

The crowd roared in amazement. "Wrong way! Wrong way!" Benny Lom, a fast Cal halfback, started after Riegels who was headed straight for the opponent's goal. "Roy, Roy, stop!" he cried.

But the noise was so great that Riegels thought the crowd was cheering him on. Just as he reached the goal, his teammate pulled him down.

The California team tried to punt from their one-yard line. But Tech blocked the kick and pounced on the ball behind the goal. The play was scored as a two-point safety for Georgia. This proved to be Georgia Tech's margin of victory.

There is a decision that, if made in haste, can affect you for all eternity. It is the claim of Jesus Christ. Jesus made the astounding claim that He is the only way to God. "I am the way, the truth, and the life. no one comes to the Father except through Me." (cf. John 14:6) A thoughtful, open-minded reading of the first four books of the New Testament may convince you of the truth of Christ's words. Don't be hasty with Christ's claim.

PRAYER

*"Lord, slow men down and help me to proceed with caution.
In Jesus' name. Amen."*

October 20

PROVERBS 20:3

"It is to a man's honor to avoid strife,
but every fool is quick to quarrel."

NEEDLESSLY QUARRELSOME

Any fool can quarrel, and most fools do! Today's Proverb is not condemning quarreling whatsoever, just those who are quick to argue.

The snapping turtle hatches from an egg the size of a ping-pong ball. From the minutes he hatches, he is an unsociable little fellow ready to bite whatever comes within reach. When he reaches three years of age, he is the size of a saucer and ever ready to bite. He has no friends, and his enemies avoid him. An adult snapping turtle can weigh as much as 150 pounds with the power to bite off a man's hand! He lives a good many years but never out grows his reputation as a snapper. The fool is quick to snap (quarrel) and never seems to see the logic of letting minor infractions pass.

Fortunately, we have those who inspire us with the way they handle an argumentative person. No one treated Abraham Lincoln with more contempt that did Edwin Stanton. He denounced Lincoln's polices and called him a "low cunning clown." Stanton went on to nickname him "the original gorilla." Lincoln said nothing. Instead he made Stanton his war minister because Stanton was the best man for the job. Years later, Lincoln lay dying from an assassin's bullet. Stanton stood nearby and with tears in his eyes he said, "There lies the greatest ruler of men the world has ever seen." Lincoln ignored Stanton's insults and consequently won him over.

Avoid life's little skirmishes; you will be happier and honored in the end.

PRAYER

"Lord, help me not to be so quick on the trigger
when a quarrel breaks out. In Jesus' name. Amen."

PROVERBS 21: 30–31

"There is no wisdom, no insight,
no plan that can succeed against the Lord.
The horse is made ready for the day of battle,
but victory rests with the Lord."

PREVAILING PROVIDENCE

The implications of this Proverb are profound. Man, in all his wisdom, skill, and power is still under the control of God. To man, it appears that what happens on a day-to-day basis is ultimately his doing. There are numerous events and activities every day which, if we do not do them, they do not get done. Feed the animals, wash the clothes, or go grocery shopping, to name a few of the more mundane. We do not see God stepping in and substituting for us. Consequently, it is hard to believe that He is ultimately ruling over this universe in such a way that no one can oppose his hand. (cf. Daniel 4:35) Yet today's Proverb states clearly that all the wisdom, insight, or planning cannot succeed against what God has determined will happen. We can do our part, but the ultimate outcome is genuinely in the hands of a sovereign God.

Before my daughter could even walk, I would stand her up and then stand behind her while holding out my two fingers in front of her. She would grip my fingers and balance herself, as she would "walk" along. I would pretty much allow her to go where she wanted to, but if she wanted to walk over to the stairs or somewhere where I didn't want her to go, I would just steer her away from it. Yes, she was walking in a sense and determining to her ability where she would go, but ultimately, it rested with her father where she would end up. God is like that. We determine how our day will be to a degree, within our human limitations, but there is a sovereign God who, ultimately, rules our day and our destiny.

⌘ PRAYER ⌘

"Lord, may we trust Your plan for our life and flow with it.
Help us not to fight Your hand of providence.
In Jesus' name. Amen."

PROVERBS 22:1

"A good name is more desirable than great riches;
to be esteemed is better than silver or gold."

WELL-EARNED REPUTATION

*P*eople talk. And what they talk about often builds reputations; like that hard-to-find restaurant in a class C setting, but the food is well worth the hunt. That crosstown mechanic who is out of your way, but you trust what he says. That dentist whose reputation you help build. Skillful living in today's world involves building a respectable name, not respectable riches.

Former Senator Sam Ervin, who presided over the Senate Watergate Committee, made this statement about former White House aide H.R. Haldeman's book, *The Ends of Power.* "A man that would commit perjury under oath (as Haldeman did) might possibly be tempted to commit it when he is not under oath . . . I would say that before I would accept his book as credible, I would want it corroborated by all the apostles, except Judas." (*Dallas Times Herald*, February 17, 1978) A old Malay Proverb says, "It is better to die with a good name, than to live with a bad one."

So, what are you building? A name that will be mentioned with fondness and admiration, or some other reputation you rather lose?

The best way to start building a respectable name is to trust Christ as Savior. (cf. John 3:16) Then the indwelling Spirit's power will enable you to build a godly character that is the basis of a noble name. (cf. Philippians 4:13)

PRAYER

"Lord, help us to build our character as zealously
as we build our estate. In Jesus' name. Amen."

PROVERBS 23:2

*"Who has woe? Who has sorrow ...
those who linger over wine ..."*

THE WOE OF WINE

A subway train crashed in London, England, killing 41 persons. A forensic expert who examined the body of engineer Leslie Newson reported the body contained the same amount of alcohol that would make a motorist legally drunk. The report also showed that Newson had been drinking before his train smashed headlong into a dead-end tunnel at Moorgate station earlier that morning! You would naturally think an engineer of a train would know the difference between a thoroughfare and a dead-end tunnel. Alcohol played a part in this tragic account.

Serious drinking has serious effects. Alcoholism is now said to be costing society around $25 billion dollars yearly. Absenteeism and low productivity of drinkers cost employers $10 million a year. A heavy drinker's absentee rate is 2½ times higher than that of non-drinkers. The cost of arresting, trying, and jailing drinkers is more than $100 million a year. Almost half the 5.5 million arrests annually in the US are related to alcoholic abuse.

Alcohol has shaped our American history more than most of us know. The last day that Abraham Lincoln lived he said, "We have cleared up a colossal job. Slavery is abolished. The next great question will be the overthrow and suppression of the legalized liquor traffic." That very evening, Mr. Booth slipped into a saloon and drank himself full to help steady his nerves. The same night, Lincoln's bodyguard left the theater for a drink at the same saloon. While he was away, Booth slipped into Lincoln's viewing box and shot him. Two drinks that changed our American heritage.

☙ PRAYER ☙

*"Lord, keep us from thinking that by abusing alcohol,
it will never abuse us. In Jesus' name. Amen."*

PROVERBS 24:10

"If you falter in time of trouble, how small is your strength!"

FALTERING STRENGTH

In 1879, a child was born to a poor Jewish family. In his early years, the child suffered a haunting sense of inferiority, primarily because of his Jewish heritage. He was shy and introspective, slow to learn, as well. His parents had him examined by a specialist to see if he was normal. In 1895, he tested but failed the entrance exam at the Polytechnic in Zurich, Switzerland. A year later he tried again and passed. Later in life he earned a doctorate from the University of Zurich, but only landed an obscure job as a patent examiner. Who is this rather slow learner? The same man who formulated the theory of relativity—Albert Einstein! He never let his early failures keep him from trying again. He did not falter in times of trouble.

Perhaps a sure sign of faltering during difficult times is to quit a noble task. To allow circumstances or a bad attitude to keep you from achieving a task God has laid on your heart. Has God been calling you to a regular time of prayer, but your weakness has found you faltering? Perhaps it's the challenge of witnessing, but your fear has sealed your lips? Perhaps it is daily Scripture reading or consistent giving? Is God calling you to service, to teach, or maybe even preach? There is a cure to faltering strength; it's in the person of Christ. "I can do all things through Christ who strengthens me." (Philippians 4:13) Don't allow your early failures to keep you from the task God is calling you to. When our strength falters, His never does.

PRAYER

"Lord, may we never give up on the strength we have in You. In Jesus' name. Amen."

October 25

PROVERBS 25:28

*"Like a city whose walls are broken down
is a man who lacks self-control."*

GAIN CONTROL

At age 16, Alexander the Great was ruler of Macedonia, at age 18 a victorious general, and king at age 20. Then he died a drunkard before age 33! He conquered the then known world, but not himself. The story of his death goes like this: Alexander began a second night of drinking and celebrating with twenty guests at a table in Babylon. He drank to the health of every person at the table. After this, he called for Hercules' cup, which had a huge capacity. Filling it up, he drank it all down, drinking to Proteas, a Macedonian in his company. Then he pledged to him again in the same manner and instantly fell to the floor. He was struck with a fever and died a few days later!

We control our finances, spending, dieting, gossiping, speeding, cursing, laziness, cleanliness, correspondence, but if we lack control in one critical area, it becomes the breach in the wall.

Do you lack self-control in some area of your life? Is it lusting, drinking, envying, stealing, procrastination, bitterness, laziness, resentment, a feel-sorry-for-yourself spirit? There is a cure for all this. Hebrews 11:34 states through faith . . . weakness {was] made strong." But my faith is so weak, I don't think I can overcome! However, Romans 10:17 teaches ". . . faith comes by hearing, and hearing by the word of God." Get to know the Bible and your faith will increase. As your faith increases, your control problem will become self-control.

PRAYER

*"Lord, remind us that self-control comes
from being controlled by You. In Jesus' name. Amen."*

PROVERBS 26:3

*"A whip for the horse, a bridle for the donkey,
and a rod for the fool's back."*

PHD IN HARD KNOCKS

When she got fed up with the frequent complaints of her 14-year-old daughter at the dining table, Mrs. Fay Young decided to do something about it.

She went down to the library for a check on what she as a girl had eaten during the London blitz in the Second World War. Then she put daughter Janet on the same diet—a week's ration of 14 ounces of meat, 3 eggs, 3 lbs. of potatoes, and 2 ounces of cheese. Sunday dinner was bread and butter and a hard-boiled egg.

"It was a good lesson," Janet decided. "I'll never complain again."

Today's Proverb teaches us that the foolish person learns the hard way, generally by breaking God's laws or man's. Like a horse that must be whipped or the donkey that must be bridled, he has to experience the rod of discipline before he submits.

PRAYER

*"Lord, help me to submit to Your laws and man's.
Keep me from the fool's discipline. In Jesus' name. Amen."*

PROVERBS 27:1

"Do not boast about tomorrow,
for you do not know what a day may bring forth."

AN EMPTY BOAST

Kobe Bryant, NBA superstar and future Hall of Famer, was dead at 41. Bryant's daughter Gianna, 13, was with her father on the helicopter and was also killed in the crash, so read the headline on CNN Monday, January 27, 2020.

Hebrews 9:27 says, ". . . it is appointed unto men once to die, after this the judgment."

Most people don't expect to die in the near future, especially one as young and famous as Kobe Bryant. The tooth and nail demand of life, the routine of daily responsibilities, and the resulting exhausting remove from us thoughts of a sudden death. But life has a way of shocking us. A prime example is the unexpected death of Kobe Bryant.

So, what is a person to do? According to the Bible, we are to be certain that we are born again. (II Corinthians 6:2) ". . . behold, now is the accepted time; behold, now is the day of salvation." Scripture urges the reader to trust Christ today, because the eternal consequences of delaying the love of God in this life is to face the justice of God in the next. Are you "born again?" Do you believe Christ bore the consequences of your personal transgressions against God? ". . . there is none righteous, no, not one" (Romans 3:10), "for all have sinned and fall short of the glory of God." (Romans 3:23) "For the wages of sin is death, but the gift of God is eternal life in Christ Jesus our Lord." (Romans 6:23) "For whoever calls on the name of the Lord shall be saved." (Romans 10:13) A sincere prayer of faith today will bring you salvation for all your tomorrows.

✦ PRAYER ✦

"Lord, help me not to boast about
what I don't know or what I don't have.
In Jesus' name. Amen."

October 28

PROVERBS 28:23

*"He who rebukes a man will in the end gain more favor
than he who has a flattering tongue."*

FAVOR VS FLATTERY

To flatter someone is to compliment them on something that is not based on reality. There are those who have elevated this to an art form. To rebuke (to correct by word or deed) a person who needs to be corrected is to risk their displeasure and possibly invite verbal or even physical abuse. So, most people avoid it. But ". . . corrections for discipline are the way of life." (cf. Proverbs 6:23) Everyone receives reproofs throughout their life. *No one* is perfectly adjusted when they are born, so corrections along the way are necessary. However, there are those timid souls who do not like the stress that comes when an individual reacts, so they prefer flattery. It reminds me of spreading cold cream on cancer!

An actor best known for his role in *Saving Private Ryan* and *Black Hawk Down* was sentenced to six months in jail and three years probation for harassing and physically abusing his ex-girlfriend. The actor was first headed for drug rehab, after which the judge would consider cutting the sentence to 90 days if he could prove that his court-ordered counseling for drugs, anger, and domestic violence were working. This was a court-ordered rebuke. If the man could turn his life around, he might have appreciated what rehab and the courts had done for him.

Perhaps you have been given your share of reproofs. At the time, it certainly did not feel like you were standing in their favor. Time has a way of changing things. The wise man will appreciate what you are trying to do for him and, who knows, he may someday thank you!

PRAYER

*"Lord, help me to be humble enough to receive a needed reproof,
and wise enough to apply it. In Jesus' name. Amen."*

PROVERBS 29:11

*"A fool gives full vent to his anger,
but a wise man keeps himself under control."*

TO VENT OR NOT TO VENT?

There are countless masses who wish they had better hold on their tempers. The jobs lost or marriages broken because someone gave full vent to their anger is staggering.

Furious at a rush-hour accident that blocked traffic in the Boston suburb of Weymouth, a motorist went ballistic at a police officer and then allegedly bumped him with her car, screaming, "I don't care who died. I'm more important."

A 43-year-old man, angry over domestic problems, barricaded himself inside an ex-girlfriend's home and hurled household items—a TV, a room air conditioner, a broomstick, and a pot of boiling water—at police officers, threatening to kill them, before he was subdued.

In contrast to those who give full vent to their anger, we have Julius Caesar. It was said of Julius Caesar that when he was provoked to anger, he would repeat the entire Roman alphabet before he allowed himself to respond.

Anyone can become angry. That is the easy part. But to be angry with the right person, to the right degree, at the right time, and in the right way, that is the hard part. It is at these times we need a wisdom that is beyond our years. The Bible says that such wisdom is ours for the asking. (cf. James 1:5–8.) This wisdom allows us to be angry to the proper degree—acceptable anger.

Today's Proverb contrasts the fool with the wise. Both experience anger, but only one enjoys success.

☙ PRAYER ☙

*"Lord, help us to rein in our anger instead of letting it run afoul.
In Jesus' name. Amen."*

PROVERBS 30:5

"Every word of God is flawless;
he is a shield to those who take refuge in him.

FLAWLESS OR FLAWED?

Can we trust what the Bible says? Are the words flawless as our Proverb teaches or do they contain serious errors?

Jesus trusted the Bible. His trust was so implicit that he said, ". . . until heaven and earth disappear, not the smallest letter, not the least stroke of a pen, will by any means disappear from the Law until everything is accomplished." (Matthew 5:17-18) His statement here is profound. The smallest Hebrew letter is the yodh, which looks like an apostrophe ('). A stroke is a very small extension or protrusion on several Hebrew letters that distinguish these letters from similar ones. Jesus is saying that every letter of every word will be fulfilled and not fail. That was our Lord's conviction regarding the accuracy of Scripture. Also, the last book of the Old Testament, the book of Malachi, had been written four hundred years before the birth of our Lord. It would have been easy for Jesus to question how accurate the copying process was from one generation to another, but He never hints at such a thing. Instead, He declares heaven and earth will pass away first. Heaven and earth disappearing would be a large-scale event, but as awe-inspiring as that might be, Jesus is saying greater still would be the failing of one written word of the Bible. (cf. v.13) I do not think Jesus was mistaken on this point. So confident was He that the Bible was flawless, that He reprimands the two disciples on the Emmaus road for not recognizing that His death and resurrection were foretold events. (cf. Luke 24:13–27) If the Bible was hopelessly miscopied and merely the words of men, He would have never scolded his disciples for missing these predictions.

We are in good company if we view Scripture as flawless. Jesus did.

PRAYER

"Lord, may our trust in the Bible be the same as Yours,
wholly and without reserve. In Jesus' name. Amen."

October 31

PROVERBS 31:10–11

"Who can find a virtuous wife?
For her worth is far above rubies.
The heart of her husband safely trusts her;
so he will have no lack of gain."

A CELEBRATED WIFE

Proverbs' wisdom for today characterizes the virtues of a noble wife. The very first character trait is what her husband feels about her! He feels he can trust her. A man can have a wife that is strikingly beautiful, but if he does not trust her, the relationship will not last. A man can have a wife who is extremely capable career wise, but if he does not trust her, the relationship will die. A man can have a wife who is a wonderful mother, but if he does not trust her, she is just a mother, not a wife. True, some men would not trust any woman. But our Proverb is addressing a woman who's first, and perhaps greatest, virtue is the peaceful trust her husband feels. Trust she has earned. A trustworthy woman behaves in a trustworthy manner. Her husband recognizes this and is at peace. When she is with the opposite sex and he is not present, he is not in a panic.

Imagine you are driving over the Glen Canyon Dam just outside of Page, Arizona, yet there are no guardrails! There is nothing to keep you from plunging 1000-feet to the river below. An individual with all his faculties intact would drive down the center of the road avoiding the edge. However, there are those who insist on driving as close to the edge as possible just for the thrill of it. A trustworthy wife does not do that, and her husband knows this.

This precious woman is trustworthy for a reason; she fears (reverences) the Lord. "Charm is deceptive, and beauty is fleeting; but a woman who fears the Lord is to be praised." (v. 30–31)

⟡ PRAYER ⟡

"Lord, we praise Your name for a trustworthy wife.
In Jesus' name. Amen."

PROVERBS 1:5

"A wise man will hear and increase learning,
and a man of understanding will attain wise counsel."

RECEIVE COUNSEL

A man was on the practice golf course when the club pro brought another man out for a lesson. The pro watched the fellow swing several times and started making suggestions for improvement, but each time the pupil interrupted with his own version of what was wrong and how to correct it. After a while, the pro just nodded his head in agreement at every suggestion. When the lesson ended, the student paid the pro, thanked him for his excellent advice, and left. The observer was so astonished by the behavior of the pro that he asked, "Why did you go along with him?" "Son," the old pro said with a smile, "I learned a long time ago that it's a waste of time to sell answers to a man who wants to buy echoes."[20]

For some people, to ask or even receive counsel is a mark of weakness. They will not ask, even when they need it, but prefer to muddle their way through a circumstance making it much more difficult than necessary. Surprisingly, excellent advice is available, and most people are more than willing to give it if asked. I am a locksmith by trade and learned a long time ago it is much better to ask for help, especially when you are just beginning. Otherwise, you will end up frustrated, embarrassed, and standing in front of a locked door a lot longer than necessary. For example, I had a co-worker who was just hired to assist me in my work. This worker was intelligent enough, but she did not have enough experience to be on her own. We were working on some difficult door locks that required knowledge of a few tricks you pick up over the years. Rather than just ask me, she struggled for quite a while. I was within talking distance, but rather than ask, she decided to learn the hard way.

PRAYER

"Lord, keep us humble enough to learn
from anyone who can teach us. In Jesus' name. Amen."

20. *Illustrations for Biblical Preaching*. Edited by Michael P. Green, pg. 18.
Baker Book House, Grand Rapids, Michigan.

PROVERBS 2:1,5

*"My son, if you receive my words,
and treasure my commands within you . . .
then you will understand the fear of the Lord,
and find the knowledge of God."*

MISPLACED TRUST

There is a lot of faith out there, some misplaced. Donald Malcolm Campbell, the British car- and boat-racer and holder of several world speed records, lost his life while racing a fast boat in Scotland. The boat exploded and rapidly sank. The only thing to surface after the explosion was Campbell's "good luck charm"—a stuffed animal. His "charm" was powerless in the final, critical moments of his life. Faith is only as good as its object.

In contrast, we learn of a boy from England who was asked if he could be lowered down the side of a cliff to recover some rare specimens. He flat out said, "No. I might have been born at night, but I wasn't born last night!" The impatient scientist offered him a handsome fee but to no avail. Finally, he agreed with one condition—that his father would be the one to hold the ropes.

Our Proverb today admonishes us to place our trust in God's Word and to treasure His commands. If we do, then we will have God's wisdom (v.6), God's shield of protection (v.7), and God's guardianship. (8) Not only is this a much better payoff, but the only object of trust that will increase our joy in this life and usher us into eternity.

PRAYER

*"Lord, keep me from trusting in the unworthy
and help me to see that receiving Your words
and treasuring them is worthy of my best trust.
In Jesus' name. Amen."*

PROVERBS 3:4–5

"Let love and faithfulness never leave you;
bind them around your neck,
write them on the tablet of your heart.
Then you will win favor and a good name
in the sight of God and man."

THE INGREDIENTS OF SUCCESS

"*A* man who had been the superintendent of a city rescue mission for forty years was asked why he had spent his life working with dirty, unkempt, profane, drunken derelicts. He said, "All I'm doing is giving back to others a little of the love God has shown to me."

As a young man, he himself had been a drunkard who went into a mission for a bowl of chili. There he heard the preacher say that Christ could save sinners, and he stumbled forward to accept the Lord Jesus as his Savior. Though his brain was addled by drink, he felt a weight lifted from his shoulders, and that day he became a changed person. A little later, seeking God's will for his life, he felt the Lord calling him to go back to the gutter and reach the people still wallowing there. The power of redeeming love enabled him to carry on his ministry for forty years."[21]

This is an excellent example of a man touched by love who, in turn, showed that same love for the following forty years! Love and faithfulness, a remarkable duet. The Bible has it right! Combine these two essential ingredients in any endeavor, any relationship, any circumstance, and you will surely find favor; God's favor and man's. What man or woman would not treasure the fond memories of a father or mother whose central behavior trait could be summed up as love and faithfulness?

Like the two sides of pair of scissors, when put together, they are irreplaceable.

PRAYER

"Lord, I need these two traits in my life. This is simple spiritual science.
Help me to come back to the wisdom of love working its wonder
through faithfulness. In Jesus' name. Amen."

21. *Illustrations for Biblical Preaching.* Edited by Michael P. Green, pg. 811. Baker Book House, Grand Rapids, Michigan.

PROVERBS 4:23

*"Keep your heart with all diligence,
for out of it springs the issues of life."*

DUE DILIGENCE

Life magazine ran story on Muhammad Ali before his fight with Joe Frazier in 1971. Ali went on a tirade about how good he was,."There's not a man alive who can whup me." He then jabbed five or six times in the air. He then bragged about how smart he was: "I'm too smart (he taps his head). I'm too pretty, striking a profile for all to see. I *am* the greatest. I *am* the king! I should be a postage stamp—that's the only way I could get licked!" Ali lost to Frazier.

The point of today's Proverb is how we think. Sometimes we do not think right. All of life's issues flow from what you are thinking. Jesus put it this way; "For from within, out of the heart of men, proceed evil thoughts, adulteries, fornications, murders, thefts, covetousness, wickedness, deceit, lewdness, an evil eye, blasphemy, pride, foolishness. All these evil things come from within and defile a man." Thoughts of evil come from within. They originate from an alienated heart from God that results in thoughts of evil, words of evil, and then acts of evil. No one commits a theft without first thinking about it. No one is deceitful unless he first thinks about it. Your environment may be awful, your home life very less than perfect, and even your genetic make-up might incline you in one direction or another, but these things do not ultimately determine what you think. What you think is in the final analysis *your* choice. Paul put it this way: "Finally, brethren, whatever things are true, whatever things are noble, whatever things are just, whatever things are pure, whatever things are lovely, whatever things are of good report, mediate (think) on these things. (Philippians 4:8) Guard your heart!

⟋ PRAYER ⟍

*"Lord, come to my aide and gently remind me
that I can't expect to live a victorious Christian life
when I choose to think on evil. In Jesus' name. Amen."*

PROVERBS 5: 4–5

"But in the end, she is better as wormwood,
sharp as a two-edged sword. "

TWO-EDGED SWORD

A wealthy couple sought to hire a chauffeur. They advertised and finally came down to four applicants who were to answer one final question. The lady of the house had each finalist come to an upstairs window that overlooked the driveway and the outside wall of the garage. "How close could you come to that wall without hitting it?" The first applicant said he could come within a foot of it. The second answered and said he could come within six inches, the third said within three inches. The final applicant said he was not sure how close he could come to the wall without hitting it, but he would instead try to stay as far away as possible. He was the one that was hired.

This story illustrates well the idea that there are some sins we need to keep our distance from. Sexual sins are one of these. If you are looking to short circuit your life, or alter the direction of your life, sexual sins will do it. What is interesting about sexual sins, whether it be sex before marriage or adultery after marriage is the altering effect sex has on the emotions and your own mind. Is it any wonder if a police officer has difficulty enforcing laws against illegal marijuana use if he himself is using? Would you trust a lecture on honesty from the Mafia? Would you trust a fireman if he himself is burning down houses? Illicit sex has the power to alter how you feel and how you think about it.

It has been well said that sex is like fire. In the fireplace, it can warm your house; outside the hearth it can burn down your house! An unplanned pregnancy can eclipse one's plans for college, or sabotage a promising relationship, or create an environment that makes you and your unborn child a burden. Illicit sex in the end is a bitter pill, sharper than a two-edge sword. What is the answer *stay clear*! Keep it in the right environment, in the committed relationship of marriage.

PRAYER

"Lord, help me not jeopardize promising plans
by a short tryst followed by a long regret.
In Jesus' name. Amen."

PROVERBS 6:6–8

"Go to the ant, you sluggard! Consider her ways and be wise . . ."

GO TO THE ANT

*J*ohn Silling, a Purdue University entomologist, stated that ants are excellent workers. The ant's entire life, which can run up to seven years, is spent working. They gather food, bring it back to the nest, and use it for day-to-day meals as well as to store for the winter. Some species of ants gather bits of grass or leaves and take them back to their nest. On this organic matter, which is used like fertilizer, they place tiny mushrooms spores and grow them for food!

The sluggard (a habitually lazy person) is admonished to get his act together. The example given him is the ant, a hard act to follow. Life, with all its responsibilities and duties, dictates that we work and work and work. It seems like if you are going to stay on top of things, you can't be shy about work. Paul puts it this way: ". . . if anyone will not work, neither shall he eat. For we hear that there are some who walk among you in a disorderly manner, not working at all, but are busybodies." (II Thessalonians 3:11) A Christian should be an excellent worker. He knows when to pause and rest, but he also knows that God has designed us to derive a sense of well-being and satisfaction from a job well done. This is God's design. Some people don't do well in retirement because that sense of purpose and well-being has been removed through retirement. That's why it's critical after retirement to find purposeful and rewarding work of some type. I witnessed a man cry because he felt so "worthless." He had been retired on a medical disability and was struggling with his lack of purposefulness.

There is a story told of a lazy farmer who was always waiting around for an earthquake. "Why on earth are you waiting for an earthquake," he was asked? "So, it can shake the taters out of the ground!"

⌒ PRAYER ⌒

"Lord, help me get back to work.
Remind me the earthquake isn't coming. In Jesus' name. Amen."

PROVERBS 7:1–5

"My son, keep my words, and treasure my commands within you . . .
that they may keep you from the immoral woman . . ."

THE HIGHWAY TO HELL

I remember while attending divinity school an encounter I witnessed while riding with a friend who was a Sheriff's deputy for Multnomah County. She was on a side street just off a main thoroughfare; young, but hard of face for her age. When my friend approached her and showed his badge, she immediately became defensive, protesting she was just waiting for a bus. After a few questions it became obvious she "hustling," as the deputy it. She argued she was putting herself through school to become a teacher. A schoolteacher? A noble goal indeed but by ignoble means.

Solomon describes this type of women as crafty (v.10), loud, rebellious, restless (v.11), liars (v.15), etc.

Proverbs characterizes the type of men who visit her as young and devoid of understanding (v.7). Solomon also describes the consequences "as an ox goes to the slaughter," "as a fool to the corrections of the stocks" (v.22), "he did not know it would cost his life" (v.23), "her house is the way to hell" (v.27).

It has always fascinated me how men who are otherwise very smart in their chosen profession can be so, should I say it, *stupid*, when it comes to this sin.

The solution is to understand the problem. This was a young man devoid of understanding (v.7). In contrast, the men who "keep my words, and treasure my commands" Proverbs 7:1) will be kept from "descending to the chambers of death" (v.27).

⇌ PRAYER ⇋

"Lord, once again the Bible is without hypocrisy
in warning us of dangers and their consequences.
Guard us from a few moments of pleasure in exchange
for a ticket straight to Hell. In Jesus' name. Amen."

PROVERBS 8:12

*"I, wisdom, dwell with prudence,
and find out knowledge and discretion."*

HOW TO CHOOSE WISELY

One day, a young president of a bank made an appointment with his predecessor.

He started by saying, "Sir, as you know, I'm young and lack many of the qualifications you have, and I was wondering if you would share some of your insights you've gained from your years that have been keys to your success?"

The older man thought for a moment and then said, "Good decisions."

Taken aback, the young man said, "But how does one come to know what a good decision is?"

The old banker said, "Experience."

"But how does one get experience?"

This time, with emphasis, the former banker said, "Bad decisions."

Prudence has the idea of carefully considering the consequences. To be cautious to danger or risk. It is wise to slow down, stop, and think before hurriedly making a decision that may have lifelong consequences.

The wise man will take the long view. Proverbs counsels us to make prudence, knowledge, and discretion (the ability to avoid an upset) our vanguard. Avoid the "act in haste and repent in leisure" mistake.

∽ PRAYER ∽

*"Lord, help us to slow down, think about consequences,
and seek sound counsel. In Jesus' name. Amen."*

November 9

PROVERBS 9:8

*"Do not correct a scoffer, lest he hate you;
rebuke a wise man, and he will love you."*

WHEN THE HAIR FLIES

To scoff is to speak about someone or something in a mocking way. If you have the unpleasant experience of having to correct a scoffer, you will pay!

A man by the name of George Albrecht, an electrician, filed a lawsuit for $25,000 against God and company. He listed about thirty houses of worship and the clergymen as co-defendants. Albrecht had sought compensation for injuries he'd received when a sidewalk collapsed under him during a rainstorm. The trial jury ruled the accident as "an act of God." Not satisfied with that ruling, he decided to sue God!

Can you imagine this man being reasonable to deal with? Hardly! The hair would fly if you tried to correct him. Our Proverb warns us that intense dislike (hate) will be the outcome. Some people are too smart to be wrong. The scoffer is one of them.

However, a wise man (one who fears God) will listen to corrective criticism. Proverbs 22:4 teaches us: "Humility and the fear of the Lord will bring wealth, honor, and life."

A man has to be humble (a modest estimate of one's own importance) in order to receive advice that will actually help. Also, a wise man recognizes good advice and appreciates deeply the help. A scoffer is too smart to be corrected, and why should he, he knows it all!

PRAYER

*"Lord, help me not to make fun of someone
who corrects me, especially when it is true.
Help me to see the good counsel and to ignore the bad.
In Jesus' name. Amen."*

PROVERBS 10:12

"Hatred stirs up strife, but love covers all sins."

THE WRECKING BALL

*H*atred has been defined as "intense dislike or ill will." When you hate, you tend to stir the pot.

A pastor in Ireland was retelling this story to a group of Protestants. A young boy by the name of Paul McGeown, who at the age of two, would love to go to the park with his mother to watch the birds. "Birdies! Birdies!" he would say with joy. One day on the way home from the park, a terrorist bomb hurled Paul across the road severely injuring his head. For sixteen days he lay unconscious in the Belfast Children's Hospital. A brain surgeon operated, and when Paul regained consciousness, he could not see. Then one month later a nurse was holding Paul near a window when the child suddenly pointed his finger and said, "Birdies! Birdies!" Paul could see again. The reaction of the people who heard the story was of great happiness for the child, calling it a miracle he had his sight restored. But one woman angrily asked, "But wasn't he a Roman Catholic?"

Amazing! I wonder if she'd feel the same way if it were her child? Some people just can't let it go. They will bring up past transgression, past mistakes, past injuries. The problem with hate is it always will distort you and eventually destroy you. Do you have someone you hate? It's time to let it go. A wise person will cover past sins and leave them alone. I admit, it's not easy to do, but it must be done. Remember, there was a time when we had injured God, and He covered our sins through Jesus.

⟡ PRAYER ⟡

*"Lord, remind us when we ask You to cover our sins
we've committed against You, that You in turn
expect us to cover those sins against us.
In Jesus' name. Amen."*

PROVERBS 11:1

"Dishonest scales are an abomination to the Lord,
but a just weight is His delight.

TRY HONESTY

"The story is told of a driver who slammed into a parked car. He got out of his car and started to write a note to put under the windshield wiper. It read: "I have just smashed into your car. The people who saw the accident are watching me. They think I am writing down my name and address. I am not. Sorry."

Funny, yes, unless of course it is your car. If you really want God's attention, be dishonest. If you want God's delight, be honest. God takes such a dim view of dishonesty He calls it an "abomination." The word abomination is defined as "a thing that causes disgust or hatred." If you want to disgust God, dishonesty will do. Those with a seared conscience have no trouble being dishonest. That is their creed. When in a tight squeeze, go to dishonesty. It will save you, at least for a while, until all the wheels on the wagon come off.

I remember the *Salt Lake Tribune* article about a man who pretended to be graduating from the University of Utah when he wasn't. He had defrauded and lied and was in general such a polished liar that he had his friends and family convinced that he was graduating and entering Medical School in the fall. When it came to graduation day, he feigned sickness, terribly sick. He even had sent out invitations to his graduation! Slick indeed. But the gig was up when his wife called the Medical School about housing. Their name was not on the housing list. A crisis ensued when she confronted him. So, being the honest chap, he was, he murdered her in her sleep! A true story.

⟶ PRAYER ⟶

"Lord, the temptation to be dishonest, in all its expressions,
is as persistent as a bad cold. Help us all to be honest.
Help us to loath what disgusts You. Help us to be a perpetual delight
in Your sight. In Jesus' name. Amen."

PROVERBS 12:24

*"The hand of the diligent will rule,
but the lazy man will be put to forced labor."*

INEXCUSABLE LAZY

The lazy man is the one who is unwilling to work or use energy. Such a person is walking down a dead-end road.

Perhaps you are familiar with the story of the dog and the rabbit. The dog boasted of his ability to run until one day a rabbit he was chasing got away! The other dogs started to ridicule him until finally he said, "You need to understand something. The rabbit was running for his life. I was only running for my supper."

Yes sir, we have all seen it. The person who excuses himself for failing to start a necessary task or failing to complete it. Unfortunately, the job just gets bigger, or passed on to someone else who is already over worked. Eventually, the lazy man will end up doing double-duty. The crisis builds until he is forced to work, and then it's the perfect "miserable" storm. A prime example is taxes. I would rather have a root-canal. However, wisdom teaches us if we will be diligent (careful and persistently work or make an effort) the dreaded task becomes manageable. Also, those loved ones of ours do not have to steer clear of us because we have buried ourselves.

Be wise, be diligent. Do not create your own crisis.

⟶ PRAYER ⟵

*"Lord, the insight of this Proverb is where we live.
Help us to work, remembering that eventually we will prevail
rather than be prevailed upon. In Jesus' name. Amen."*

PROVERBS 13:3

"He who guards his mouth preserves his life,
but he who opens wide his lips shall have destruction."

BURNING LIPS

*D*r. Albert Cantril, a professor at Princeton University, conducted a series of experiments to demonstrate how quickly rumors spread. The story goes like this: Dr. Cantril called six students into his office and said the Duke and Duchess of Windsor were planning to attend a university dance. The students were sworn to strict secrecy. In less than a week this fictitious story was all over campus. Town officials were calling asking why they were not informed, the press frantically phoned for details. Now here is the point: this was a pleasant rumor. Can you image how fast a slanderous rumor moves? Almost at the speed of light!

Those original six students had some explaining to do. This Proverb emphasizes the reality that those who strive to guard what they say, especially while under pressure, fair far better than those who open wide their mouth. The formidable power of controlling what you say can even make a fool look good. "Even a fool is counted wise when he holds his peace . . . (Proverbs 17:28) Some of us, me included, need to just close our mouths. This saintly habit will rescue us from a cartload of crises.

Here's the formula: A closed mouth preserves your life; open it wide and court destruction!

⁕ PRAYER ⁕

"Lord, we plead for your help in controlling our mouth.
May we never play Russian roulette with what we say.
In Jesus' name. Amen."

PROVERBS 14:29

"He who is slow to wrath has great understanding,
but he who is impulsive exalts folly."

FEELINGS CHANGE,
CONSEQUENCES DON'T

You are young only once, but you can stay immature indefinitely. Today's Proverb warns us against being impulsive—acting on instincts without thinking decisions through. We tend to think this is a mark of the young, but many adults suffer from the immaturity of impulsiveness. We have all made our impulsive decisions and have paid dearly for them. The old saying, "act in haste and repent in leisure" strikes a familiar chord in us all. But the mature soon learn that you cannot keep making these sudden decisions without giving careful thought to the consequences.

Being impulsive can be like leaping into a wonderfully responsive sports car, gunning the motor, taking off at a high speed, and then discovering the brakes are out of order. Such behavior exalts folly—a lack of good sense.

The answer to exalting folly is also prescribed in this Proverb: ". . . slow to wrath." Slow down and bring your feelings of anger under control. Think through what is happening and especially the consequences. Feelings change! Consequences often do not!

Another note needs to be sounded. There must be restraint. You will always lose something if you slow down and not say or act on first impulse. You lose the satisfaction that comes from "telling someone off." There is a certain amount of fun in that. However, what you gain far outweighs the satisfaction of "giving someone a piece of your mind." What you often gain is "saving face." As we mature, we understand that often the incident is *not* worth acting or speaking on impulse. What we learn over *time* is most of our first impulses are wrong. We learn to be "slow to wrath," take it all in, and then act with a clear view of the consequences.

❦ PRAYER ❦

"Lord, help me keep my foot on my impulsiveness.
In Jesus' name. Amen."

November 15

PROVERBS 15:4

*"A wholesome tongue is a tree of life,
but perverseness in it breaks the spirits."*

THE TREE OF LIFE

A man and his wife were on a long road trip when he stopped at a full-service gas station. After the attendant filled the gas tank, checked the oil, and washed the windshield, the man said the windshield was still dirty: "Wash it again, please." So, the attendant washed it again. After which the man said the windshield was still dirty. Just then, his wife reached over and took her husband's glasses and cleaned them with a tissue. After the husband put them back on the *windshield* was clean!

Proverbs teaches us that a tongue that reflects a wholesome heart is a tree of life. If we have a bleak and negative attitude, everything we look at will be dirty! Paul says it this way: "Finally, brethren, whatever things are true, . . . noble, just, pure, . . . lovely, . . . of good report, . . . meditate on these things." (Philippians 4:8) If we discipline our minds to dwell on these things, the tongue will follow. To speak a kind and gracious word creates an atmosphere around you that is positive, thankful, and uplifting. A little bit of heaven right here on earth. A tree that gives life. But some people are always on the negative; nothing is right! It is hard to be around them. This use of the tongue is perverse— "to behave in a way that is unreasonable or unacceptable." The result is a broken spirit. Imagine living in a household where this was the atmosphere. Children raised in this environment soon learn that life is one giant claw or one giant tooth. Nothing is good or wholesome.

Your tongue can be trained. Start with your own attitude. *What do I spend my time thinking about? Is it always on the negative? Do I really praise people and thank God?* Start small. Start encouraging people. Be more thankful. You will soon find people will enjoy being around you, and you will start enjoying life too. You will be eating from the "tree of life."

PRAYER

*"Lord, You invite us to eat from 'the tree of life.'
Help us to encourage and 'life' up. In Jesus' name. Amen."*

Pastor Dan Butcher | 319

November 16

PROVERBS 16:9

"A man's heart plans his way, but the Lord directs his steps."

PARADOX

A paradox is defined as "a contradiction between two beliefs or conclusions that are in themselves reasonable."

Modern physics faces a paradox in its study of light. There is ample evidence that shows that light consists of waves; likewise there is ample evidence that light consists particles. The paradox exists in that light is both waves and particles at the same time. You cannot rule out one in favor of the other. Neither can it be reduced to the other or explained in terms of the other; the two seemingly incompatible positions must be held together, and both must be treated as true. —J.I. Packer, *Evangelism and the Sovereignty of God*, p. 19.

This is the position of our Proverb today. Man acts freely in his day-to-day choices; some unconcerned about God or any intervention of God in his little world. The believer, however, is very concerned about God's intervention. For the believer, there are certain paradoxes in his own life that defy explanation. Good faith effort, sacrifice, and plans for the good sometimes turn out to be the opposite of what is hoped for. The believer has a resource in these times of conundrums. His trust is in a loving God who can work ". . . all things together for good to those who love God . . .." (Romans 8:28) Like all the raw material that enters the receiving dock of a car manufacturer—wire, glass, cloth, leather, metal, rubber, etc.—and at the opposite end rolls out a sleek and shiny car ready to be shipped to foreign and domestic customers. As these items don't come together by chance, but highly skilled men and women assembly them, likewise, God is able to bring together the raw materials of our lives—broken homes, sickness, disappointments, and even death—together for good. Only God can do this. The Lord is at work in the process. If you want peace and contentment in your life, trust that God is doing the driving while allowing us to have our hands on the wheel.

✦ PRAYER ✦

"Lord, we trust You as the director of our lives, and praise You for allowing us to write some of the script. In Jesus' name. Amen."

PROVERBS 17:14

*"The beginning of strife is like releasing water;
therefore, stop contention before a quarrel starts."*

BULLDOGS AND SKUNKS

Vance Havner said, "A bulldog can whip a skunk, but it's just not worth the fight!"

When I was a young Christian, I thought I had to argue every "jot" or "tittle" for God. As I matured (and that took a while), I realized that I was heading down the wrong track and ended up at the wrong stop. Some people, by disposition, like to contend (assert a position in an argument). But you soon learn that the energy and general bad mood that result are hardly worth it. Solomon teaches us that many contentions are just not worth the effort. Stop the breach at the beginning. We learn, hopefully, that the issue at hand is just not worth the flood that follows bad feelings. Mind you, some items are doubly worth contending for, i.e. the "love of God," "forgiveness through Christ," "salvation through faith," etc. When the gauntlet involves these, we have to take a stand. Jude says it this way: ". . . I found it necessary to write to you exhorting you to contend earnestly for the faith which was once for all delivered to the saints." (Jude 3) Pray earnestly that we learn the difference between the trivial and the transforming.

Likewise, some do not contend when they should be slugging it out! Do not take that literally, but some curl up into an emotionally ball when challenged. All things being equal, some need to bite their tongue and some need to embolden them.

PRAYER

*"Lord, help us to pull back the reins when it's not time to contend,
the courage to let the horse run when it is,
and the wisdom to know the difference.
In Jesus' name. Amen."*

PROVERBS 18:7

*"A fool's mouth is his destruction,
and his lips are the snare of his is soul."*

PADLOCKING THE MOUTH

On May 21, 1941, the German battleship, the *Bismarck*, was sighted in the North Atlantic. This ship was dubbed "unsinkable" by the Germans. At the sighting, the Royal British Navy raced to the scene. The *Bismarck* headed toward the French coast, controlled by the Germans, when suddenly the ship swung around and reentered the area where the British ships were massed in their greatest strength. Suddenly the pride of the Germany Navy started to zigzag erratically off course, which made it an easy target. Apparently, a torpedo had damaged her rudder and without its control the unsinkable ship was sunk.

The tongue is the rudder of our life. It has the power to control our future, our present joy and happiness, and any real hope of success. It also can sink our dreams. James put it this way: "Look also at ships: although they are so large and are driven by fierce winds, they are turned by a very small rudder wherever the pilot desires. Even so the tongue is a little member and boasts great things." (James 3:4)

This concept is so easy to understand; the practice is so hard to undertake. As in so many difficult tasks, start slow and build momentum. First, make it your goal to restrain your tongue one time in one conversation in one day. Build from there. We soon learn that much of what we say really is not necessary. Second, ask God for His favor to put into practice James' words: ". . . beloved brethren, let every man be swift to hear, slow to speak, slow to wrath; for the wrath of man does not produce the righteousness of God." (James 1:19-20)

✒ PRAYER ✒

*"Lord, I have often short-circuited my success
by just opening my mouth! I desperately need Your favor
in speaking when I should, what I should, and how I should.
In Jesus' name. Amen."*

November 19

PROVERBS 19:3

*"A man may ruin his chances by his own foolishness
and then blame it on the Lord!*

THE SHAME OF BLAME

This is Proverb's version of the blame game. However, it did not start in the book of Proverbs but in Genesis with Adam and Eve, my parents and yours! Adam blamed God for his naughtiness due to the woman's influence on him. "The woman you put here with me—she gave me some fruit from the tree, and I ate it." The woman, not to be outdone, blames the serpent. "The serpent deceived me, and I ate." (cf. Genesis 3:12-13) Adam and Eve now display all the heartache that bequeaths their rebellion, the first being blaming others for their own wrongdoings. This phenomenon did not just stay in the pages of Genesis or with the characters of the Old and New Testament, but it appears in our daily papers with commonplace regularity.

As I wrote about this Proverb, Salt Lake City was grinding through the humiliation of a trial over the Olympic Bribery Scandal. Bribing members of the International Olympic Committee with lavish and varied favors (college scholarships to I.O.C. members' children) to land the Olympics in Salt Lake City. Salt Lake City was dubbed *Slick* Lake City as a result. Yet, as you read the papers, the principle players were not to blame! This less than noble trait of dodging accountability while simultaneously assigning blame is not something we just read about in the papers, we ourselves struggle with this tendency, too!

Much of the wrong doings in our personal lives is our own creating. We cannot blame God. James 1:13 states, "Let no one say when he is tempted, 'I am tempted by God'; for God cannot be tempted by evil, and He Himself does not tempt anyone.'" The reality is we bring on most of our own unhappiness!

The solution to all this is in the Son of God. Jesus said in John 8:36, "If therefore the Son shall make you free, you shall be free indeed."

⌘ PRAYER ⌘

*"Lord, help us to stop blaming others
and to own up to our own faults. In Jesus' name. Amen."*

PROVERBS 20:7

*"The righteous man walks in his integrity;
his children are blessed after him."*

AN INSPIRATIONAL INFLUENCE

Through Rochester, New York flows the Genessee River, between steep and crooked banks. On one occasion, a man had just arrived by train from an extended stay away. While walking home he heard the excited voices of some men along the bank. "What's the matter?" he shouted. They replied, "There's a boy in the water!" Instantly, the man took off his coat and dove in the water. He was able to grasp the youth's arms and pull him to safety. After clearing his face of water, he shouted, "Heaven, it's my boy!" He had plunged in for the boy of somebody else and ended up saving his own!

Question? How do you think the boy felt about his father from that day on? Hero! *My dad is a hero!* Yes. Most likely none of us will be in that circumstance, but you can still be a hero. You can be a hero in the minds of your children every time they think of you. All fathers can walk in righteousness (the quality of being morally right). Being morally upright is not as dynamic as saving a boy from drowning, but it can have an influence that will far out live your life; it will live on in the lives of your children. If you want to give your children true riches, try integrity (the quality of being honest with strong moral principles).

You may not have much money, fame, or influence, but through Christ, you can have a reputation for honesty and a good name.

⚬ PRAYER ⚬

*"Lord, keep us from winning at the wrong game
(fame, power, wealth), and instead concentrate
on the true game of life; a life in fellowship
with You that will bless our children afterward
when the clock runs out on us. In Jesus' name. Amen."*

PROVERBS 21:1

*"The king's heart is in the hand of the Lord,
like the rivers of water; He turns it wherever He wishes."*

FREEDOM TO CHOOSE
AND GOD'S SOVEREIGN RULE

"An ocean liner leaves New York bound for Liverpool. Its destination has been determined by proper authorities. Nothing can change it. Onboard the liner are several scores of passengers. These are not in chains, neither are their activities determined for them. They are completely free to move about as they will. They eat, sleep, play, lounge about on the deck, read, talk, as they please; but all the while the great liner is carrying them steadily onward toward a predetermined port.

Both freedom and sovereignty (God's supreme rule) are present here, and they do not contradict each other. So it is, I believe, with man's freedom and the sovereignty of God. The mighty liner of God's sovereign design keeps its steady course over the sea of history. God moves undisturbed and unhindered toward the fulfillment of those eternal purposes which He purposed in Christ Jesus before the world began. We do not know all that is included in those purposes, but enough has been disclosed to furnish us with a broad outline of things to come and to give us good hope and firm assurance of future well-being.—A.W. Tozer, *The Knowledge of the Holy*

Today's Proverb teaches us that as powerful and influential as a king is over those in his kingdom, the king is subject to the Lord's direction. He has no power to resist, even though he moves through his day exercising his free will to choose as he wills, the majesty of God operates according to His predetermined ends for all of mankind. Meanwhile, God is still able to justly hold every man accountable for his choices, both good and ill.

❦ PRAYER ❧

*"Lord, help me to trust Your ultimate control of my life
and that of everyone I love. Help me to trust that You are to wise
to make a mistake and too deep to explain Yourself.
In Jesus' name. Amen."*

PROVERBS 22:6

*"Train up a child in the way he should go,
and when he is old, he will not depart from it."*

PRECIOUS MEMORIES

"Children brought up in Sunday School are seldom brought up in court!" —*Our Daily Bread*

Adelaida Blanton tells this story about her mother. When she was a child, they had a "five-minute rule" in their house. What this meant was the children had to be ready for school five minutes before they had to leave. They were a large family and that extra five minutes was prayer time with their Mother. The place was wherever their mother happened to be when they were all ready to leave. Sometimes it was the kitchen, other times the living room or bedroom, or even out on the porch. They would kneel and each child's name was mentioned with some special blessing asked. From time to time a neighbor child would drop by, and they were included in the prayer circle as well. When the prayer was over, they all stood up, received a kiss and were off to school.

Is there any wonder why this precious five minutes lingers in their minds as the years passed, and their mother went to be with the Lord?

You may not have had this privilege growing up, but you now have the *opportunity* of setting your family history straight with your own children. Start young and be consistent. Keep before your children the place of prayer, Bible reading, and Sunday School. A short Bible story in the morning followed by a short prayer will cast over your children's character the mind of God. This is especially critical since there will be a day when they will face life without you! But they can always face life with the Lord.

✧ PRAYER ✧

*"Lord, of all that I must do, help me not
to rob them of Your Word. In Jesus' name. Amen."*

PROVERBS 3:4–5

"Do not overwork to be rich . . .
for riches certainly make themselves wings;
they fly away like an eagle toward heaven."

MONEY TALKS—IT SAYS GOODBYE

*T*oday's Proverbs teaches that "riches make themselves wings; they fly away like an eagle." Since this is the case, and indeed it is, why do men and women cling to it like it like it will never leave them? I have done enough funerals as a Pastor, and I have never seen a U-Haul following a hearse! *You cannot take it with you.*

Benjamin Franklin is credited with the following observation: "Money never made a man happy yet, nor will it. There is nothing in its nature to produce happiness. The more a man has, the more he wants. Instead of its filling a vacuum, it makes one. If it satisfies one want, it doubles and triples that want in another way." Proverbs 15:16 offers this as a solution: ". . . better is a little with the fear of the Lord, than great treasure with trouble."

The following is well thought out and appropriate:

Money will buy:
A bed BUT NOT sleep.
Books BUT NOT brains.
Food BUT NOT appetite.
Finery BUT NOT beauty.
A house BUT NOT a home.
Medicine BUT NOT health.
Luxuries BUT NOT culture.
Amusement BUT NOT happiness.
A crucifix BUT NOT a Savior.
A church-pew BUT NOT heaven.

PRAYER

"Lord, help us to accumulate reverence for God and service for man.
Keep us from thinking that money is the end all game of life.
In Jesus' name. Amen."

November 24

PROVERBS 24:29

*"Do not say, 'I will do to him just as he has done to me;
I will render to the man according to his work.'"*

ITCHING FOR REVENGE

I like what the old country preacher said about revenge: "I'm not going to get even. I'm going to tell God on you." Sound advice. Then, of course, there is this approach. I was working at a Fred Meyer store years ago while going through Seminary. I recall one of the sales associates telling me she didn't get mad, she just got even. Most people choose to get even! They lay in wait, consuming their mental and physical health while they plot out their revenge. But it is a heavy toll. Revenge usually is not as sweet as they'd hoped for and generally shows itself in poor health years down the road.

God says He'll take care of business. "Vengeance is mine, and recompense; their foot shall slip in due time; for the day of their calamity is at hand, and the things to come hasten upon them." (Deuteronomy 32:35) The problem we have with this verse are the three little words "in due time." If truth be known, most revenge taken by man is immediate, impulsive, and disastrous. We just do not want to wait on anybody, not even God! But waiting on God is always best. We learn this as adults, whether it be airline tickets, food made from scratch, or a duly earned raise. However, it does not satisfy our anger to wait when comes to justice; but a wise man soon learns that waiting on God always brings the best. We know this when it comes to the circumstances of life. It is time we learn it with God: ". . . for the day of their calamity is at hand . . ."

So, don't grab the wheel out of God's hands. He has it under control.

✎ PRAYER ✎

*"Lord, help me to wait on You for any retribution;
don't let me ruin the ingredients by stirring too quickly.
In Jesus' name. Amen."*

PROVERBS 25:15

*"By long forbearance, a ruler is persuaded,
and a gentle tongue breaks a bone."*

GENTLE PERSUASION

A pilot by the name of Edmund Gravely had died at the controls
of his small plane while on the way to Georgia from North
Carolina. His wife, in a panic, kept radioing for help. "Help, help,
won't someone help me?" Authorities who picked up the distress
signal were flustered because the wife kept changing channels while
radioing for help! She finally made a very rough landing on her own
and had to crawl for three-quarters of mile to a farmhouse for help.

Today's Proverb emphasizes the wisdom of gentle persistence
when asking for a request. This Proverb has multiple applications,
one of which is prayer. The temptation is to give up after a while if
no immediate answer comes from God. Oh well, the answer must
be *no*! *Not necessarily!* I sometimes wonder if God is testing me to
see if I really believe He is the only true source of help. So, He
draws out the answer to see if I will persist! Persist, my friend, until
you know God has said *no*.

Also, this Proverb is a general principle for all requests of sig-
nificance. Have you been seeking a raise? Do you have a difficult
child, or a spouse who refuses the right? Try forbearance, but try
it in a gentle way. Not with threats, not with angry yelling, not
with a whining spirit, but in a gentle manner that eventually has
the strength to break the bone of resistance. Gentle persuasion will
prevail!

PRAYER

*"Lord, I need a gentle tongue and persistence.
May I use these two sisters for my help and Your glory.
In Jesus' name. Amen."*

PROVERBS 26:11

"As a dog returns to his own vomit, so a fool repeats his folly."

FOLLY

A man and his wife were traveling home after dinner when passing through a green light, he noticed a flash from the traffic signal. He commented to his wife he was going the posted speed limited, so he turned around and again went through the light five miles below the speed limit. Again, a flash was seen. Angered, he tried a third time well below the posted speed limit, and for a third time saw flash. Flustered and confused he went home. Four days later he received in the mail three citations for failure to wear a seat belt!

This man is a victim of life, sometimes funny, sometimes not! The tendency to repeat mistakes is almost inborn. It has been said that having experience means you recognize a mistake the second time you make it. Our Proverb is a little more serious in nature. Some mistakes are tragic, such as a fatality due to a second DUI. Strong desire or passion often drives us to repeat our folly. We act almost instantly without thinking, and then we are back to the vomit.

A sound cure for such folly is to memorize the above Proverb. These are short sayings and easy to remember. After memorizing it, call it to mind and chew on it like a cow does her cud. I do much better about repeating my previous folly when the Holy Spirit immediately calls to my mind this verse. Also, the sight of a dog returning to its own vomit tends to sear the concept in my memory.

⟶ PRAYER ⟵

"Lord, I'm through with the vomit pile.
Help me to recognize my previous folly
and not to repeat it. In Jesus' name. Amen."

PROVERBS 27:20

*"Hell and Destruction are never full;
so the eyes of a man are never satisfied."*

SWEET CONTENTMENT

Coming downstairs one morning, Lord Congelton heard his cook say, "If I only had five pounds, I would be content! Congelton thought the matter over and gave her the five pounds. She thanked him repeatedly. He paused outside the kitchen door and then heard her say, "If only I had asked for ten pounds!"

Contentment has been defined as "feelings of satisfaction with one's possession, status, or situation." Paul the Apostle said, "Now godliness and contentment is great gain." (I Timothy 6:6) A great gain, indeed. The truth is many Christians are not content. They think contentment comes from without—a newer car, better looks, a different spouse, more money, elevated status. Wrong! Contentment is resting in God's personal plans for you. "There are many plans in a man's heart, nevertheless, the Lord's counsel—that will stand." (Proverbs 17:21) God has a plan, and you will be much happier if you stop rebelling against it with a discontented heart. I remember watching a parade, when down the street trots a mare with her colt tied by rope to her saddle. That colt was having a heck of a time, fighting that halter and rope all the way down the parade route. How we often fight God's careful and loving plans with a heart of discontent.

Contentment comes from thanking God for his sovereign plan for our life. Remember, contentment is something that must be worked at, but like any worthy habits, it becomes second nature after a while and then come the benefits.

PRAYER

*"Lord, the Way of Wisdom is to be content
with Your plans for our lives.
Help us not to substitute our own.
In Jesus' name. Amen."*

PROVERBS 28:6

"Better the poor who walks in his integrity,
than one perverse in his way though he be rich."

BETTER TO BE POOR

The FBI agent said to the bank teller after the bank had been robbed for the third time, "Did you notice anything special about the bank robber? "Yes; he seemed to be better dressed each time."

Funny, but the story illustrates what some will do to get rich. The gaining of riches is the main pursuit of many, even if it means losing their soul. Jesus said it this way: "What will it profit a man if he gains the whole world; and loses his own soul?" (Mark 8:36)

It will profit you nothing! The lost will be for eternity. Most things in life you can recover from, but not the loss of your soul when you die. Our Proverb today speaks in opposites. Most people would choose riches over poverty, a little dishonesty and cheating here and there over integrity. Why not, they say? No one is looking. The problem is, many years down the road, the soul becomes perverse (to behave in a way that is unacceptable, regardless of consequences). Now a little cheating has morphed itself into cheating as a way of life with no twinge of regret. God prefers you to be penniless. Rags over riches, honesty over hoarding, poor over perversity. Strange what God prefers. Even stranger are those who trade eternal hell over an eternity in heaven. Christ said, "It is better to be lame in this life than to be cast whole into hell." (Mark 9:45)

⟶ PRAYER ⟵

"Lord, help me to remember that often less in this life
is more in the life to come.
In Jesus' name. Amen."

PROVERBS 29:6

*"By transgression, an evil man is snared,
but the righteous sings and rejoices."*

A SNARE AND A CURSE

"The story is told of a time when Sir Arthur Conan Doyle decided to play a practical joke on twelve of his friends. He sent them each a telegram that read, "Flee at once . . . all is discovered." Within twenty-four hours, all twelve had left the country."[22]

In this case, it was their "secret sins." Put it this way: ". . . be sure your sin will find you out." (Numbers 32:23)

There is a predator that stalks all Christians—sin. If it entangles us, it will eventually bind us as slaves. Jesus said, "Most assuredly, I say to you, whoever commits sin is a slave of sin." Jesus' solution is to become a "son," because slaves do not abide in Heaven, only sons. He also promises to set you free: ". . . if the Son makes you free, you shall be free indeed. (John 8:34–36)

The Way of Wisdom teaches us that righteousness will deliver us and leave us singing. We need to be reminded from time to time that what "glitters is not gold." Sure, righteousness has its challenges—always doing what is right, the sacrifice, extra work, even isolation, but in the end, we usually are pleased. It might even leave us singing. Guard especially against the secret sins. God does see. "For the eyes of the Lord run to and from throughout the whole earth, to show Himself strong on behalf of those whose heart is loyal to Him." (2 Chronicles 16:9) Why forfeit all you've labored for? Stay on the right side of circumstances and in the end, you will not be fleeing town because "all is discovered."

PRAYER

*"Lord, help me not play with sin. It is the mark of an evil man.
Keep me instead rejoicing with the righteous,
for that is the Way of Wisdom. In Jesus' name. Amen."*

22. *Illustrations for Biblical Preaching.* Edited by Michael P. Green, g. #627, p. 181. Baker Book House, Grand Rapids, Michigan.

PROVERBS 30:20

*"This is the way of an adulterous woman:
she eats and wipes her mouth,
and says, I have done no wickedness."*

A CRAZY EXCUSE

*H*ere are a few choice excuses offered to police officers as explanations for their car accident:

"An invisible car came out of nowhere, struck my car and vanished."

"I pulled away from the side of the road, glanced at my mother-in law, and headed over the embankment."

"Suddenly a tree was there, where no tree had been before!"

We love our excuses, especially our own. This flaw originated with our forefather Adam: ". . . the woman, whom *You* (emphasis) gave to be with me, she gave me of the tree, and I ate." Adam was blaming the Lord for his sin.

Our tendency to cover our tracks by blaming others is serious business, but the individual who does not even attempt to excuse himself but goes beyond to redefine the nature of wrong has stepped into a moral twilight zone. Our Proverb exposes the adulterous woman as one who does not even offer an excuse but declares herself innocent of any wrong. Travel down this slippery slope for a while, and you end up with no conscience, like a hand calloused to touch and feeling. The conscience becomes silent. Standards of right and wrong only become personal preferences. You like vanilla, and I like chocolate. There is no moral standard of right and wrong. But we do live in a world of absolutes. Two plus two equals four here in the United States and in the United Kingdom. Gravity has the same effect in India and in Indonesia. Wickedness is still wickedness and adultery is still adultery according to the Bible. No excuses, no blaming, and no other so-called "truth."

⁓ PRAYER ⁓

""Lord, deliver us from deceit's deceptions. In Jesus' name. Amen."

PROVERBS 1:19

*"So are the ways of everyone who is greedy for gain;
it takes away the life of its owners."*

INSATIABLE GREED

The story is told of a great ship that had struck a reef and was quickly sinking. The people on board had only a few minutes before the ship was lost, so all possessions were abandoned as they fled to the lifeboats. That is, except for one. This man ran from one stateroom to the next filling his pockets with abandoned gold pieces. This took just long enough for him to miss the last lifeboat. So, in desperation, he put on a life jacket and jumped overboard. To the horror of the passengers in the lifeboats, the man hit the water and plummeted to the bottom like an anchor, never to surface. His new treasures had become his undoing.

Greed has been defined as "intense and selfish desire for something, especially wealth." So many strive and exhaust themselves for what they believe is the answer to their problems. Often all is lost as we sacrifice time, health, family, and our standing before God, just so we can have our prized obsession. Proverbs teaches that such pursuit takes away from the pursuer. The sad note is these possessions and the imagined joy they will bring often fade with time, leaving the individual hungering for the next selfish pursuit. In the meanwhile, our family suffers, our relationships suffer, and especially our relationship before God. Proverbs warns us ahead of time to give up such pursuits. The Way of Wisdom is to realize that we are consuming ourselves in such blind pursuits, all the while neglecting our true wealth—God Himself. Jesus teaches us in Matthew 6:33, ". . . seek first the kingdom of God and His righteousness and all these things will be added to you."

⟶ PRAYER ⟵

*"Lord, the Way of Wisdom is to pursue You,
not our plastic dreams of wealth.
In Jesus' name. Amen."*

PROVERBS 2:1–5

"My son, if you receive my words, and treasure my commands within you, so that you incline your ear to wisdom, and apply your heart to understanding, yes, if you cry out for discernment and lift up your voice for understanding, if you seek her as silver, and search for her as for hidden treasures; then your will understand the fear of the Lord and find the knowledge of God."

A WORTHWHILE PURSUIT

*I*f we work upon marble, it will perish; if on brass, time will efface it; if we rear temples, they will crumple into dust; but if we work upon immortal minds, and imbue them with principles, with the just fear of God and love of our fellow men, we engrave on those tablets something that will brighten to all eternity.—Daniel Webster

A knowledge of the Bible without a college course is more valuable than a college course without the Bible.—William Lyon Phelps

The above quotes highlight the value of seeking the fear of the Lord and the knowledge of God over any other knowledge. Our Proverb today highlights the same thought. But it comes at a price. Solomon tells us that we must receive God's words, treasure his commands. (v.1) We must incline our ear to wisdom and apply our heart to understanding.(v.2) We must cry for discernment and lift our voice for understanding. (v.3) We must seek her as silver and search for her as for hidden treasures (v.4), *then* we will understand the fear of the Lord and find the knowledge of God. (v.5)

Looking for reality in your relationship with God? Try these eight verbs: receive, treasure, incline, apply, cry, lift, seek, and search. *Then* you will experience God actively involved in your life.

PRAYER

"Lord, Solomon describes the Way of Wisdom as a relationship with You in receiving, treasuring, inclining, applying, lifting, and seeking Your commands. In Jesus' name. Amen."

December 3

PROVERBS 3:5

*"Trust in the Lord with all your heart
and lean not on your own understanding . . ."*

UNFALTERING TRUST

Faith is not credulity. It is not believing in something you know is not true. Neither is faith a substitute for knowledge. Christian faith operates in the realm of meaning, not in the realm of fact. Faith recognizes fact, but it is not out to obtain, contradict, or prove facts. Saint Augustine knew this when he said, "I believe in order that I may understand."

I believe God can be trusted. To trust God means a conscious dependence on God's love, wisdom, and strength. If God has said it, then we can trust it. When I need wisdom, God said he'd give wisdom. "If any of you lacks wisdom, let him ask of God, who gives to all liberally . . ." (James 1:5) If I need strength, God gives it. "I can do all things through Christ who strengthens me." (Philippians 4:13) If I need direction, God gives it. "I will instruct you and teach you in the way you should go, I will guide you with *my* eye." (Psalm 32:8) Trusting God for the confusing, disheartening, and sad, means letting go of trying to understand the perplexing events in my life. There are just some experiences in life that are beyond finding out or understanding. We simply trust God with these and move on. When I try to "lean on my own understanding," I am saying that I really don't trust God. Our experience then becomes one weary round of confusion after another.

PRAYER

*"Lord, may I count You as reliable (trust)
and stop my periodic spells of trying to understand
every confusing incident in my life. In Jesus' name. Amen."*

Pastor Dan Butcher | 337

PROVERBS 4:18–19

"But the path of the just is like the shining sun,
that shines ever brighter unto the perfect day.
The way of the wicked is like darkness;
they do not know what makes them stumble."

TWO ROADS, TWO DESTINIES

Recently a Sunday supplement in our Nation's Capital carried excerpts from a sermon entitled, "Why I Know There is a God." The sermon had been delivered on Laymen's Sunday last year in an Arlington, Virginia, church. It was a message in simple terms of belief in God and in Christian principles. It concluded with the thought that man is placed on earth as a free agent. He is given freedom of choice, and only he can make the decision as to whether he will or will not live by the guidelines which Christ followed throughout His days on earth.

The parishioner who delivered that sermon on Laymen's Sunday was American Astronaut John Glenn. The rugged and unshakable faith expressed in the title by the author of the sermon permeated the whole.

Our Proverb teaches there are two paths a man can walk. One road is a path of light, the other of darkness; one leads to promise, the other to a stumbling destruction. The Way of Wisdom says that life exists because God exists. On this road is love, contentment, and purpose in ever increasing portions, ". . . that shines ever brighter unto the perfect day." (v.19) The way of the wicked says there is no God; man makes his own way. On this road, there is often misery, lack of meaning and purpose, and ends poorly. As the Proverb says, "They do not know what makes them stumble." (v.19)

Two roads, two destinies—one is ever-increasing light; the other ever-increasing darkness.

⟶ PRAYER ⟵

"Lord, we trade our darkness for Your Light.
In Jesus' name. Amen."

December 5

PROVERBS 5:21

"For the ways of man are before the eyes of the Lord,
and He ponders all his paths."

EXHILARATING KNOWLEDGE

There is a small arctic sea bird called the guillemot. It lives on the rocky cliffs of northern coastal regions. These birds flock together by the thousands in rather small areas. Because of the crowded conditions, hundreds of the females lay their pear-shaped eggs side by side on a narrow ledge in a long row. All these eggs look alike, so it's incredible that a mother bird can identify those that belong to her. Research has shown that the female guillemot knows her own eggs so well, that when even one is moved, she finds it and returns it to its original location.

Today's Proverb teaches us that God is intimately acquainted with us! He sees us and ponders our ways, our habits. He knows if we are selfless or selfish, if we are kind or unkind, merciful or merciless. Such knowledge is beyond our understanding. Jesus put it this way: "But the very hairs of your head are all numbered." (Matthew 10:30) Such knowledge encourages us that "No temptation has taken you except such is common to man; but God is faithful, who will not allow you to be tempted beyond what you are able, but with the temptation will also make the way of escape, that you may be able to bear it." (I Corinthians 10:13) God sees, God knows, and God will help. Trust Him by faith to sustain you during your times of temptation, sorrow, or disillusionment. God has it together, and He will help you to get it together as well.

⁓ PRAYER ⁓

Lord, to believe that an all-powerful, all-loving,
and all-knowing God sees and ponders our life,
lifts our hopes when we feel hopeless.
In Jesus' name. Amen."

PROVERBS 6:1–5

"My son, if you become surety (co-signer) for your friend,
if you have shaken hands in pledge for a stranger . . .
deliver yourself like a gazelle from the hand of the hunter . . ."

DELIVERANCE

A young man who lived on Chapline River, Kentucky, was out setting traps one evening for coons, when, by an accident, he got his finger caught in his own trap. It was an ingenious trap made by a hole bored into a large log and nails driven in so that if the animal put his paw in for the bait, he would catch on them, and the more he tried to get away, the worse he would be off. The boy caught his own finger and found it impossible to get it out.

He stayed all night on the log and, to his horror, found the next morning that the water was rising in the river, and he would soon be swept out on that log, and that would mean drowning. So, he took his knife in the other hand and cut off his finger to save his life.—Current Anecdote

Do not get your finger caught in co-signing for the loan of another. The temptation becomes particularly troubling when you know the individual asking for your signature—a brother, a sister, or close friend. Our Proverb says *don't.* Our Proverb presents this trap with such urgency, it almost pleads with us to undo such an agreement if you already have. The dangers are obvious. Steer clear. You'll be able to preserve the relationship better if you say no early on, rather than later when the conflict of nonpayment has bloomed into outright hostility.

⁓ PRAYER ⁓

"Lord, keep me from allowing my compassion
from running contrary to Your Word's counsel.
In Jesus' name. Amen."

PROVERBS 7:27

*"Her house is the way to hell,
descending to the chambers of death."*

A FAST TRACK TO HELL

San Francisco (AP)—Actress Jane Fonda proposed at the Second Annual Hookers' Convention that prostitution be decriminalized or that laws against it be enforced equally against prostitutes and their clients.

Ms. Fonda addressed a panel audience of about 200 persons. She pledged at a news conference to support the organization's drive to decriminalize prostitution.

The actress said the unfairness of the prostitution laws was evident in Hollywood where customers, who included heads of studios, executives, and politicians, were seldom charged, though the prostitutes catering to them were arrested.

In the eyes of some, prostitution is just another way of making a living. However, the warning our Proverbs provides for us today is clear—being a prostitute is a fast track to hell. Our Proverb describes the prostitute as:

- Immoral (v.5)
- Appeals to the young who are devoid of understanding (v.7)
- She is crafty of heart (v.10)
- She is loud and rebellious (v.11)
- She is bored with the home life (v.11)
- She does not show due respect for another (v.13)
- She flatters and uses enticing words (v.21)
- Her steps lead to the chambers of death and hell (v.27)

Not the type of woman you write home about! Need I say more? If you are looking for shame and dishonor and a one-way ticket to hell, visiting a prostitute will do it. The good news is God's grace (his unearned favor) cleanses us from all sin through the sacrifice of Jesus Christ.

❧ PRAYER ❧

"Lord, remind us that we cannot improve on Your plan for our lives, therefore, we pray we will be holy and obedient, especially with the woman of Proverbs Chapter 7. In Jesus' name. Amen."

December 8

PROVERBS 8:11

"For wisdom is better than rubies,
and all the things one may desire cannot be compared with her."

SCHOOLED IN WISDOM

I recall hearing of a man with a PhD who ran an elevator in a downtown Louisville, Kentucky, office building. Just prior to my oral examination for the same degree, the faculty examining committee failed to pass a philosophy student. I was concerned, thinking the faculty committee was getting tougher. I asked one of the professors why they failed to pass the man. He said the student was able to answer all the questions about the philosophy of others, but he had no philosophy of his own. Both the elevator operator and the student had knowledge; neither had wisdom.

Knowledge is a mental accumulation of facts. Wisdom is the ability to use knowledge properly in the ordering of one's life. Wisdom has been defined as the successful application of knowledge. What good is a degree if you are unable to apply that knowledge wisely?

Today's Proverb teaches us it is not enough to have knowledge. A man may have an earned PhD in physics, but may deny that there is a God. He may acknowledge the world has intricate design but no designer! He may comment on earth's orderliness but deny there is any intelligent power that maintains that order. He may even agree with Einstein's Theory of Relativity, that matter had a beginning, but deny that there is a cause (God) to that beginning.

It is true, wisdom is superior to knowledge and nothing can compare with her.

⟨⟩ PRAYER ⟨⟩

"Lord, our society pursues knowledge at breakneck speed,
but has passed by wisdom in so doing.
Keep me focused on the true values in life.
In Jesus' name. Amen."

PROVERBS 9:10–12

"The fear of the Lord is the beginning of wisdom,
and the knowledge of the Holy One is understanding."

HOW WILL YOU VOTE?

A colored minister was once asked to explain the doctrine of election. Said he, "Brethren, it is this way: The Lord, He is always voting for a man; and the Devil, he is always voting against him; then the man himself votes, and that breaks the tie!"

So, my friend, how will you vote? Our Proverb today tells us that true wisdom begins with reverence for God. It also teaches that true understanding about life comes from knowledge of the Holy One. However, verse 12, teaches that if you scoff (speak about something in a scornful or mocking way), you will bear the penalty.

A deck hand aboard RMS *Titanic* boasted, "God Himself could not sink this ship." It is reported when the Captain gave the orders to abandon ship, many of the passengers simply could not believe the *Titanic* could sink and refused to board the lifeboats! As a result,1502 men, women, and children plunged into the icy depths.

So, my friend, how will you vote? Is your vote for the Christ? II Corinthians 5:21 states it plainly: "He (God) made Him (Christ) who knew no sin to be sin for us that we might become the righteousness of God in Him?" Or will you mock and vote for the devil, "and bear it alone?" (Proverbs 9:12)

PRAYER

"Lord, may I always vote to reverence Your Word
and Your way. Keep me from the rocky road of scoffing.
In Jesus' name. Amen."

PROVERBS 10:19

"In the multitude of words sin is not lacking,
but he who restrains his lips is wise."

BABBLING LIPS

R. G. LeTourneau was for many years an outstanding Christian businessman—heading a company which manufactured large earth moving equipment. He once remarked, "We used to make a scraper known as "Model G." One day somebody asked our salesman what the "." stood for. The man, who was quick on the trigger, immediately replied, "I'll tell you. The "." stands for gossip because like a talebearer this machine moves a lot of dirt and moves it fast!""

If you want a daily challenge, learn to restrain your lips! It is so easy to speak up, to speak out and speak too much. Eventually, one of these will end you up in the outhouse. Our Proverb directs us in the light of restraining our words when speaking, casually at home or cautiously at work, the art of restraining your lips will pay high dividends. Once something is spoken, you cannot take it back, though you wish you could. Those people who are favored naturally in this area of restraining their words, usually hold on to what is said, only to strike back later when you are gone. Nobody is without sin.

The Way of Wisdom is to restrain the lips, too many words will end up poorly, especially when tempers are flaring.

⟶ PRAYER ⟵

"Lord, teach us to not only count our days,
but to count our words. In Jesus' name. Amen."

December 11

PROVERBS 11:2

"When pride comes, then comes shame;
but with the humble is wisdom."

THE BOY WHO SPIT A MILE

Grantland Rice was the greatest man I have known, the greatest talent, the greatest gentleman."This is the appraisal of the late Red Smith. Many felt the only thing greater than his talent was his generous heart. Rice was the epitome of courtesy.

The story goes that the noted journalist's working pass ticket for the Army-Notre Dame football game went astray. This man, who virtually created that classic game, did not complain. Instead he went down Broadway, bought a ticket from a scalper, and watched the game from the stands with his typewriter on his knee. Afterwards, he went to the press box to complete his story. Hearing of the experience, a friend asked, "Why didn't you throw some weight around?""Tell you the truth," Granny came back, "I don't weigh much."

Humility has been defined as "low in ran."like that of a Private in the Army. A Private does not have much influence and in general is ordered rather than give orders. Grantland's response to the advice of "throwing some weight around" reflects such an attitude. A man of pride, however, sees himself with an "assume superiority."This assumed superiority does not mean he deserves it, it's just assumed.

True wisdom is to see God as creator and 'us-ins' as the created. Pride, however, spits off the edge of the Grand Canyon to the river a mile below and gives himself the credit for spitting a mile!

⸻ PRAYER ⸻

"Lord, keep us from living up to an exaggerated idea of our-self, all
the while looking down on others.
In Jesus' name. Amen."

PROVERBS 12:25

*"Anxiety in the heart of man causes depression,
but a good word makes it glad."*

WHAT'S YOUR WORRY?

*T*homas Carlyle was an anxious, serious, searching type of person. He had a soundproof room built in his London residence so he could work in unbroken peace. However, a neighbor had a cock that crowed rather vigorously during the early mornings. Carlyle complained to the owner about it. Whereupon the neighbor replied that the rooster crowed only three or four times at most. "But" answered Carlyle, "if you only knew what I suffer waiting for that cock to crow!" Like Carlyle, many harassed and suffering people spend their days waiting for something dreadful to happen!

What is your worry? Worry has been defined as "getting on a wooden horse and trying to make a fast get away!" Such worry, our Proverb teaches, only weighs the heart down. It's a burden to be constantly waiting for the "cock to crow!" When, our worried expectations often do not play out, there is a solution. Paul has a "good word" for us: "Be anxious for nothing, but in everything by prayer and supplication, with thanksgiving, let your requests be made known to God; and the peace of God, which surpasses all understanding, will guard your hearts and minds through Christ Jesus." (Philippians 4:6-7) Now that's a good word that make us glad: " . . . the peace of God which surpasses all understanding . . ."

PRAYER

*"Lord, keep us from sabotaging the future with anxiety
that spoils the present. In Jesus' name. Amen."*

PROVERBS 13:20

"He who walks with wise men will be wise,
but the companion of fools will be destroyed."

UNDESIRABLE COMPANIONS

There are localities in Switzerland where the canary is caged with a nightingale so that the canary may catch the sweetness of the nightingale's song and melodious harmony that delights European tourists. This is a demonstration of the power of association. The canary may be trained by a nightingale. Likewise, men and women may make their lives strong, pure, and sweet in thought, word, and deed by unbroken association with those who live on a higher plane.

Likewise, a fool's association with other fools will only hasten the day that fool's end. As "iron sharpens iron" (Proverbs 27:17), one's companions have a tremendous influence on how we think, speak, and act. Walk with the wise, as our Proverb teaches, and learn to be wise. Choose to walk with the fool who says there is no God (Psalm 14:1), and don't be surprised if you end up profane, godless, and corrupt. We can sing with the nightingale or crow like the crows.

⁓ PRAYER ⁓

"Lord, keep us close to You and close to those
who are so inclined. In Jesus' name. Amen."

PROVERBS 14:8

"The wisdom of the prudent is to understand his way,
but the folly of fools is deceit."

UNPRINCIPLED DECEIT

After several pastors had failed to win a condemned criminal to Christ by preaching down to him, a layman went to visit the man. Entering the death row cell, he sat on the cot alongside the man, took him by the hand, and said, "We are in a bad fix, aren't we?" The man broke into tears and soon yielded to Christ. He needed somebody to understand and care.

There is another way to approach life, not with an understanding heart as the above illustration shows, but by way of deceit.

President Walter G. Clippinger of Otterbein College in Ohio enjoys the story of the fake blind man. The pitiable creature, with dark glasses and his little tin cup was standing on the street corner, patiently waiting for some small contribution. A kindly man passed by and generously dropped a dime in the poor old fellow's cup. Then for some reason he turned around, and to his surprise, saw the blind man's glasses pushed up on his forehead and his eager eyes closely examining the recent gift.

"I thought you were a blind man," said the disgruntled donor.

"Oh, no," was the answer. "I am only substituting for the regular blind man today. I'm not really blind at all."

"Well, where is the regular blind man?" asked the other.

"Oh, he's gone to the movies; it's his afternoon off."

⇌ PRAYER ⇌

"Lord, may we value honesty as much as You do.
In Jesus name. Amen."

December 15

PROVERBS 15:3

"The eyes of the Lord are in every place,
keeping watch on the evil and the good."

THE ALL-SEEING EYES

Gatlinburg is a tourist city buried deep in the Great Smoky Mountains of Tennessee. This city of 1,764 inhabitants all but rolls up the sidewalks in the winter but is literally working alive in the summer. In and around Gatlinburg are many beautiful scenes and many photos are taken in these parts. But the most photographed sight in Gatlinburg is the sculptured head of Christ in the Christus Gardens. This breathtaking marble figure of Christ is sculptured in such a way that the eyes appear to "look" in every direction. Regardless of where you stand, the eyes are upon you.—Carl C. Williams

It's good for the soul to know that God sees everything. It comforts the person who has been abused and forsaken, the broken hearted, the downtrodden. It also comforts the soul that your service, sacrifice, and devotions are noted. However, it chills the heart of the evil. Those who are constantly running from their conscience or those who no longer even hear their conscience. "For His eyes are on the ways of man, and He sees all his steps." (Job 34:21) It's good for the soul to be watched by God, for the righteous, this is their delight; for the wicked, this is their doom.

PRAYER

"Lord, remind us that as we see all we do,
that You see all. In Jesus' name. Amen."

PROVERBS 16:3

*"Commit your works to the Lord,
and your plans will be established."*

A DIVINE SUBMISSION

The verb commit is from a word that means "to roll." The idea is to "roll your cares onto the Lord." Trusting the Lord with our concerns and decisions frees us from worrying about them throughout our day.

To celebrate an old man's seventy-fifth birthday, an aviation enthusiast offered to take him for a plane ride over the little West Virginia town where he spent all his life. The old man accepted the offer. Back on the ground, after circling over the town for twenty minutes, his friend asked, "Were you scared, Uncle Dudley?" "No-o-o," was the hesitant answer. "But I never did put my full weight down."[1]

It is difficult to trust (to count as reliable), but the Bible is clear; if you want God's intervention in your life, you must learn to trust Him with your cares. I like the little boy's rendition of the song, "Trust and Obey" which he sang as, "Trust and okay." If we commit our worries, concerns, and plans to the Lord, and hold that trust, things will be okay.

PRAYER

*"Lord, I have a long and hard day ahead of me.
I commit my plans to You. Please establish them for me,
for I trust You. In Jesus' name. Amen."*

December 17

PROVERBS 17:3

*"The refining pot is for silver and the furnace for gold,
but the Lord tests the hearts."*

A SUPREME TEST

The A.C. Nielson Company, which measures television audiences and their behavior, revealed that in the average American home the TV is on six hours and fourteen minutes a day, every day of the year. Significantly, this is two hours per day more than the daily average ten years ago, which is approximately the same point in time that the Standard Achievement Test scores began to decline.

This time frame is significant because the first generation to cut its teeth on television began taking the SAT's in the early 1960's, which is, of course, when the decline in scores started. *Media and Methods* in its April 1975 issue reported that while the television set in the average American home is on approximately 2100 hours per year, the average American spends only five hours per year reading books.[1]

I believe God is testing His saints constantly on the use of their time! One such test is illustrated above. It seems to me that God's people have time to watch TV but no time to read the Bible. God's people have time to view violence and sex, but no time for prayer. God's people have time for the distasteful and ridiculous, but no time for service. So, my friend, what do you have time for?

⟶ PRAYER ⟵

*"Lord, keep us from the sensual, the silly, the sad;
instead may our hearts be tuned to the Spirit,
our Savior, and our Sword. In Jesus' name. Amen."*

PROVERBS 18:9

"He who is slothful in his work is a brother
to him who is a great destroyer."

LAZINESS HAS A BROTHER

A farmer was sitting on the porch of his house when a stranger came by and asked, "How's things?" "Tolerable," said the farmer. He continued by saying, "Two weeks ago, a tornado came along and knocked down all the trees I would have had to chop down for this winter's firewood. Then last week lightning struck the brush I had planned to burn to clear the fields for planting. That's remarkable." "What are you doing now?" The farmer answered, "I'm waiting for an earthquake to come along and shake the taters out of the ground."[23]

Are you waiting for some taters to be shook out of the ground? Granted, it's easy to put off unpleasant tasks, it will keep until tomorrow, we say. However, these little projects keep waiting until one day we are forced to gather up "the taters." By then the unpleasant task has grown to be many unpleasant tasks. It best to take on those tasks that are priorities first and get them done, and it's best do them immediately. It's a joyous feeling to know that you've accomplished a task of high priority. It is surprising what a relief it is, a burden you didn't know you were carrying.

There is a task that laziness triumph's over many, many times. It is our quiet time before God. Laziness strikes this high priority down regularly. The "Way of Wisdom" is to recognize that such laziness is a brother to him who destroys. It is a brother who can destroy our walk with God. That is one brother we all need to disinherit!

⟋∾ PRAYER ∾⟍

"Lord, we all struggle with laziness. Help us to get after our priorities,
especially our daily quiet time with You. In Jesus' name. Amen."

23. *1000 Illustrations for Biblical Preaching*. Edited by Michael P. Green, g. #746, p. 212-213. Baker Book House, Grand Rapids, Michigan.

December 19

PROVERBS 19:23

"The fear of the Lord leads to life, and he who has it will abide in satisfaction; he will not be visited with evil."

LASTING SATISFACTION

Sometime ago there appeared in a newspaper a cartoon showing two fields divided by a fence. Both fields were about the same size and each had plenty of the same kind of grass, green and lush. In each field there was a mule, and each mule had his head through the fence eating grass from the other mule's pasture. All around each mule in his own field was plenty of grass, yet the grass in the other field seemed greener or fresher, although it was harder to get.

And in the process, the mules were caught in the wires and were unable to extricate themselves. The cartoonist put just one word at the bottom of the picture—*Discontent!* [1]

This Proverb speaks to satisfaction (fulfillment of one's wishes or expectations) as being found in "The fear (reverence) of the Lord . . .." How few would believe that walking with God would bring true satisfaction? Jesus put it this way: "I have come that they may have life, and that they may have it more abundantly." (John 10:10) The pursuit of God through the knowledge of the Bible and submission to His will, tends to wean out of us the constant yearning to find satisfaction in some other form. Strange as it may sound, but to follow the admission to give generously tends to free us from the love of money. To strive to love others tends to free us from hating them and to serve our fellow man. And humble sacrifice tends to keep the focus off ourselves and our own puny problems. There is another benefit to this wise counsel: "He will not be visited with evil." God's judgment will not fall on him. That is a sure plus.

PRAYER

"Lord my satisfaction in life be You.
In Jesus' name. Amen."

Pastor Dan Butcher | 353

PROVERBS 20:24

*"A man's steps are of the Lord;
how then can a man understand his own way?"*

OUR BEWILDERING MYSTERIES

A beautifully touching story emanated from Phoenix, Arizona, a few years ago. It was the account of a seven-year-old boy who accidentally fell into a two-hundred-seventy-five-foot well. For forty-five minutes the lad was trapped in darkness, having suffered multiple fractures.

"Daddy get me out of here," he yelled.

"Don't worry, son, and don't be scared. We will get you out. Just push against the sides of the pipe so you don't sink."

Eventually, proper rescue equipment arrived. A rope was lowered into the well. Mr. Stage, the lad's father, gave specific instructions how to place the rope over his shoulders and beneath the arms, and to hold on. The boy obeyed and was lifted to safety. The father commented: "He always did mind good." Irrespective of grammar, there existed a trustful relationship between father and son.[24]

A similar rapport should exist between a Christian and God.

The beauty of the above Proverb and the illustration that follows teaches us that much of life is an issue of trusting God. It also teaches us to stop trying to understand the personal mysteries in your past or present life. All things may not go as planned, good or bad, but God is still in control. We generally do not have problems with those issues that are a mystery to us that ended favorably. The real rub comes with those that do not. Like a cat that chases its own tail, we must learn to *trust* God for the incidents in our life that are past understanding. If we cannot trust *Him*, we'll end up dizzy about life.

PRAYER

"Lord, how I love to understand all things related to my walk with You. Teach me to trust You and stop the useless activity of chasing myself! In Jesus' name. Amen."

24. *1000 Illustrations for Biblical Preaching.* Edited by Michael P. Green, p. 189, Trust and Triumph.. Baker Book House, Grand Rapids, Michigan.

December 21

PROVERBS 21:3

*"To do righteousness and justice
is more acceptable to the Lord than sacrifice."*

FRACTIONAL OBEDIENCE

*R*ighteous living and a life of justice is more important than religious rituals with neither. The Old Testament prophet Samuel reproves King Saul by saying, "Has the Lord as great delight in burnt offerings and sacrifices, as in obeying the voice of the Lord? Behold, to obey is better than sacrifice, and to heed than the fat of rams." (I Samuel 15:22)

How tempting it is for some to throw money at the Lord, and then to continue to live in disobedience to God's commands.

How tempting it is to volunteer at the Homeless Shelter at Christmas and then to continue in a life of stubborn rebellion against God's laws.

How tempting it is to attend an Easter Service and then call it good while returning to a life of dissipation.

A grandfather was visiting his six-year-old grandson when his mother called, "Tommy, it's time for your shower!" Grandfather asked, "Do you use the shower downstairs or the one upstairs?" Tommy replied, "Momma says that I can't take a shower upstairs, and when Momma says *no*, we'd better do *no*!"[25]

It is best to do *no* when God says *no*. Do not be fooled into thinking that occasional obedience and justice in some form will erase a life of stubborn disobedience. That is not the "Way of Wisdom."

～ PRAYER ～

*"Lord, how tempting it is to throw You some sacrifice
hither and yarn, when humble righteousness
is the order of our days. In Jesus' name. Amen."*

---

25. Jones, G. C. (1986). *1000 Illustrations for Preaching and Teaching* (p.137). Nashville, TN: Broadman & Holman Publishers.

PROVERBS 22:2

*"The rich and the poor have this in common,
the Lord is the maker of them all."*

THE UNDESERVING POOR

God makes both the rich and the poor. To favor the rich over the poor is to despise their Creator. "Listen, my beloved brethren: Has God not chosen the poor of this world to be rich in faith and heirs of the kingdom which He promised to those who love Him?" (James 2:5)

Some hold the doctrine that a poor person is poor because they refuse to work. This is shortsighted. Proof of this is the term "working poor." It is not my intent to discuss why people are poor, but the fact that there are poor people, and lots of them. So, this Proverb teaches us to respect them and not to favor the rich (who often are rich because of inheritance), but to treat them as equals, because both are human beings made in the image of God.

An ancient king made a great feast and invited a company of poor people who were Christians. He also invited his nobles. When the poor Christians arrived, he had them seated in his presence; but, when the nobles came, he set them in the hall.

The nobles demanded the reason why. He answered, "I do not do this as their king. But, as I am going to another world, I must honor them as God's dear children, who shall be kings and princes with me hereafter. I would have you esteem them according to their worth—and show it."[1]

This king had it right! How we pass by what God honors and honor what God passes by.

❧ PRAYER ❧

*"Lord, how often we value what You oppose
and oppose what You value.
Help us to readjust our thinking and our focus.
In Jesus' name. Amen."*

PROVERBS 23:13

"Do not withhold correction from child,
for if you beat him with a rod, he will not die,
you shall beat him with a rod, and deliver his soul from hell."

SPARE THE ROD, SPOIL THE CHILD

The Organization of American States has closed its central Washington office because the area, just one mile from the White House, is a hotbed of crime. The Library of Congress is now closing a half-hour early so its employees can get off the streets before dark—the time when muggers become most active.

Nowhere in the nation is the crime rate more drug-related than it is in Washington, DC. The Nation's Capital has become a center for narcotics traffic.[1]

Some will feel I am naive to believe that an old-fashioned spanking would help in such cases as the drug-related crimes in Washington, DC, but I believe it would. I understand that the breakdown of the family through divorce, poverty and the absence of either one or both parents contribute to such environments, but when a child is lovingly corrected for directly disobeying their parents, they soon learn that "no" means "no." One of the most urgent needs a child has is to learn to obey authority. To be trained to obey authority will set him well for the rest of his life. This form of self-control will serve him well as he navigates life's many challenges. I understand that authority sometimes is abusive, and there is a host of laws and ordinances that guard against that, but I am referring to the character habit of self-control that expresses itself in respecting and obeying authority. A child is often too young to understand why "no" means "no," but he does understand pain. A controlled, reasoned, and loving trip to the "woodshed" will not distort his personality, but instead will teach him to control that personality when he is tempted to hit, steal, or otherwise disobey.

⌘ PRAYER ⌘

"Lord, may we learn that our obedience to Your command now
will encourage our children's obedience to You later.
In Jesus' name. Amen."

PROVERBS 24:19–20

"Do not fret because of evildoers,
nor be envious of the wicked;
for there will be no prospect for the evil man,
the lamp of the wicked will be out."

STABBED WITH ENVY

It was Sir Winston Churchill's standing order that when he returned by train from a trip that his dog Rufus should be brought to the station to meet him. Rufus would be let off his leash to dash to his master and be the first to greet him.

One day, I happened to be standing close by. Rufus ignored his master and came leaping all over me instead. Of course, Sir Winston loved Rufus too much to blame him. Instead, he turned to me with a hurt look and said quietly, "In the future, Norman, I would prefer you to stay in the train until I've said hello."[1]

Our Proverb for today is not quite as humorous, but the thought still applies. How we often envy the wicked, wishing we had their type of attention. The Bible, however, takes a dim view of the wicked, regardless of their wealth, beautiful wife, and name. God's perspective is often so different from our own. There is no "prospect for the evil man," no happy future or inspiring ending to his life. Unless true faith and repentance enter the picture, the "lamp of the wicked will be put out." Hardly worth envying.

Jesus put it this way: "For what will it profit a man if he gains the whole world, and loses his own soul?" (Mark 8:36)

A man or woman who pursues wealth, fame, and influence, all the while ignoring God, will find God ignoring them when they die. The end of such a life is nothing worth envying.

⇌ PRAYER ⇌

"Lord, keep us from admiring the wicked,
for in the end we'll end up just as they are. In Jesus' name. Amen."

December 25

PROVERBS 25:6-7

"Do not exalt yourself in the presence of the king,
and do not stand in the place of the great;
for it is better that he say to you, come up here,
than that you should be put lower
in the presence of the princes . . ."

AN EGOTISTICAL BOAST

Voltaire, the noted 18th century French philosopher, said that it took centuries to build up Christianity, but "I'll show how just one Frenchman can destroy it within fifty years." Taking his pen, he dipped it into the ink of unbelief and wrote against God.

Twenty years after his death, the Geneva Bible Society purchased his house for printing the Bible. And it later became the Paris headquarters for the British and Foreign Bible Society. The Bible is still a bestseller; an entire 6-volume set of Voltaire's works was once sold for 90¢.[1]

It's best not to mock God. "Do not exalt yourself in the presence of the king . . ." especially the King of kings. Galatians 6: 6 says, "Do not be deceived, God is not mocked . . ." The proper approach is this: "Humble yourselves in the sight of the Lord, and He will lift you up." (James 4:10)

Seek God and seek His kingdom, then God will honor you as He sees fit. I plead with you, don't make the mistake that God is unaware of our arrogant boasts again Him.

⟶ PRAYER ⟵

"Lord, keep us humble before You,
even if it means humbling us. In Jesus' name. Amen."

PROVERBS 26:4–5

"Do not answer a fool according to his folly,
lest you also be like him.
Answer a fool according to his folly,
lest he be wise in his own eyes."

CRACKED-BRAINED FOOLS

These two Proverbs appear to be contradictory, but they are not. There are times when talking to a fool (one devoid of morals) when it is best not to respond to his comments lest you lower yourself to his level. There are other times when it's best to respond to him lest he goes off convinced that his bias and unreasonableness is reasonable.

My wife and I were taking our daily walk when we noticed the neighbor across the street was loading up a U-Haul. We introduced ourselves by name, had the usual small talk, and then I wished him a Merry Christmas and said the two of us were Christians. He said that he did not believe all that, stating the Bible was just the words "of man." I responded by saying, "Jesus Christ believed they were the Words of God." He backed off and then said that religious people follow God "out of fear." I said, "You are judging me when you say that because I follow Christ out of love for Him. To say that we follow Christ out of fear is just a 'straw man,' easy to push over." He became even more aggressive, stating he could not follow the God of the Bible because it condemns the homosexual lifestyle, using his neighbors next to him, two gay men, as examples. He said that they were born with those chromosomes, and they could not help their lifestyle. My response to that statement he liked even less. A thief who stole his car could claim he didn't have the right chromosome, to be honest. At this point, he was visually angry and went back to loading the U-Haul. So, the question is asked, should I have engaged him in his clear bias against Christians and the Bible? I believe so. There are many people who believe Christians are just plain stupid and fearful; people who have no real clue about life, so they hide fearfully behind their beliefs. To leave this man unchallenged would only convince him that his bias was well-founded.

∽ PRAYER ∽

"Lord, help us not to live to fight, but be ready to
when called upon by Your Spirit. In Jesus' name. Amen."

PROVERBS 27:4

*"Wrath is cruel and anger a torrent,
but who is able to stand before jealousy?"*

SELF-HARMING JEALOUSY

I remember reading somewhere in a Grecian story of a man who killed himself through envy. His fellow citizens had reared a statue to one of their number who was a celebrated victor in the public games. So strong was the feeling of envy which this incited in the breast of one of the hero's rivals that he went forth every night in order, if possible, to destroy that monument. After repeated efforts, he moved it from its pedestal, and it fell, but in its fall, it crushed him.[1]

Yes, jealousy can destroy you. Jealousy is basically the thought of being replaced by a successful revival. The feeling of being rejected, not measuring up, or being considered second best causes a rage that, as the Proverb teaches, "Who can stand before it?" It leaves in its wake heartache, broken homes, and fractured relationships. Also, jealousy is not an amiable companion. Not only does it destroy others, but it also consumes and destroys the bearer, such as the above story illustrates. What then is the cure? I believe Henrietta C. Mears had it right: "The man who keeps busy helping the man below him won't have time to envy the man above him—and there may not be anybody above him anyway."—Ibid, #2676

So, watch your focus. You can always find someone better than you. It is better to help the man next to you or someone who is *actually* below you.

PRAYER

*"Lord, remind me that jealousy consumes
the one who harbors it. In Jesus' name. Amen."*

PROVERBS 28:23

*"He who rebukes a man will find more favor
afterward than he who flatters with the tongue."*

The same man cannot be both friend and flatterer.
—Benjamin Franklin.[1]

REBUKE

On the island of Sicily in the fourth century B.C., there ruled a tyrant named Dionysus (the elder). He had in his court a certain "yes" man named Damocles who sought advantage by flattering the cruel king.

One day, he extolled the virtues of Dionysus so eloquently that the tyrant proclaimed a magnificent banquet in his honor. During the festivities, however, Damocles happened to look up and discovered to his dismay that a naked sword hung suspended over his head by a single hair.

The word "rebuke" means "to express sharp disapproval of someone because of their behavior."

How we all love the feeling of being admired! To be held in "high esteem." We crave it as the body does its necessary air. However, the cowardly act of flattery (excessive and insincere praise, given to further one's own interests) is to abuse this natural need and turn it into a weapon for personal gain. What we really need at times, for our own help and that of others, is to express the dreaded words of rebuke. Such constructive criticism may even save a life, such as the rebuke a police officer offers gives when he hands us a ticket for speeding through a school zone.

We need to be careful about our insincere praise. We may find a sword dangling over our head by a single thread!

⟶ PRAYER ⟵

*"Lord, give us the courage to rebuke when necessary
and the restraint from flattering. In Jesus' name. Amen."*

PROVERBS 29:1

"He who is often rebuked, and hardens his neck,
will suddenly be destroyed, and that without remedy."

AN END TO PATIENCE

The world is always twenty minutes ahead of one man in Coventry, England.

"In 1922," he said, "the clocks were advanced twenty minutes. I never accepted this. Nobody was going to take twenty minutes out of my life."

So, he kept his watch set for the old time. He is twenty minutes late for every appointment. As a result, the determined man has been fired from half a dozen jobs.

"They won't beat me," he declared. "I'm going to die twenty minutes late to show them I was right."[1]

So, have it your way! The problem with stubbornness, or "hardness of neck"as our Proverb puts it, is you "sow the wind and reap the whirlwind." (Hosea 8:7) If you find yourself often rebuked (to express sharp disapproval of someone's behavior), you'll find yourself broken with no solution, especially if it's God doing the rebuking. If God is doing the rebuking, and you are doing the resisting, your ultimate destination is Hell, broken and beyond repair. If God has been speaking to you, and you will know when He does, do not harden your heart in disbelief and rebellion. Turn to His Son for salvation from your sins. Simple faith in the sacrifice of Christ will bring you to God (II Corinthians 5:21) otherwise, be aware, there is an end to God's patience.

PRAYER

"Lord, may we not presume on Your good nature
or on Your patience. In Jesus' name. Amen."

PROVERBS 30:17

*"The eye that mocks his father, and scorns obedience
to his mother, the ravens of the valley will pick it out,
and the young eagles will eat it."*

UNDESERVED

A father had told his son he would send him to sleep in the attic, with only bread and water for his supper if he broke the laws of the home once more. The child disobeyed again and was sent to the attic: The father could not eat. He had the boy on his mind and his heart. His wife said, "I know what you are thinking. But you must not bring the boy from the attic. It would cause him to disobey again. He would have no respect for your word. You must not cheapen your relation as his father by failing to keep your promise."[1]

To which her husband replied, "You are right. I will not break my word. To do so would cause my son to lose his respect for my word. But he is so lonely up there." He kissed his wife good night, entered the attic, ate bread and water with the boy, and when the child went to sleep on the hard boards, his father's arm was his pillow.

He who knew no sin suffered for the sinner.—Wilbur Nelson

The above Proverb may seem severe, but there's good reason. God Almighty is our Father. His love is well-illustrated with this story, to disrespect our earthly father or mother is to disrespect God's nature as loving. Yes, your parents may have been horrible, they do not deserve your respect, or love, but does anyone deserve God's love? No, but He still extends it to us.

∙ PRAYER ∙

*"Lord, help us not to relate to people
based on merit but based on mercy. In Jesus' name. Amen."*

PROVERBS 31:30

"Charm is deceitful, and beauty is passing,
but a woman who fears the Lord, she shall be praised."

THE DECEIT OF CHARM

Many years ago, I met a lady whose outward appearance was practically devoid of beauty. But as I came to know her, I witnessed character traits that sparkled like many diamonds. Through the years I have remembered her as one of the most beautiful persons I have ever known. That surely was what Peter had in mind when he wrote in I Peter 3:3-4, "Do not let our adornment be merely outward—arranging the hair, wearing gold, or putting on fine apparel—rather let it be the hidden person of the heart, with the incorruptible beauty of a gentle and quiet spirit, which is very precious in the sight of God."

I think it significant and insightful for this Proverb to combine the two words, "charm" and "deceit." Charm is defined as "the power of giving delight or arousing admiration." Deceit is defined as "concealing or misrepresenting the truth." A woman of beauty can use her "charm," her power of delight, to conceal evil intentions. A beautiful woman can be very self-centered with objectives in mind that only serve her interests. How much better is a plain-looking woman who has character traits such as kindness, long suffering, humility, and forgiveness. This woman has beauty for sure, but a strange thing happens when you meet such women; they actually become better looking! Their inner beauty outshines their plain features, giving them an attraction all their own right.

Oh, how happy is the man who has *this* kind of a wife.

PRAYER

"Lord, keep us from the deceit and charm of a beautiful face
devoid of a beautiful heart. In Jesus' name. Amen."

*P*astor Dan Butcher is a man dedicated to God and serving His children. He has a love for the book of Proverbs and feels God's children have much to learn on a daily basis from this book of Scripture.

Dan Butcher has served in Utah as a Christian minister for forty years. He has pastored churches in Kanab, Kamas, Sandy, and Tooele. He received his education at Southwestern Baptist Bible College (now called Arizona Christian University) and Western Seminary in Portland, Oregon. He is married to Lani, and together they have four children.

If you would like to contact Dan, he can be reached through Book-Wise Publishing, Riverton, Utah or his email at dlbutcher2@aol.com.

www.ingramcontent.com/pod-product-compliance
Lightning Source LLC
LaVergne TN
LVHW011342080426
835511LV00005B/103